SailingActs

SailingActs

FOLLOWING AN ANCIENT VOYAGE

LINFORD STUTZMAN

Good Books

Intercourse, PA 17534
800/762-7171
www.GoodBks.com

Credits
The anchor/cross icon used throughout the book was an early Greek Christian symbol
found in archeological excavations. It incorporates the Roman symbol of execution, the cross,
into a positive symbol of security, the anchor, by the seafaring Christians.
We mounted a replica of this symbol on the cabin wall of *SailingActs*.

All photos are provided by Linford and Janet Stutzman, except for Photo
31 (by Aram DiGennaro) and Photos 52 and 56 (by Byron Gingrich).

Cover photo by Michael Hostettler.

Maps and boat diagrams are by Matthew Styer/EMU Marketing Services.

All scripture references are taken from the HOLY BIBLE, NEW INTERNATIONAL
VERSION®. NIV®. Copyright © 1973, 1978, 1984 by International Bible Society.
Used by permission of Zondervan. All rights reserved.

Design by Dawn J. Ranck
Cover design by Dawn J. Ranck. Inspired by Kristen Parmer with EMU Marketing Services.

SAILINGACTS
Copyright © 2006 by Good Books, Intercourse, PA 17534
International Standard Book Number-13: 978-1-56148-546-8
International Standard Book Number-10: 1-56148-546-2

Library of Congress Catalog Card Number: 2006023363

Library of Congress Cataloging-in-Publication Data

Stutzman, Linford, 1950-
  SailingActs : following an ancient voyage / by Linford Stutzman.
    p. cm.
  ISBN-13: 978-1-56148-546-8 (pbk.)
    1.   Mediterranean Region--Description and travel. 2.   Stutzman, Linford, 1950---Travel--
Mediterranean Region. 3. SailingActs (Ketch) 4. Sailing--Mediterranean Sea. 5. Bible. N.T. Epistles
of Paul--Geography. 6. Paul, the Apostle, Saint--Travel--Mediterranean Region. I. Title.
  D973.S89 2006
  910.9182'2--dc22   2006023363

Table of Contents

To Janet, first mate in every sense of the word; creative gourmet cook; courageous friend, whose faith, hope, and love endured throughout the journey, motivating, challenging, encouraging, blessing, and giving life. The greatest of these, truly, is love.

To my mother, Arla, who not only let me look at the maps in her Bible, but who, like Paul, demonstrated how to travel difficult journeys in life with joy and contentment.

Paul's First Missionary Journey (47-49 A.D.) and His Journey to Rome (59-60 A.D.)

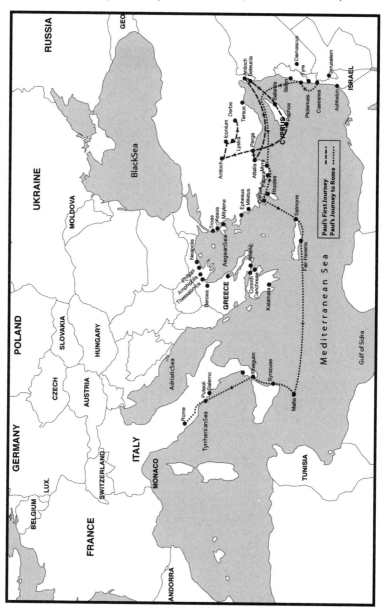

Paul's Second (50-53 A.D.) and Third (53-57 A.D.) Missionary Journeys

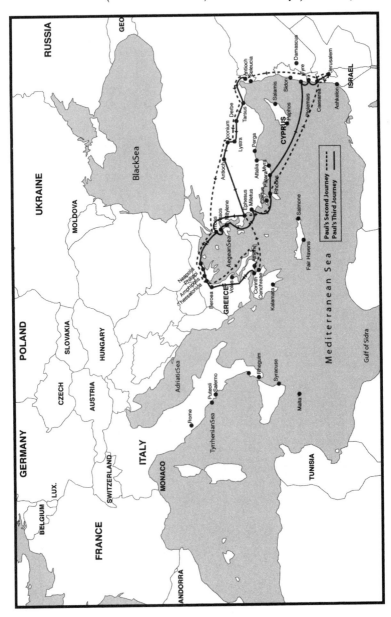

SailingActs' Journeys in 2004

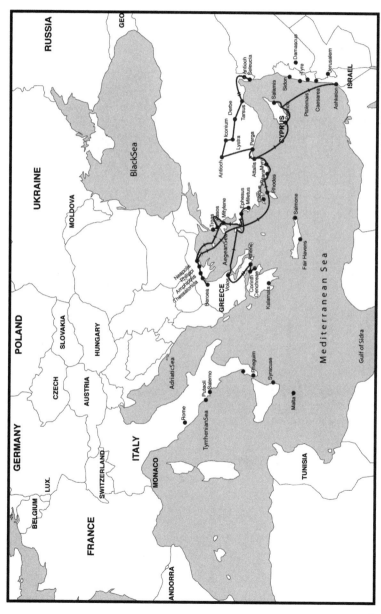

SailingActs' Journey to Rome in 2005

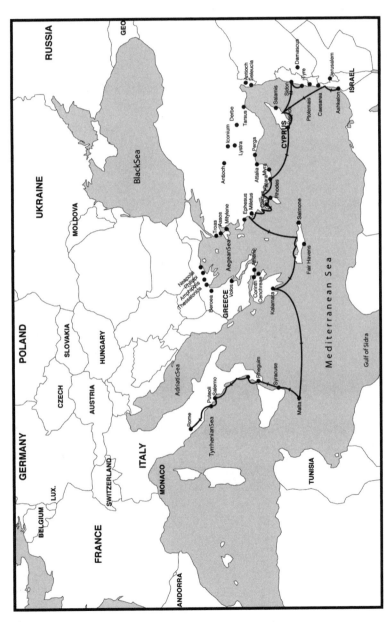

Itinerary of Places Visited

	Date *Visited*	Modern *Name*	Biblical *Name*	Acts *Reference*
2004				
1	05/10	Volos, Greece		
2	06/10	Athens, Greece	Athens	17:15-16; 18:1
3	06/11	Corinth, Greece Cenchrea, Greece (arch. harbor)	Corinth Cenchrea	18:1; 19:1 18:18
4	06/18	Palaio Trikeri, Greece (island)		
5	06/19	Skiathos, Greece (island)		
6	06/22	Skopolos Greece (island)		
7	06/24	Stena Valia, Greece (island)		
8	06/25	Skiros, Greece (island)		
9	06/26	Psara, Greece (island)		
10	06/27	Chios, Greece (island)	Kios	20:15
11	06/28	Samos, Greece (island)	Samos	20:15
12	07/04	Kuşadasi, Turkey	near Ephesus	18:19, 21, 24; 19:1, 17, 26, 35; 20:16-17
13	07/06	Miletus, Turkey (arch. site/harbor)	Miletus	20:15, 17
14	07/10	Çesme, Turkey		
15	07/11	Oinousses, Greece (island)		
16	07/12	Lesvos, Greece (island)	Mytilini	20:14
17	07/15	Ayvalik, Turkey		
18	07/18	Behramkale, Turkey	near Assos	20:13, 14
19	07/18	Daylan, Turkey	near Troas	16:8, 11; 20:5-6
20	07/22	Limnos, Greece (island)		
21	07/28	Samothraki, Greece (island)	Samothrace	16:11
22	07/30	Thasos, Greece (island)		
23	08/01	Kavalla, Greece (port)	Neapolis	16:11
24	08/03	Philippi, Greece	Philippi	16:12; 20:6
25	08/04	Amphipolis, Greece (arch. site)	Amphipolis	17:1

SailingActs

	Date Visited	Modern Name	Biblical Name	Acts Reference
26	08/04	Thessaloniki, Greece	Thessalonica	17:1, 11, 13
27	08/04	Veria, Greece	Berea	17:10, 13; 20:4
28	08/05	Apollonia, Greece	Apollonia	17:1
29	08/07	Thasos, Greece		
30	08/08	Limnos, Greece		
31	08/10	Lesvos, Greece	(see above)	
32	08/11	Chios, Greece	(see above)	
33	08/12	Samos, Greece	(see above)	
34	08/14	Kuşadasi, Turkey	(see above)	
35	08/16	(arch. harbor, Turkey)	Trogyllium	20:15 (some manuscripts)
36	08/16	Agathonissi, Greece (island)		
37	08/17	Kos, Greece (island)	Cos	21:1
38	08/19	Simi, Greece (island)		
39	08/20	Rhodes, Greece (island)	Rhodes	21:1
40	09/04	Kalkan, Turkey	near Patara	21:1
41	09/06	Finike, Turkey	near Myra	21:1 (some manuscripts); 27:5
42	09/08	Antalya, Turkey	Attalia	14:25, 26
43	09/11	(arch. site)	Perga	13:13, 14; 14:25
44	09/13	Yalvaç, Turkey	near Antioch (Pisidia)	13:14
45	09/14	Konya, Turkey	Iconium	13:51; 14:1, 19, 21; 16:2
46	09/14	(arch. site)	Lystra	14:6, 8, 21; 16:1, 2
47	09/15	Karaman, Turkey	near Derbe	14:6, 20; 16:1; 20:4
48	09/16	Tarsus, Turkey	Tarsus	9:11, 30; 11:25; 21:39; 22:3
49	09/17	Antakya, Turkey	Antioch	6:5; 11:19, 20, 22, 26, 27; 13:1
50	09/17	Seleucia, Turkey	Seleucia Pieria	13:4
51	09/22	Paphos, Cyprus (Greek)	Paphos	13:6, 13
52	09/23	Limassol, Cyprus (Greek)		
53	09/24	Salamis, Cyprus (Turkish)	Salamis	13:5
54	09/26	Ashkelon, Israel		

	Date Visited	Modern Name	Biblical Name	Acts Reference
2005				
1	03/26	Damascus, Syria	Damascus	9:2, 3, 8, 10, 19, 22, 27; 22:5, 6, 10, 11; 26:12, 20
2	04/05	Herzliya, Israel	near Caesarea	8:40; 9:30; 10:24; 11:11; 12:19; 18:22; 21:8, 16; 23:23; 24:1; 25:1, 4, 6, 13, 24
3	04/08	Larnaca, Cyprus		
4	04/09	Tyre, Lebanon	Tyre	12:20; 21:3, 7
5	04/09	Sidon, Lebanon	Sidon	12:20; 27:3
6	04/13	Paphos, Cyprus	(see above)	
7	04/15	Finike, Turkey	(see above)	
8	04/19	Kekova Roads, Turkey		
9	04/20	Kalkan, Turkey	(see above)	
10	04/21	Kapi Creek, Turkey		
11	04/22	Bozuk Buku, Turkey		
12	04/23	Cnidus, Turkey (arch. harbor)	Cnidus	27:7
13	04/23	Bodrum, Turkey	near Cnidus	
14	04/27	Altinkum, Turkey		
15	04/28	Kuşadasi, Turkey	(see above)	
16	05/19	Samos, Greece	(see above)	
17	05/20	Patmos, Greece (island)		
18	05/21	Kos, Greece	(see above)	
19	06/03	Astipalaia, Greece (island)		
20	06/06	Santorini, Greece (island)		
21	06/08	Dhia, Greece (island)		
22	06/09	Rethimnon, Crete (Greece)	Crete	27:7, 12, 13, 21
23	06/11	Khania, Crete (Greece)		
24	06/13	Kali Limenes, Crete (Greece)	Fair Havens	27:8
25	06/13	Loutro, Crete (Greece)	Phoenix	27:12
26	06/15	Kithera, Greece (island)		
27	06/16	Kalamata, Greece		
28	06/22	Valleta, Malta (island)	Malta	28:1
29	06/29	St. Paul's Bay (shipwreck site on Malta)		27:39-44

7

SailingActs

	Date Visited	Modern Name	Biblical Name	Acts Reference
30	06/30	Siracuse, Sicily (Italy)	Syracuse	28:12
31	07/04	Catania, Sicily (Italy)		
32	07/07	Reggio di Calabria, Italy	Rhegium	28:13
33	07/08	Tropea, Italy		
34	07/12	Cetraro, Italy		
35	07/13	Cape Palinuro, Italy		
36	07/14	Salerno, Italy		
37	07/16	Pozzuoli, Italy	Puteoli	28:13
38	07/17	Salerno, Itlay		
39	07/20	Tropea, Italy (*SailingActs* in marina for winter of 2005-2006)		
40	07/24	Rome, Italy (on the Appian Way)	Rome	28:14 ff.

Acknowledgments

While I admire Paul, I also note that he apparently had no family who loved and supported him—no wife, no sons—at least that we know about.

It's with deep gratitude and appreciation that I mention our sons. David read much of the manuscript and gave suggestions on how to improve the narrative in places. Jon's interest in the project never flagged, even though it meant he was the only member of the family living in the United States for the duration. And my admiration and respect for my wife Janet ranks up there with my admiration and respect for St. Paul himself.

Then there is Captain Steve and his wife Jenny, the Greek sea-captain who sold us the *Aldebaran*, then watched over us with concern and assistance whenever we ran into difficulty.

And the Eastern Mennonite University (EMU) sabbatical-review committee, who overcame its reluctance to allow a 15-month sailing adventure to qualify as a sabbatical. A special thanks to Paul Sauder, whose encouragement resulted in the EMU Web site, and to Mike Eberly and Marci Gineris of the EMU communications department, who faithfully posted the photos on the Web site.

Others, like seminary students Aram DiGennaro and Josef Berthold, who joined us on parts of the journey, endured endless discussions about Paul, shared insights, and asked tough questions; Mike and Ginny Hostettler of Nazareth Village, who enthusiastically believe in the value of first-century insights; and Dave Landis and Eric Kennel, who joined us as crew and fellow learners on *SailingActs* for six weeks of their own round-the-world pilgrimage. The 29 students who went with Janet and me to the Middle East in spring 2004 were wonderful in their support and enthusiasm for the venture. The 12 EMU students on the summer 2005 Greece/Turkey cross-cultural study program provided an inspiring forum for discussing the impact of Paul in the Greek world.

The international sailing community is incredible. We're grateful for the expertise and friendship of people like Moshe and Panne, and Rueben, who wintered with us in Ashkelon, Israel; for Henry and Chippy from the nearby *moshav* (an agricultural cooperative community unique to Israel), whose optimism and enthusiasm kept us going; for Michal of the Ashkelon Marina; and Raffi, whose tragic loss of his son in a sailing accident less than a year earlier did not hinder him from giving so much technical assistance. We'll never forget any of these and other wonderful people we met along the way: Pam and Bruce, Rick and Tsipy, and countless others who have been cruising for far longer than we have or, for that matter, than Paul did.

I wish to thank those who sent e-mails of encouragement and interest. One of the goals of the sabbatical was to share the experience in some way with as many people as possible. The encouragement we received from all those who not only logged on, but responded to, the Web site was invaluable. Thank you.

Finally, the superb navigational skills of Merle and Phyllis Good, who piloted this book through the wind and waves of publishing, is deeply appreciated. Thanks to editor Delphine Martin, whose patience and care made the voyage a pleasure.

Prologue

August 20, 2004, Mandraki Harbor, Rhodes

I lie exhausted on my bunk in the forepeak of *SailingActs*, trying to relax while next to me, in the stuffy front cabin on the V-berth, Janet is sleeping peacefully. Although it's 2:00 in the morning, vacationers still stroll by on the wharf of the crowded Mandraki harbor on the island of Rhodes. I listen, suddenly alert, as several tourists stop near *SailingActs*, talking too loudly. Their British accents are slightly slurred by alcohol.

"Look at these sailboats. Fantastic way to go. Forget hotels, Love. Next time let's charter a boat and sail when we come on vacation," a man is trying to persuade his partner. I can't understand her reply, but she must have expressed some reservations about the capabilities of her would-be sailor. The man counters by talking even louder, extolling not only the obvious virtues of sailing on the Mediterranean, but his own competence. They wander off into the night and I realize with some alarm that something seems vaguely familiar with that little audio drama.

They don't have a clue, I think to myself. *They don't know that earlier today our genoa was destroyed, that we had to place an order for almost $4,000 worth of new sails for which we couldn't pay. They are completely unaware that the foam mattresses on which Janet and I are lying were saturated by countless gallons of salty seawater by a freak wave, and are still a little clammy in spite of being hung out to dry for hours. They are blissfully ignorant of the fact that I had mangled the propeller on a hidden anchor chain as I tried to back into a berth on the wharf of Mandraki Harbor just hours ago, and that we'd need to have the boat hauled out and the propeller replaced before sailing any further. No, this would-be sailor is not only drunk, enthusiastic, and confident. He is utterly ignorant.*

Had I been the same when I decided to sail the routes of the Apostle Paul? What possessed me to consider spending a sabbatical

SailingActs

sailing the journeys of the Apostle Paul in the Mediterranean? If Paul described his sailing experiences as full of hardship and peril, what made me think that the same sea routes would somehow be pleasant and fulfilling?

Eventually I fall asleep and dream of stability, flat spaces, and home.

July 1955, Cascadia, Oregon

My father was preaching his Sunday-morning sermon in the small church in our logging community in the foothills of the Cascade Mountains in Oregon. As usual, I was seated by my mother, fidgeting on the hard, hot, sticky bench. It was the same every week: two church services on Sunday and, in order to keep up the momentum, one on Wednesday nights for "prayer meeting."

This was a lot of sitting for a marginally hyperactive five-year-old whose mother in the 1950s was not burdened with modern tools of diagnosis and diversion. Instead of providing medication and coloring books, she provided me, without feeling any sense of guilt whatsoever, with all the treatment I needed—a stern reminder to behave.

That Sunday morning, not yet able to read and desperate for amusement, I paged through my mother's Bible, looking for pictures. To my disappointment there were none, but there were some colored maps in the back. On those maps, with bits of whispered help from my mother, I met Abraham drifting southward through the Promised Land, Moses leading the Children of Israel out of Egypt through the desert, Jesus wandering around the Sea of Galilee, and Paul sailing up and down the Mediterranean Sea.

In the weeks that followed, I studied those maps and eventually became aware that God's people, especially the important individuals in the Bible, seemed to travel a lot, leaving long, colored trails behind them.

The routes of the Apostle Paul fascinated me most, for his travels were so extensive that the map makers had to use a bewildering assortment of colors or styles of lines just to keep the various journeys separate. This was difficult because he seemed to backtrack and repeat certain routes a lot. Paul's travels provided the most entertainment as I tried to trace each of his separate journeys, from beginning to end, without ending up in Antioch instead of Jerusalem. I liked Paul a lot.

In my 50s now, I'm still fascinated by these maps. I think the Bible must be the only sacred book in the world with maps of real places inside the back cover. These are unusual maps, depicting not just the changing borders of countries through history and locations of cities, but also actual routes traveled by people like Abraham, Moses, Jesus, and Paul. All of the maps and the routes, except Paul's, are exclusively on land. (The Sea of Galilee on which Jesus sailed occasionally on a small boat doesn't really qualify as a sea.) Of the heroes of faith, Paul was the only seafarer. Paul was different.

Seafarers have always been different from their land-bound contemporaries, and in their differences, seafarers have changed the world. They've demonstrated that there is more—always more—people, places, gold, languages, and land. Seafarers have expanded their own, and everyone else's, universe. They've taught people to think globally. They've provided connections between isolated societies, and in the process, empires became larger, trade and war expanded, and ideas spread.

Seafarers were the forerunners of the Internet and globalization. They introduced alcohol, weapons, education, new food, germs, and ideas to people who couldn't resist even when they tried. They carried gold away and left corpses behind. Many never returned from their ports of departure but died on the sea or in the lands they discovered. Others survived to grow obscenely wealthy, to enslave their hosts, and to build mansions that are now registered as National or World Heritage Sites. Whether seafarers brought hope or tragedy to their destinations, they always brought change.

Seafaring exploration and change go together like wind and waves. Men on ships, like seeds carried on winds or attached to animal fur, plant strange new ideas into the fertile fields of culture where they fall. If they take root, they may cross-fertilize, flourish, and eventually dominate and replace the indigenous varieties before they've had time to develop resistance. When seafarers return to their homes, they often bring the fruits of these cross-fertilized ideas back with them.

What follows is a sailing story, following one of the most influential explorers of history who, traveling by land and sea, succeeded incredibly to introduce an idea—the "good news," Paul called it—into the pagan world dominated by the Roman Empire with its ancient and modern gods. Paul's efforts changed history. Our voyage in this book was motivated from the beginning by a desire to better understand this unique and controversial man— a former terrorist turned seafarer, explorer, innovator, missionary, theologian, and saint—the Apostle Paul.

Explorers are easily admired or despised but not easily understood without going along on the trip. To really appreciate the experiences, drama, and development of Paul the explorer, you need to sail with him to Cyprus, up the Turkish coast, and among the Greek islands of the Aegean. You need to voyage from Caesarea to Rome and travel the dusty, rugged interior of Turkey and Greece. On the Mediterranean Sea that is both terrifying and idyllic, on the long, parched roads of those biblical maps, you will discover Paul, not only as the tireless missionary or the controversial theologian, but as an explorer and experimenter whose influence continues to shape the world.

Over the years, while serving as a missionary and pastor overseas, I read all the books I could find about Paul the missionary. As a theologian of sorts, I followed the theories and debates about the meaning of Paul's writings. As a traveler I visited many of the places Paul preached. But following the routes of Paul through storms, darkness, cold, and heat, listening to the roar of the waves or the flapping of sails, approaching the legendary islands of the Aegean, anchoring in ancient harbors with their ruins of theaters and temples along the Greek and Turkish coastlines, viewing the fascinating cultures of the Mediterranean from sea level, following the voyages that changed the world, it is as a traveler and especially as a sailor, that I have come to better understand and appreciate Paul.

I invite you on board *SailingActs* to sail with Paul.

CHAPTER 1

Dreaming of Sailing Acts

We were standing at the ancient harbor of Caesarea, on the coast of Israel between Tel Aviv and Haifa, gazing out across the Mediterranean in the direction of Rome, when suddenly, as if being surrounded by a light brighter than the midday sun, it hit me. I was due for a sabbatical from Eastern Mennonite University (EMU) where I teach courses on religion, culture, and mission. Standing there in Caesarea, looking toward Rome, it was crystal clear that I'd spend that sabbatical following the sea routes of Paul marked on the maps in the back of my mother's Bible which I had studied 50 years earlier.

This was in February 2001. Janet and I were in Caesarea leading a group of students for a semester-long study program in the Middle East. In Israel, where we were spending about six weeks, the students were taking an intensive two-week course from the Jerusalem University College called "Biblical Geography, History, and Archeology."

We marveled at Herod's Caesarea as we clambered over the well-preserved aqueduct, the remains of pagan temples, and the hippodrome. It was at Herod's most impressive engineering feat of all in Caesarea, the artificial harbor that was constructed using the new invention of concrete, where everything came together. Looking out toward Rome over the Mediterranean from that ancient harbor, my admiration for the Apostle Paul, the opportunity for a year-long sabbatical, the attraction and interest Janet and I have for the rich cultures and fascinating history of the Mediterranean, and our shared love of sailing—and possibly just some plain short-sighted optimism—all formed a question with only one possible answer. Why not spend the year sailing the Mediterranean, tracing the routes of Paul's missionary travels, visiting every site mentioned in the book of Acts? Why not?

I had just finished reading two books, Bruce Feiler's *Walking the Bible,* and *We Followed Odysseus* by Hal Roth. I was ready to explore ancient voyages just like they had. I wanted to sail all the routes, visit all the harbors, and travel all the roads that Paul had traveled in Acts. The prospect of Janet and me sailing in the Mediterranean, digging up new insights into Paul and his contribution to the world, seemed not only completely logical, but irresistible.

I suspected Janet was not struck with the same life-changing revelation there at Caesarea. I now faced the delicate task familiar to seafaring men since the invention of boats: persuading their wives to let them go, or perhaps even accompany them on their "life-enriching," "completely safe," "horizon-expanding" journeys. Men have (foolheartedly?) scoffed for centuries to their shocked wives and loved ones as they confidently prepared for insane voyages: "Don't be ridiculous!"

Fearing categorical rejection, I outlined the plans to Janet, which went roughly like this: Save up money during the next couple of years. Buy an old but seaworthy boat somewhere in the Mediterranean. Fix it up. Sail the Acts routes of Paul in the Aegean in the 2004 sailing season. Winter in Israel and write. Sail the route from Caesarea to Rome in the summer of 2005. Sell the boat at the end.

To my amazement and delight, Janet actually supported and improved the ideas.

So began two years of reading. I read books about the Mediterranean, sailing, and regional travel and history. I read books on Paul's thought and his travels, and a novel called *Paul,*

and books on first-century culture, life, and travel in the Roman Empire.

We also began saving money. The sabbatical, if approved, would pay me two-thirds of my salary for a year. We figured this would cover our living expenses. All other expenses, such as buying and outfitting a sailboat, would be our own responsibility.

We started Googling the Internet, researching sailboats suitable for cruising the Mediterranean and living on for over a year. We combed the "boats for sale" sites, looking for the best boat we could buy on a limited budget.

I sent $48 to a company that produces gigantic charts of the Mediterranean Sea and, when they arrived a week later, taped them together and fastened them to a wall in our basement. They formed a 6x12-foot mega-chart for plotting routes and dreaming.

I spent evenings looking at the amazing variety of countries around the rim of the Mediterranean—Spain, France, Italy, Greece, Slovenia, Croatia, Montenegro, Albania, Turkey, Syria, Lebanon, Israel, the Gaza Strip, Egypt, Libya, Algeria, and Morocco. I thought about the way the Roman Empire once tied them all together, how Christianity did the same, and how Islam attempted to do so. We'd be sailing history, religion, and cultures when we sailed the Mediterranean, the liquid center of an incredible empire.

We tied rope to objects in the basement and, in front of that huge chart, practiced our bowlines, clove hitches, sheet bends, and other knots. We hung another smaller chart of the Mediterranean in our library above the desk with the planned routes boldly drawn. This one was to impress our guests. I figured the more people who knew of our plans, the harder it would be for us to back out if we got cold feet.

Janet and I gave each other presents like foul-weather gear and safety harnesses for three Christmases in a row. For Christmas 2001, Janet and I gave each other a "Comprehensive Sailing Course" to be taken the following summer. We made it increasingly difficult to change our minds. We were giving each other gifts of commitment.

Two years of thinking through the implications the idea would have on our future forced us to face some tough issues. One of the most difficult decisions concerned Janet's position as EMU's director of parent and alumni relations. She spent 12 rewarding and challenging years in this position, and wanted to continue. She proposed a leave of absence, which was denied. If Janet wanted to be part of the sabbatical project, she needed to resign her position with no guarantees of a future position at EMU when she returned. We talked about it often. "Maybe you could continue," I suggested, "and join me in the summers for a while."

But Janet wanted to take part in the whole thing and so, after weighing the options, she resigned from a position she loved and informed a tearful staff. Doubts, tears, fears, euphoria, excitement, uncertainty, and occasional struggles with depression went into this tough decision.

In the summer of 2002, Janet and I took the sailing course we'd given each other as presents the previous Christmas. It wasn't that we didn't know how to sail. We'd learned during the years we lived in Perth, Australia, from 1986-1990. We had arrived in Australia just as the America's Cup races were finishing in Perth, and the excitement moved us to take advantage of the vast sailing waters in and around Perth. We bought a small sailboat and learned to sail. After moving to Virginia in 1991, we bought a small "pocket cruiser," a 16-foot, trailerable Compac Yacht in which we explored the Chesapeake Bay for a number of summers.

What Janet and I had never done was prolonged cruising, passage-making, and living aboard a sailboat for more than three days at a time. Now we were planning 15 months in foreign cultures, unknown seas, and new living conditions.

The intensive American Sailing Association course took us through three levels in one week: Basic Keelboat Sailing Standard, Basic Coastal Cruising Standard, and Bareboat Chartering Standard. During this week aboard a 41-foot Benentau, we became familiar with the abundance of skills needed for extended cruising: boat and sail handling under all kinds of conditions; navigation; mechanics; maintenance; and living in claustrophobic, tiny spaces with others.

Captain Joe, the instructor, was adamant about the value of this course. "If one of you falls overboard," he lectured Janet and me, "the other has to be able to rescue that person without any help."

Then he made Janet and me practice with a life jacket he'd fling into the water without warning, yelling, "Man overboard!" He'd let whichever one of us was at the wheel at the time turn the 41-foot monster around by ourselves and rescue the life jacket. This isn't an easy task for one person in a stiff breeze under sail. To put it bluntly, I'm fortunate it was just a life jacket being rescued that first time and not myself—or I wouldn't be writing this book! Later, sailing in the Mediterranean, we'd appreciate the value of that excellent course over and over again. At the end of the week, we passed the exam and each received a little log book documenting our success.

Two years before our planned departure in May 2004, we designated a cabinet in our library as our "sea chest" into which we put anything we planned to take with us for the voyage. It gradually filled with books, instruments, boating gear, and documents. We proudly added the log books to this growing collection.

But we were preparing and saving for a sabbatical that wasn't yet approved by the university. EMU is a wonderful place to work, with administrators who care about faculty and staff. However, it is still an institution and, like all institutions, it has procedures and schedules for making decisions. The deadline for applying for a sabbatical for the following academic year is September 15. But how could I make concrete plans to move ahead on buying a sailboat in time to be ready to sail in May 2004 if the sabbatical was not certain until October 2003?

So on May 21, 2003, I submitted a proposal long before the deadline with a letter of explanation. Having submitted the letter, there was nothing to do but to plow ahead with preparations as if the proposal would be approved. Better to have made plans and be disappointed if they cannot be implemented, I reasoned, than to wait until it's too late to implement plans if and when the proposal is approved.

If timing was one issue, approval was another. Writing the proposal to be reviewed by a faculty proved challenging. I was afraid that the project would sound to the landlubbers on the decision-making committee like far too much fun rather than serious academic research. This needed to be remedied but it couldn't be done by trying to persuade the nonsailors that sailing is often demanding work, uncomfortable living, and a downright terrifying endeavor when it's not boring, frustrating, expensive, and slow. No, the proposal would need to address thesis, goals, methods, and outcomes. It needed to argue that the only way to learn how Paul's experiences in travel shaped his thinking and his message would be to sail the routes he did.

Feeling pleased about submitting a well-reasoned thesis rather than "we are going to enjoy life on the sunny Mediterranean aboard a yacht," I waited all summer for the response. But, of course, there was none. The sabbatical committee of solid, academic, earth-dwelling types wouldn't meet until fall, no matter how desperate I was.

The fall semester of 2003 began as usual. I was teaching a full load and trying not to worry. The committee was scheduled to meet to make the decision sometime in October. On October 9, walking across campus in the perfect weather and magnificent colors of fall in the Shenandoah Valley, I happened to meet one of the committee members who said nonchalantly, "We're going to decide on your sabbatical proposal this afternoon."

I gulped. Really? This was earlier than I had thought. Now, the possibility of *not* getting approval loomed menacingly. "When will I find out?" I quavered to the committee member.

"Oh, the provost will send you a letter soon."

So the decision will be made and I will be the last one to find out, I thought. *It will be hard not to worry.*

Hard? It was impossible. I began building scenarios of rejection, how I would appeal, negotiate, apply again. *No, I'd tell myself, the answer will be yes. It has to be! If not, we won't be able to afford a leave of absence for a year without shifting my research topic from Paul to something like piracy.*

For the next three days I couldn't convince myself more than a few minutes at a time before the doubts would return. *Surely if they approved it they'd tell me right away,* I thought one moment. Then in the next, *No, they'd tell me immediately if I didn't get approval. They'd inform me of the good news with a proper letter.*

On the third day of this pitched, mental battle, I met the academic dean coming out of the auditorium. She said, "Have you had any feedback from your proposal?"

"No," I said my heart pounding, "can you tell me something?"

"Well," the dean hedged, "you have more in it than you can do."

But it is approved?! I screamed mentally. Orally, it came out something like, "Would you be able to tell me whether or not it is approved at this point?"

"Yes, with a few modifications, which the committee recommended. It is approved."

I'm not really the type of person who hugs academic deans on a regular basis, but at that moment I couldn't help myself. I threw my arms around her as I realized that, after almost three years of dreaming and preparing, *we were going to sail the Mediterranean with Paul!* Paul himself, commissioned by the church to sail from Antioch to Cyprus in 47 A.D. for his first mission journey, could not have been happier.

Janet was coordinating the EMU homecoming events that weekend and was not available to discuss our plans at length, but I caught up with her long enough to share the good news. Alone that evening I got out a calendar and realized that life had not gotten easier with the news of that day. Here it was, already October. In January, Janet and I were scheduled to take another group of students to the Middle East for the semester, returning to campus in late April. In addition to my regular full teaching load that fall, we had to finish preparing for that cross-cultural semester and had already started to meet regularly with the 29 students who were going along. Then we would be with the students in the troubled Middle East. This did not seem like the ideal conditions for carefully planning and preparing for a sailing sabbatical.

Since ancient times, and even today, the summer sailing season in the Mediterranean for most people starts in May and runs through September. In order to meet our voyage goals, we needed to start sailing in the first summer by June at the latest, preferably in May. But not only did we have no boat, we hadn't even *started* the boat purchase process. Yes, I had spent many hours intently surfing the Internet looking at sailboats listed for sale in the Mediterranean, but the promising ones were clearly for people who owned computer companies, and the cheap ones looked like their mooring lines were all that kept them above the water line.

We decided roughly what we wanted: something about 33 to 34 feet long, old enough to be affordable yet well designed, in good enough shape, and built ruggedly enough to be seaworthy in all kinds of weather. Speed under sail wasn't too important. She shouldn't look too modern; a charter-type, sleek party boat just wouldn't fit the image for the project. She should have plenty of space for living for 15 months, with room to take guests along occasionally.

So looking at the calendar that October, I realized, soberly, that we had only about eight weeks left to finalize *all* of the plans, including buying a sailboat, before leaving for the Middle East. I had no clue of the legal hurdles of buying, as an American, a boat with a foreign flag. This was good, because if I had known, I might have given up right then.

November arrived and I spent every day teaching and planning for the semester in the Middle East, and every evening in front of the computer, searching the Internet for boats for sale and regulations for buying them. I wrote to brokers in Greece, Cyprus, England, and the United States. If they responded at all, they seemed to have nothing promising.

The pressure mounted. Maybe we need to postpone for a year, we thought as Thanksgiving approached. Maybe we need to buy a boat in the United States and ship it to the Mediterranean. Maybe we could *sail* one from the United States to the Mediterranean.

"No!" said Janet with the authority of the first mate.

"Why not?"

"Figure it out," she said. "You don't have enough time for that even if you did know what you were doing."

I figured it out. She was right.

Just before Thanksgiving, a picture of a boat in Volos, Greece, a place I had never heard of before, appeared on a Web site. The picture showed a rugged, rather traditional looking boat with two masts—a ketch—sailing smartly along with its three brilliant white sails filled with wind, heeling slightly in sparkling blue water with white spray flying, silhouetted against a perfect blue sky. Sitting in the cockpit were three relaxed sailors. I looked closely. One looked a little like me.

I read the advertisement. "For Sale: Westerly 33, Sailing Yacht *Aldebaran* built 1979. One owner. 35,000 euros. Located in Volos, Greece." The price in U.S. dollars was $41,500.

I carefully looked over all the information on the Web site again and again, which included several sketches of the British-built Westerly 33 inside and out. The description, sketches, photos, and price were all attractive. Something about this boat seemed right, a feeling I'd never had looking at the hundreds of boats for sale in the Mediterranean. I printed the information and showed it to Janet. Her response was exactly the same as mine.

"Write to him right away."

I did. "Dear Captain Steve Hadjistamatiou," I wrote, carefully spelling out his last name. "I have seen your boat advertised on the Web and am very interested in it. Could you answer a few questions?" I hit "send" and shut off the computer.

All of my correspondence about prospective boats up until that point had been with boat brokers, not the actual owners. From this experience, and because I was writing to a Greek sea captain across six time zones, I didn't expect a reply for at least a week. But when I opened my e-mail at work the next morning, there was a reply from Captain Hadjistamatiou. I didn't know it at the time, but I was entering the strange new world of buying a boat I had never seen, from a man I had never met, in a place I had never visited (Volos, Greece).

But wanting as many options as possible, I kept looking for boats on the Internet. As December approached, the urgency of having a boat in place before leaving for the Middle East in January increased every day. A few days later, I spotted another Westerly 33 for sale in Greece, listed with a British brokerage, and sent an e-mail requesting further details. I was impressed with another quick response describing the boat. *Another good possibility,* I thought as I read the description. *Now we have two good options.*

The information did not include the name of the boat, but the description seemed very similar to the *Aldebaran*, except that the price was about $3,000 more. I was attracted to the *Aldebaran* because of the price, but was a little wary of doing business by e-mail with someone on the other side of the planet whom I had never met and didn't know if I could trust. I began corresponding seriously with the broker.

So with two good prospects, I began to relax just a little. Maybe we'd be able to find a decent boat and begin the process of buying before we left for the Middle East in January. The

British brokerage put me in touch with Gregory, an independent Greek yacht broker in the Athens area who handled the boats listed in Greece. I was impressed by the helpfulness and competence of the brokerage and Gregory, and decided that I'd buy their boat instead of the *Aldebaran* directly from the owner.

"Where is the boat located?" I wrote to Gregory.

"Volos," came the reply. Suddenly it dawned on me that there was only one Westerly 33 for sale, not two. The owner and the broker were both advertising the same boat! I was corresponding to both about the *Aldebaran* without knowing it. Now we were back to one boat and two Greek sellers. This was not an improvement.

This was the first of many times that I was bungling into very unfamiliar territory. Should I buy from Captain Steve and save $3,000? But what about the legal work? What if he cheats me? Maybe I should spend the extra $3,000 and go through the broker. He could walk us through the steps and would likely look after our interests. Janet agreed.

"Dear Captain Steve," I wrote on December 10. "We are very, very interested in moving ahead with the purchase of the *Aldebaran*, but I have decided to work with Gregory because of the red tape involved."

Captain Steve wrote back. "That's okay with me but you will pay $3,000 more than you need to."

I continued to send and receive e-mails almost daily to and from either Gregory or Captain Steve about the *Aldebaran*. Gregory sent me a list of steps that needed to occur to buy a boat in Greece and warned me that each step involving an official stamp from a governmental office could take considerable extra time.

"The purchase process will go something like this," Gregory explained in an e-mail. "First you and the owner agree on a price. Then both the buyer and the seller will sign the memorandum of agreement. You can then have the boat surveyed and make the final deal contingent on the boat being in roughly the condition the seller claims it is. When you and the seller reach an agreement, you put down a deposit and that finalizes the deal. When further paperwork is completed and full payment is received by the lawyer, the boat must be de-registered in Greece and clear customs. You will then have to re-register the boat in the United States. She will fly the U.S. flag and you can rename the *Aldebaran* at that time if you want to. All of this from the Greek side will take about 90 days if everything goes well."

Gregory did not say precisely what each step would cost. He hinted fairly often about inevitable delays and I realized we had no time to waste. If we wanted to sail by June, we'd need to keep moving ahead with the purchase process and preparations.

With only weeks before departure for the Middle East, we decided to proceed with the purchase of the *Aldebaran* and committed to this by e-mail. Gregory wrote back, "Send 10 percent for a deposit, and the *Aldebaran* cannot be sold to someone else in the meantime."

We decided to take the risk of the *Aldebaran* being sold to someone else; we'd wait until we got a chance to see her before committing the deposit. We agreed that I would fly to Athens from Tel Aviv during the spring break in March when we were in the Middle East. I would look at the *Aldebaran* and a number of other boats in Greece, and make the final decision at that point. We'd either buy the *Aldebaran* if she hadn't been sold to someone else in the meantime and if she appeared to be in the same good condition as she looked on the Internet. Or, we'd buy another boat that might be a better purchase.

We started thinking about a name for whatever vessel we'd sail. "How about a Greek word connected to the Apostle Paul?" I asked Janet.

"You mean the Greek word for shipwreck?"

"No, I had in mind something like *Apostolos* (apostle). Or how about *Aggelos* (messenger) or *Klaytos* (called). All seemed too theological for a boat name. How about *Hermes*? Too pagan. *Paulus*? Too masculine. How about keeping the name *Aldebaran*—the name of a huge star? Too irrelevant.

Paul's journeys are recorded in detail in the New Testament book, The Acts of the Apostles, or Acts for short. We'd been talking about "sailing Acts" for some time as the name of the project and a possible book title.

"Why not use 'sailing Acts' as the name of the boat, too?" I suggested to Janet one day. So *SailingActs* became the name of the future boat. This name, we reasoned, could be interpreted two ways. For people familiar with the voyages of Paul in the book of Acts, the name would fit in a literary sense. For those with no familiarity with Acts, it would also describe what we'd be doing in a literal sense—*acting* as if we knew what we were doing as we sailed the Mediterranean.

A few days later, just before Christmas, I ordered a set of decals with the name *SailingActs* and the port of registration as Alexandria, VA, estimating the size and the color of the wording to fit with what was visible on the photograph of the *Aldebaran* posted by Captain Steve on the Internet. This order, as well as charts, almanacs, cruising guides, and airline tickets back to Greece in May, all needed to be placed and received before we left for the Middle East in January. We'd have exactly 10 days between the time we'd return in April from the Middle East and May 6, when I would fly to Greece to begin the sabbatical.

In December 2003, the month of finals, grading, reading papers, submitting grades, and Christmas vacation, we met for the final orientation for the Middle-East students just before they left for Christmas break. They'd return in January, eager for the Middle East and, hopefully, well prepared.

On Christmas Eve, as is our tradition since living in Germany, we carefully lit the real candles on the tree and sang a few carols, including "Oh Little Town of Bethlehem." "The hopes and fears of all the years, are met in thee tonight," we sang and I thought of the future, of leaving for the third trip to the troubled Middle East with 29 students, of continuing to plan and prepare for the sabbatical venture immediately following the semester, of needing to purchase a boat by March at the latest or call off the whole thing for another year.

The hopes and fears of the sabbatical are with me tonight, I thought, *and will likely be with us for the whole time between now and when we actually begin sailing Acts. I sense that hopes and fears will be with us during many points of the voyage itself. It will likely be a way of life during the 15 months of sailing Acts.*

I looked around at the warm traditions, happy faces, and safe home in the soft glow of candlelight and realized that the coming year would be so unlike that moment. We'd be sailing. We'd be challenged and confused and afraid.

We were at home that Christmas Eve, but the voyage had already begun with the planning; the plans had already started to change before we even implemented them. We were, I realized, no longer in control of our project. The project would be taking us far beyond our plans and expectations. What happened from here on would be even less predictable than anything up to that point. We had not begun the voyage of sailing Acts, but on that night, Christmas Eve 2003, I felt I was already beginning to understand sea people, explorers, and the Apostle Paul just a little better in preparing to do so.

On Christmas morning, we gave each other sailing gifts again. I gave Janet and myself identical sailing caps with *SailingActs* and a sailboat logo embroidered on the front. We would not wear them, we agreed, until we were in the Mediterranean, sailing Acts on *SailingActs*.

CHAPTER 2

Buying the *Aldebaran*

The Christmas holidays ended. On January 10, 2004, the 29 students we were taking to the Middle East returned to EMU with their crisp, clean passports, new luggage, and great anticipation. Janet and I had battered passports, well-used luggage, and nagging trepidation.

We were taking a group of students to the Middle East for the third time since the *intifada* began in Israel/Palestine in the fall of 2000. We would, as usual, be living and studying in both Israel and the West Bank. The students would become friends of people who hated and feared each other. We'd endure endless security checks and go through tense border checkpoints. We'd experience that the Middle East has not changed very much since the days of the Roman Empire. "Peace," when there has been any in the Middle East, has been won when one side was powerful enough to dominate the other into sullen submission, or, as is more often the case in history, when an outside empire brutally imposes peace through military occupation.

We flew to Frankfurt, then on to Cairo, crossing the Alps, then the Mediterranean. Looking down we could see the islands and could even make out the shape of the boot of Italy. Looking carefully we saw tiny dots on the surface of the water, boats, looking small and stationary from the airplane. Janet and I exchanged glances; we'd soon be on a small speck, looking up at airplanes.

We approached the brown sand of Egypt that met the azure-blue waters of the Mediterranean. We spotted large vessels clustered around the Mediterranean mouth of the Suez Canal, cargo ships heading for the Red Sea and on to the Orient. The transportation of goods across the Mediterranean has a history of thousands of years. In the first century, the largest ships were those carrying grain from Egypt to the hungry Empire, especially to the city of Rome. Travel and shipping were not easy in the first century, but at least there were no problems with hostile nations. We'd be crossing tense borders, waiting at military checkpoints, traveling through tiny countries carved out through violence and unilateral decisions of outside powers. We'd be using pounds, dinars, shekels, and euros, and learning to say "thank you" in four languages as we made our way around the Mediterranean—sea of blood and empires, faith and hatred, power and glory.

I thought about Paul, looking down at this sea of history, the "wine-dark sea" of Homer's Odysseus, the terrifying sea of the biblical Jonah, the useful sea of the Phoenicians, and especially Paul. When he traveled, Rome dominated. Rome did what no other empire accomplished. It imposed a form of peace completely around the Mediterranean and introduced promising new possibilities for those who cooperated with its power, and fearsome consequences for those who did not. Rome finally destroyed the pirates that plagued sea travel on the Mediterranean for centuries. People of the Empire could sail the entire rim of the Mediterranean and could communicate in Greek everywhere. There were no borders, no currency problems, and no language barriers that restricted travel.

Janet and I have loved the Mediterranean ever since traveling through Italy, Greece, Turkey, and Israel for several extended times in the 1970s, which included living for almost a year in Israel during the Yom Kippur War of October 1973. We love the intensity and variety of cultures, cuisines, and religions. We find no place as fascinating as the Mediterranean, cradle of Western civilization, the sun-baked lands of faith and fear circling this sparkling sea.

The plane landed at the Cairo airport. We disembarked in the shocking January heat of the desert. Our Egyptian friend and guide, Osama ("of no relation to bin Laden," he joked to the students), was waiting. We climbed aboard the bus, drove through the frantic streets of Cairo, and checked into the Ambassador Hotel. It was good to be back but this time we couldn't help thinking about our next flight to the Mediterranean, when we would begin the voyage by sailboat. *Next time there will be no Osamas to help us,* I thought. *We'll be on our own.*

In free moments we slipped into Internet cafés and checked our e-mail. Everywhere we went, no matter how remote the village, it seemed the students could find an Internet café within about 30 minutes after arriving in a new place. By e-mail we stayed in touch with sons David and Jon; EMU colleagues; the students living in our house; Captain Steve, the owner of *Aldebaran*; and Gregory, the yacht broker.

E-mails from either Captain Steve or Gregory inevitably caused my heart to race. Were they writing to say that the *Aldebaran* has been sold? Had the deal derailed in some other way? Have they changed the price? "I will definitely come to see the *Aldebaran* in March," I wrote several times.

By the end of January, we moved through Jordan and were crossing the Allenby Bridge into the West Bank and up to Jerusalem. This time we were all concerned, because several days before arriving to the border we received news from several sources that the Israelis were refusing entry to groups and individuals who were planning to visit the West Bank.

At the border, the Israelis grilled us about our travel plans but never asked if we were planning to go to the West Bank, a fact we did not volunteer. Having cleared the passport control, we boarded the chartered bus and wound our way past the tip of the Dead Sea, Jericho, and up the steep ascent through the Judean hills toward Jerusalem. Then, following a brief stop on the top of

the Mount of Olives for a view of the magnificent Dome of the
Rock and the ancient city of Jerusalem, we continued south
toward Bethlehem.

The Alternative Tourism Group which organized our time in
the West Bank had, as usual, lined up a variety of organizations,
speakers, and experiences to immerse the students in the realities
of the region. For three weeks the students would live in
Palestinian homes, take Arabic language classes, and listen to
Palestinians analyze, describe, and explain their experiences,
their struggle, the conflict, their hopes, and their fears.

In spare moments the students began to make travel plans for
spring break during the first week in March. I made my own
plans and purchased a round-trip flight from the Ben Gurion
Airport in Tel Aviv to Athens. Janet would stay in Jerusalem to be
available to students needing assistance during their travel. But I
had a boat to buy. The closer we got to March 1 without an e-mail
from Captain Steve or Gregory saying the *Aldebaran* had been
sold, the more I dreamed of buying her. In my imagination, she
became a thing of beauty and I could see her sailing, white sails
full, spray flying. I imagined sitting in the cockpit in the port of
some quaint Greek island. It would be morning and I'd be sip-
ping a cup of steaming coffee while reading the *Herald Tribune.*
The decks would be spotless, the teak glowing. People would
pause and admire *SailingActs* as they walked by on the wharf.
"Where did you get that beautiful boat?" they'd ask. I would nonchalantly glance up and take another sip of coffee. "I picked her
up in Volos," I'd say.

Two weeks before spring break, we left the West Bank with
the students and moved to Jerusalem to begin a two-week intensive course at the Jerusalem University College called "Biblical
Geography, Archeology, and History," taught by Dr. Paul Wright.
For two weeks we clambered up tells, hiked through *wadis* (dry
gorges), investigated ruins, descended into caves, felt our way
through black tunnels, struggled up mountains and down cliffs,
visited churches, and formed a long, pale, American line as we

pushed our way through the crowded streets in the old city of Jerusalem. We memorized maps, soil types, and weather patterns. And in the end, the students recognized a whole new dimension of the historical accuracy and the contemporary power of the familiar biblical stories. "To understand the Bible," Dr. Wright often told the students, "you must read it with your feet."

How about the book of Acts? I'd think to myself. *To understand that part of the Bible, to understand the Apostle Paul, wouldn't you have to read Acts by sailboat?*

Dr. Wright had been describing the land of Israel as "the land between." Israel's geographical location between Babylon and Egypt, Asia and Africa, the sea and the desert, the Fertile Crescent and the Nile Delta, make it a land bridge. And as all important bridges, it has always carried the trade, traffic, and armies of empires, making this bridge a precarious place to live.

"If Israel is the 'land between'," I asked Dr. Wright the day we visited the port city of Caesarea, "couldn't Paul be called the 'man between'? Didn't he serve as a bridge between monotheistic Judaism and polytheistic paganism? Didn't he seek to bring Jew and Greek together? Didn't that make him vulnerable like the land and the people of Israel in history?"

"Yes," Dr. Wright agreed, "Paul was extraordinary, a pioneer with amazing stamina, vision, and courage, a Jew who traveled, not because he had to or because of business, but because of the faith he wanted to share with everyone, including the pagan peoples of the Mediterranean. He was the first follower of Jesus who had the vision of taking the message of Jesus of Nazareth to all the peoples of the entire Roman Empire."

Standing in Caesarea that day, I gazed toward Rome, the Empire's center of political, military, economic, and administrative power in Paul's day. It was invisible across the waters. I looked back toward Jerusalem, the religious, administrative, and social center of Judaism. Jerusalem also was hidden, not by water, but by land. Why did the aging Paul have such a strong desire to go to Rome instead of retiring in Jerusalem, his work accomplished? I hoped to find some answers sailing Acts.

The Jerusalem University College course ended on Saturday, February 28. At 2:00 the next morning, the alarm rang. My flight, as do most flights from Ben Gurion Airport to Europe, was scheduled to leave in the wee hours of the morning. I quickly checked in the campus computer lab for any e-mails from Gregory or Captain Steve. Both had sent last-minute information. I printed the e-mails and stuck them in my daypack. It was time to leave for the airport and fly to Athens.

A shuttle picked me up at the Jerusalem University College gate for the one-hour ride from Jerusalem to Ben Gurion. We meandered through the dark streets of Jerusalem, picking up other passengers: a Hassidic Jewish couple with eight pieces of luggage, Orthodox businessmen, and American students. *I bet I'm the only person going to buy a boat in Greece,* I thought.

By 4:50 a.m., I was through all the security checks and was waiting in the lounge, groggily rereading the last e-mails from Gregory and Captain Steve. Gregory had e-mailed the name of a budget hotel near the Acropolis in Athens, with instructions to call him when I arrived.

At 5:30 a.m., the sleep-starved passengers shuffled on board the Olympic flight. I dozed as we took off, then awakened when an Orthodox Jew stood up in the aisle, donned his prayer shawl, and began rocking back and forth for his morning prayers just as the plane began its descent. The Greek flight attendants frowned and rolled their eyes at one another behind his back, grunting their exasperation every time they squeezed past. The praying man paid no attention

Jew and Greek, I thought. *What would Paul have acted like if he were on this airplane from Israel to Greece? Paul, too, was a Jew sur-*

rounded by impatient Greeks on the ships he sailed back and forth between Palestine and the Aegean.

We landed at the gleaming new Athens airport and the taxi driver who took me to the hotel charged double what the meter showed, but I was too tired and excited to protest more than a minute or two. I hoped this wasn't indicative of the way my other business transactions in Greece would occur.

The "budget" category of the hotel became apparent as soon as I checked in. The television didn't work and the toilet leaked water all over the floor, though the price and location were excellent. But I had come to buy a boat, not stay in a hotel room watching TV with dry feet.

February 29 was a beautiful Sunday morning in Athens. The sun shone on the Acropolis, and the *agora* (ancient marketplace) lay just across the street. After being up all night, I was ravenous, so I found a sidewalk café in the vicinity and enjoyed an omelet and coffee while feasting my eyes on the Acropolis and the Aeropogus next to it. Paul's territory—only two blocks away!

I was transfixed thinking of the gods and the gospel meeting almost 2,000 years ago right in this area. Church bells began to ring and I noted the difference between the church bells in Athens and the electronic voices of mullahs declaring Allah's greatness back in Jerusalem. *Paul was here.*

Back in the hotel room I called Gregory and received a recorded message in gentle, Greek-accented English informing me that he was not in at the moment but that I could call back later. This was fine. Now I had time to explore the Acropolis again, and to spend time in the *agora* reconstructing the scenario from Acts 17 when Paul preached his famous sermon at the Aeropogus.

Athens in the spring of 2004, five months before the summer Olympics, was a huge site of frantic construction. I thought about the effort and expense for ancient Athenians to build the Acropolis, and the effort and expense for modern Athenians to host the Olympics. *Is modern Athens any different than ancient*

SailingActs

Athens? Did Paul's visit here really change anything in Athens other than the bells on Sunday morning?

It was afternoon, and the two hours of sleep the night before were beginning to catch up. I dragged myself to the last site of the day, the ruins of the once mighty Temple of Zeus, and observed the ever-present stray dogs sleeping in the shade of the pillars. *Homeless dogs sleeping in the shade of homeless, sleeping gods,* I thought. *Yes, Paul's visit did change Athens, at least for the gods. Paul was here.*

Back at the hotel again I called and spoke to Gregory for the first time. We agreed to meet on Tuesday. This gave me a much-needed day to meet with Anwar, our travel agent in Athens, in order to finalize the arrangements for when the students would arrive in the city in April.

I fell asleep the instant I lay down on the saggy bed. But in the middle of the night I woke in a slight panic. *If I put my life savings into a boat, what if I can't sell it at the end of the voyage? What about taxes? Where am I to register it? How do I transfer funds? Can this all be done in time to start the voyage in May?* I thought of the challenges I'd face the next few days, of Greek sellers and weak dollars, of taxes, customs, and regulations. It's funny how things you've successfully dealt with in the light of day return in the middle of the night to haunt you. I forced myself to think of other things, like sailing effortlessly in perfect conditions, and eventually fell asleep.

Today I'll meet Gregory and begin ship-shopping, I thought the moment I woke Tuesday morning. *May this start well,* I prayed.

I was waiting in the lobby/breakfast area of the hotel when a bearded, T-shirted man walked in. "Hello, I'm Gregory," he said, "let's go." We climbed into his little Suzuki vehicle, a half-miniature truck, half-compact car so popular in Greece. I noticed that the back was filled with papers, rusty tools, and partly eaten bags of potato chips—not a good sign. Gregory appeared gentle and patient until he slipped behind the wheel of his truck/car and became, in an instant, a weaving, tailgating madman.

"I'm the broker in Greece who does the most business with foreigners," he explained, between yelling at other drivers who—in a way not apparent to me—were impeding Gregory's progress. "And I'm showing boats to several others all this week. I'm very busy."

This much was clear. I mentally diagnosed Gregory with severe attention deficit disorder within three minutes of meeting him. "Will you be taking me to see some boats today?" I asked between near collisions, a steady cacophony of honking, and Greek expletives.

Gregory began to answer, yelled at a driver, cut off another one, all the while fishing around in the back seat for a paper. I was sure he'd never find it, but I had underestimated his ability to rummage on the go. Somehow, after handing me what looked like a grocery list in Greek, then possibly a traffic ticket also in Greek, he snagged a sheet of paper with a list of about 30 boats, along with their lengths and prices. I looked over the list. Most of the boats he highlighted on the list were in the size range I requested, but only three or four were in the price range.

"We'll look at a couple of these today," Gregory promised as he inched impatiently through the congestion of Athens' port of Piraeus. "I'll show you one boat before I meet my other clients today."

At last we reached the large marina where most of his clients' boats were moored. I was a little troubled that Gregory kept mentioning all of the other clients to whom he was showing boats.

The sight of what appeared to be thousands of masts in the marina seemed promising. *Maybe I'll find a boat I like even better than the Westerly,* I thought. Gregory aimed the Suzuki down one of the narrow pontoons and stopped beside one of the most decrepit looking sailboats I've ever seen floating.

"How about this one?"

It was on the list of possibilities, a Gin Fizz, once a sleek, racy boat, now a sleek, racy disaster. The ragged sails were heaped haphazardly on the deck. Tattered ropes draped from sagging lifelines. I noticed the broken hatch locks and years of accumulated grime covering everything. I sneaked a look at Gregory to see if this might be some kind of Greek boat-broker joke, but he was completely serious. The owner drove up with the key and proudly showed me through the mangled interior, into which he had thrown all of the boat's broken equipment.

"I've just put 10,000 euros into this boat," he boasted, "and I'm not finished yet."

You are so right, I thought, *but I'm finished. You'd have to pay me at least 10,000 euros to take this thing off of your hands.* "Great boat," I said, feeling guilty for the bald-faced lie, "but I'd like to see what else Gregory has before making a decision."

"What time is it?" Gregory wanted to know.

I glanced at my watch. "Twelve-thirty."

He shot off backwards down the pontoon in his Suzuki to make a telephone call from a pay phone in the marina, leaving me alone amid the forest of masts. I noted with concern that this "successful international yacht broker" neither wore a wristwatch nor carried a cell phone. Minutes, then hours, went by as I waited for Gregory. I wandered aimlessly through the marina, filling my pockets with rocks to ward off the snarling, hungry dogs that slunk everywhere, and looked at the gleaming boats. All of the ones I saw for sale were at least $100,000 above my budget.

I began to wonder if maybe I was at the mercy of an incompetent broker, and that all the boats for sale in Greece within my budget would be floating, money-eating monsters like the one Gregory just showed me. A wave of doubt and helplessness rolled in. More would continue to roll in and out with tidal regularity all the rest of the week.

The next day was a repeat of the first: A full day with Gregory with one or two inspections of awful boats sandwiched between hours of waiting as he showed beautiful yachts to buyers with huge budgets. All these buyers had rental cars; I was stuck with Gregory and his Suzuki as he charged back and forth between marinas. This presented an additional challenge to Gregory, for all the roads around Athens were under massive construction due to the Olympics later in the year.

All the boats Gregory showed me for those two days were neglected, trash-filled, dirty disappointments. The one boat that looked somewhat promising was tightly locked and, despite trying for a very long time, Gregory could neither find a way to break in nor track down the owner who had the key. The Westerly up in Volos I had been looking at on the Internet remained the only hope.

"Tomorrow," Gregory promised on Wednesday evening, "we will go to Volos."

Gregory brought me to spend the night in Loutraki, a town outside of Athens where he lived, and checked me into a hotel so we could leave for Volos the next day without needing to fight the Athens traffic in the morning. Worry was pushing in like a high pressure system that evening.

Thursday in Volos to look at the last possibility, the Aldebaran, I thought as I tossed about in bed, trying to get some sleep. *Friday I will fly back to Jerusalem, with or without a boat. I'm not sure if the sabbatical will happen.* I thought of the Apostle Paul on his journeys, at the mercy of Greek sailors. He, too, likely waited on wharfs for Greeks, uncertain if and when he would be able to move ahead. *Maybe I'm learning something here, something good.* But I wasn't sure what it was.

I awoke early Thursday morning. *Will Gregory show up? Will today end in huge disappointment, just mild disappointment, or maybe even success?*

We were to meet at 9:00. At 9:15, Gregory called the hotel. "I'll be 15 minutes late." Based on experience during the past days, I doubled that immediately. At 9:45 he showed up and we worked our way slowly out of town as he carried on shouted conversations with friends on the street through the open car window. We dropped off a roll of film to develop ("I'll have to get a digital camera sometime," he said. *And don't forget the cell phone and watch,* I added to myself), and paid his electric bill.

At 10:30 we were finally on the road toward Volos. The route from Loutraki to Volos winds through fantastic, ancient scenery and takes five hours. We climbed over rugged mountains, through forests and rich fields, and along the sea coast. We discussed religion, culture, boats, and life. It began to rain. We arrived in Volos at dusk, the clouds low and dark. Everything was dripping wet.

Captain Steve met us on the wharf. I looked eagerly past him and there she was, tied to the wharf, gently rocking, the *Aldebaran*! She was grungy, battered, and worn, but I immediately saw something about her I hadn't seen in the other boats. She appeared sturdy, solid, with good lines. Ten seconds after arriving in Volos, while still shaking hands with Captain Steve, I saw a possibility (see Photos 1 and 2 showing the *Aldebaran* and Captain Steve).

Captain Steve was short and rotund, a former sea captain, and it showed. He'd been everywhere. He knew everything. He spoke English with command. And he was in charge. I was wary of him from the beginning. Captain Steve invited me aboard the *Aldebaran*. He opened the hatch and we descended into the cabin, which smelled strongly of diesel and stale cigarette smoke. The water dripped through the open hatch. "Go ahead, look at everything," he said, then lit a cigarette and smoked non-stop as I poked around.

I saw the sagging fabric on the ceiling, and the head (toilet) was completely rusted shut. I stepped across the piles of equipment on the floor and looked under the cushions at the lockers crammed full with junk. I noted the once beautiful teak and holly floor and the solid teak interior. It would take work; it would cost money. But this boat had potential.

I inspected the rigging (very good condition), the sails (pretty old and worn—might make it), and the ropes and halyards (all would need replacing). The diesel engine sprang to life and throbbed smoothly when Captain Steve turned the key. He flipped a switch and something below the floorboards howled, and eventually a small stream of water spurted into the sink where it remained. The drain was clogged.

I looked over the instruments above the chart table, an impressive array of gadgets added over the years with wires dangling everywhere. "Just like an airplane cockpit," Captain Steve boasted. It was completely dark by the time we went back up on deck. Gregory was waiting on the wharf the whole time. I stalled, thinking, weighing the options as I poked around on the damp deck in the darkness, considering the problems and potential. *I will definitely make an offer contingent on a survey,* I thought. *Should I call Janet? Didn't she tell me to use my own judgment and that she'd support any decision I'd make?* I needed to make this decision alone.

We crossed the street and sat in one of the many seafood restaurants that line the waterfront in Volos. Captain Steve ordered a massive, delicious meal from a variety of local fish dishes and chatted with Gregory. I realized, as I pondered the options, that if we were going to proceed as planned for the sabbatical, I'd need to decide on the *Aldebaran* during the meal. There were no other options, and there simply was no time to start over with the process without delaying the sabbatical by a whole year.

The asking price was 38,000 euros, about $44,000 at that time. My budget was 45,000 with another $5,000 for restoration and upgrading. I was pretty sure that $5,000 wouldn't be enough for the *Aldebaran*. *Maybe Captain Steve will come down on the price,* I thought. *He seems to be in a pretty good mood after a bottle of wine and several glasses of ouzo.*

"I'll give you 37,000 euros for the *Aldebaran*," I offered.

Captain Steve laughed loudly. "No, I can get far more than I'm asking. There's an Englishman coming to see her in a few days. If you don't want the *Aldebaran*, that's okay." Captain Steve was holding all the cards and he knew it.

I tried another tack. "There are so many things that need repair." I listed several of the obvious ones.

"What you see is what you get," Captain Steve replied.

Back and forth we went. At one point Gregory and Captain Steve held a lengthy conversation in Greek and I tried to read body language for clues. Gregory seemed exasperated and Captain Steve appeared insulted, shocked, and wounded, but in the end he did not budge. Dinner was over. I was being worn down. I got bolder in my desperation.

"How many dinners do you want to buy for prospective customers?" I asked Captain Steve. "Maybe the Englishman will not like what he sees. I'll take the *Aldebaran* right now if you come down at all on the price and agree to cover the expense of some repairs."

"Okay," Captain Steve finally said, "I'll come down 250 euros and cover certain repairs. You may have it surveyed if you want to, and you can then change your mind and get out of the deal if you find a major problem with the boat, but I will not agree to additional repairs even if the survey shows they are necessary."

We shook hands. I had just purchased a sailboat! Captain Steve immediately became jovial and expansive and regaled Gregory and me with sea stories and opinions on religion and life. *Why is he so happy?* I wondered.

I excused myself and walked back to the *Aldebaran*, rocking gently on her moorings. *Janet's and my boat!* I looked back across the street and saw Captain Steve pontificating to Gregory. *These are the people Paul risked his reputation for to get included into the church. "Wild olive branches," he called the Greeks, "grafted in by God through Jesus into the true faith." Well, they have been grafted in all right. I may have been taken in by one or both of those two Greeks sitting over there. Thanks, Paul.*

I looked again at the *Aldebaran* there in the damp darkness and imagined her taking Janet and me over 3,000 miles across the unpredictable Mediterranean. She would be our home for 15 months. *Thanks, Paul.*

Back in the restaurant, Gregory finished up the verbal agreement and outlined the next steps that would finalize the purchase.

We shook hands again, and then we were off for the five-hour trip back to Loutraki. A dense fog had added to the dark dampness of the night. Gregory, always tense behind the wheel, seemed almost terrified as he searched for, then took, "shortcuts" over high, winding mountain roads. I spent three hours in the darkness, pretending to sleep, guessing how Janet would react to the purchase of the *Aldebaran,* and then, as the trip progressed, how she'd receive the news of my tragic death on the narrow Greek mountain road.

I dozed during what seemed like the depths of the night, only to be awoken as Gregory pulled into a deserted parking lot in what appeared to be the middle of nowhere. He got out in the driving rain and began to beat on the door of a small shop, trying to get the owner to open up. I watched with amazement as Gregory shopped—several kilos of sheep cheese and goat cheese, numerous bottles of wine, and a variety of other delicacies which, he explained, were the best in Greece. We loaded everything into the Suzuki and then once again—with Gregory fighting sleep, rain, fog, and every other driver on the road—continued toward Loutraki.

It was well after midnight when we arrived. While Gregory apparently got rejuvenated anticipating the delights of the cheese and wine he had bought, I was exhausted and was anticipating the comfort of a bed. But Gregory suddenly remembered that he wanted to show me an old church—the Church of St. Andrew. So, even though it was pitch-dark, raining steadily, and we were shivering in our T-shirts, we clamored about, peering through the broken windows of a church that appeared to be in a state of abandonment and ruin. I peered, shivering, into the blackness, and was reminded of all the derelict, depressing boat interiors I had seen the past few days. Gregory excitedly showed me a cave next to the church where Christians had hidden during a time of persecution in the 14th century. Then, at last, Gregory was satisfied and drove me to the hotel where a dry, warm bed was waiting.

The next morning, Gregory had arranged to pick me up and take me to his home where we worked on the memorandum of agreement, the document that formalized the deal we had shaken hands on the night before. I wasn't surprised, when entering his apartment, to see that it was in total chaos, with piles of papers, documents, magazines, half-finished lumps of sheep cheese, and empty wine bottles. We negotiated dates for the survey, the money transfers, and taking possession of the *Aldebaran*.

I wanted to fix the dates for completion as early as possible. "Things take time in Greece," Gregory insisted, and entered a delivery date which he thought was realistic: the end of April. I signed the documents, said goodbye to Gregory, whom I had grown to trust (at least in matters of boat-buying), and returned to the hotel to check out in order to catch the flight to Tel Aviv late that evening.

At the bus station in Athens, Anwar, my Palestinian friend who arranges the Greek travel for EMU's Middle East study program, met me with his car for the trip to the airport. He laughed when I told him about the experiences of the previous couple days. "I really like it here in Greece," he revealed, "but it has taken me years of doing business to figure out how to get anything done."

I thought about how Greeks, Palestinians, and Americans cooperate and compete, how we view each other and do business together. Paul dreamed of the radically different Greeks and Jews being united by faith in Jesus. He referred to the Greeks as "wild olive branches" that were, or could be, grafted into the olive tree, domesticated in a sense, by God himself through faith in Jesus.

What an appropriate image. The Mediterranean is almost completely surrounded by cultures that have domesticated a variety of olive trees and have cultivated them for centuries. Olive production has been so vital to life in the region historically, that even victorious armies, plundering the lands they conquered, would refrain from destroying their enemies' olive groves. I thought of two exceptions: when the Crusaders destroyed the olive trees of their Muslim and Jewish enemies as they violently sought to establish Christianity. And, in more recent history, when thousands of olive trees were uprooted by the Israeli military forces seeking to counter Palestinian terror.

In the first century, the variety of peoples around the Mediterranean was united under the heavy hand of the Roman army. Paul's vision was that these same peoples of the Mediterranean would be peacefully united through faith in the good news of the new kingdom. Had this vision ever really been fulfilled?

On the nighttime flight back to Tel Aviv, I slept and dreamed of our *Aldebaran*, rocking gently on the wharf in Volos. I went through customs as the sun rose in the east, then caught a *sherut* (shared taxi) up to Jerusalem. I walked inside the walls of the Old City through the New Gate to Knights Palace Hotel where Janet was staying during my time in Athens, arriving just as she was getting out of bed. Over breakfast, and for the rest of the day, we discussed the *Aldebaran*. I showed her the photos I took. She asked about every detail of the boat and was completely enthusiastic about the purchase. We spent the rest of the day making plans. That night I slept for 11 hours straight.

With several days left of spring vacation, we decided to rent a car, drive the length of Israel's coastline from south to north, stopping at each of the six marinas in Israel. We wanted to compare the facilities, location, and prices, then decide which marina to winter in that fall. So, on a warm Sabbath morning we drove down from Jerusalem to Ashkelon and began rating the pros and cons of each marina on the coast.

Ashkelon—beautiful, friendly, high security (the closest marina to Gaza), and mostly empty.

Ashdod—similar to Ashkelon but less impressive, and too close to the commercial harbor.

Jaffa—crowed and dirty with no facilities.

Tel Aviv—large, impersonal, modern, and bustling.

Herzlia—too upscale and resort-like.

Acco—very attractive in the old harbor, close to markets, but overcrowded and without modern facilities.

The choice was clear after that long day. We'd sail our boat into Ashkelon when arriving in Israel in the fall.

We spent several enjoyable days in the beach town of Nahariya, one of our favorite places to relax in Israel, then drove back to Jerusalem to meet the 29 students returning from their own independent travels. As usual, they were delighted to be back and entertained each other with their adventures.

"Did you buy a boat?" they asked, then cheered when I passed the boat photos around and told them the stories of Gregory and Captain Steve.

During the days following, between lectures, tours, and travel, I'd dash into the closest Internet café and check the latest developments. Each time an e-mail from Gregory or Captain Steve appeared, I'd get suddenly anxious. Was the deal still on track? It was. The survey was completed, and Captain Steve unexpectedly agreed to take care of some of the problems that were discovered. He was ready to sign the memorandum of agreement and make everything legally binding.

We were scheduled to leave Jerusalem and begin our two-week program on Kibbutz Afikim close to the Sea of Galilee around noon of March 15. Knowing it would be more difficult to communicate from the kibbutz, I checked my e-mail early in the morning for the last time at Mike's Center, a combination Internet café and Laundromat in the Old City of Jerusalem. The memorandum of agreement was attached to an e-mail from Gregory! Just in time! I was to sign it and fax it to Gregory immediately. I printed off the attachment, then signed and faxed it. *That takes care of the paperwork for a while,* I thought to myself.

Two hours later I decided to check my e-mail once more. Another e-mail from Gregory was waiting. "Please resend the fax," Gregory instructed. "My fax machine ran out of paper during the transmission." I wasn't really surprised. With only minutes to spare before the bus left, I frantically printed the memorandum of agreement for the second time, signed it again, and took it to the man at the desk of the Internet café to fax.

"Sorry," he said, "the fax machine just broke."

I sprinted down the exotic streets of Jerusalem's Old City to another Internet café where I faxed the document. Then I dashed down the Via Dolorosa, startling a group of Christian pilgrims carrying a huge wooden cross toward the Church of the Holy Sepulcher and, panting like a marathon runner at mile 26, burst into the Ecce Homo Convent where the group was staying. I collected the luggage and students, and we boarded the waiting bus to Galilee.

More e-mails arrived during the next several days on the kibbutz. I transferred funds from my bank in the U.S. to a lawyer in Greece, as instructed by Gregory. I signed more documents. The Greek bill of sale arrived by e-mail on a Monday and I needed to sign this very important document in a Greek consulate. That required a trip to Tel Aviv to the only Greek consulate in Israel. The sooner I could get these documents back to Gregory, the less likely there'd be a delay. I decided to go the next day, Tuesday, and called the Greek embassy to find out their office hours.

"We are open two hours a day, 10:00 in the morning to 12:00 noon," the Greek-accented voice explained on the phone, "Mondays, Wednesdays, and Fridays only."

I imagined the consulate staff sitting around smoking and drinking Greek coffee for the other 34 hours a week. "Okay," I said, "I'll come in on Wednesday."

"Sorry, we're closed Wednesday. It's a Greek holiday. You'll have to come Friday." Almost a week of waiting!

On Friday morning at 5:35, as dawn was breaking, I waited outside the entrance of Kibbutz Afikim for the *sherut* that ran to Tel Aviv. We arrived in the city by 7:30. Consulting my tourist street map of Tel Aviv, I estimated roughly where I should get off to walk to the consulate. I found the office building with the Greek consulate by 8:00. With two hours to wait, I bought a

SailingActs

Jerusalem Post and a *Herald Tribune,* ordered breakfast in a nearby café, and caught up on world news.

At 10:00 I was waiting in line at the consulate. At 10:15 I was called to the little window and the man behind the glass took my two documents and stamped them with a flurry. "That will be 240 shekels ($60) please."

It was now 10:20 and I began to understand why being open six hours per week was enough for the consulate to be economically viable. At that rate, one Greek stamping documents could take in $4,320 during those six hours. I express mailed the documents to Gregory before returning to Galilee.

The final week in Israel with the study semester was spent, as always, in Nazareth Village, a first-century, reconstructed interpretive center about Jesus in the heart of Nazareth. One of my primary sources of inspiration for following Paul's journeys by sailboat came from the experiences at Nazareth Village. If Jesus can be understood better by experiencing his environment, then one should be able to understand Paul better by experiencing his.

April arrived and we left Israel for Athens. I called Gregory from the hotel, and he assured me that things were moving ahead, just a little slower than anticipated. "What's the problem?" I asked.

"There's no problem," he explained. "This is Greece."

Five days later we boarded a ferry from Patras, Greece, to sail to Bari, Italy, where we took a bus to Rome for our final week of the semester. "The next time we're on the Mediterranean," Janet and I told each other, "it will be on board our own sailboat!"

On the flight home to the U.S. a week later, we made a list of things that I urgently needed to do in the 10 days before flying back to Athens: Go to West Marine and buy a GPS, an off-shore life-jacket, and a safety harness for Janet (she already gave me one for Christmas earlier). Send off for flags of all the countries we'd visit. Order copies of pilot books for the Aegean Sea and the Turkish coast. Get a new computer. Sell our car. Make arrangements for the Web site. Turn in the grades for the Middle East semester and write the final administrative reports. Set up bank accounts and automate all bill-paying. Check on registering the boat in the U.S., and inquire about insurance.

For some reason, flying high above the Atlantic, having left the stress of the Middle East and the challenges of Greece and boat-buying behind, this all seemed feasible. We ate, read, dozed, and dreamed of the *Aldebaran* at the Volos wharf, waiting for our return.

CHAPTER 3

Conversions

Arriving home at Dulles International Airport in Washington, D.C., with a group of students after being away for three-and-a-half months in a part of the world known for its violence and tension is an emotional experience for everyone. Janet and I watched the teary, noisy, celebrating chaos. As usual, we stood aside and celebrated inwardly, thankful that another semester in that troubled, fascinating region had ended safely, grateful for the incredible experiences, and the growth and learning that the students demonstrated. We said goodbye, knowing we would miss them.

A group of students was staying in our house during the semester and we wondered, as we pulled into the driveway, what things would look like. A hand-lettered sign on the door greeted us: "Welcome Home, Lin and Janet!" Because the semester was not quite over and with graduation celebrations a few days later, some of the students were still there. But we were home, and it was good to be back. We relaxed for a few hours, then collapsed into bed.

One of the first tasks the next morning after breakfast was to go through the collection of mail the students had saved in a large cardboard box during our absence. I was especially careful as I sorted the mail into three piles—important, to open later, and junk mail. There were several documents for the *Aldebaran* that were mailed for completion and signatures, so I carefully placed them in a special folder and set them to one side. That evening I placed the unopened junk mail into the recycle bin at the end of our street where it would be picked up the following day.

The next day, long after the recycle truck collected our junk mail, I began looking for the boat documents to sign. As I searched with increasing concern, the awful thought began to build toward panic: No, it couldn't be true! I had just recycled the documents for the *Aldebaran!*

I can't remember how that problem was solved, but I must have asked the agent to send new documents. My precise recollection of this event is clouded by an even greater disaster which threatened that same day. I'd begun e-mailing the U.S. Coast Guard from Israel, getting information on the requirements and recommendations for documenting a boat that would sail in international waters. Everything I read recommended that we document the boat with the U.S. Coast Guard, rather than register the boat in our home state. Application forms were available online for downloading—a simple, clerical task.

I called the Coast Guard's toll-free number for additional information that awful morning. The woman was helpful and friendly and I began to feel better. *How nice to be back in the United States,* I thought, *with clear instructions in English, with efficient, friendly, and low-cost bureaucracy.*

"How long will it take to receive the documentation after I submit the application?" I asked almost as an afterthought.

"Let's see," she replied. "It's now April. We should have everything ready for you by August or September."

I chuckled, knowing I had either heard wrong, or the woman thought I had asked when the U.S. Coast Guard celebrates Labor Day. "No," I repeated slowly and distinctly. "When will the documents for the boat be ready?"

"I just told you," she replied, very slowly and distinctly. "There's at least a four-month backlog of applications. We're working on applications now dated December of last year."

Stunned, I weakly hung up the phone, my stomach in knots. *There goes the sabbatical,* I thought, *or there we go on sabbatical to somewhere like Nebraska.* I went back online. *Maybe this is something I can point and click my way out of,* I thought grimly. I looked for "boat documentation" on Google, and a site for an "express boat documentation" outfit appeared. This looked promising. I called the number and poured out my heart to a sympathetic man on the line in Kentucky. It felt good just to unload my dilemma.

"Our service is very quick," the man said, "it's the Coast Guard's process that takes time. You have two options. One, you can check out the possibility of documenting the boat in the Virgin Islands, or two, for a fee of $300, I can submit a request to the Coast Guard to expedite your application. Under your circumstances, I'm pretty sure they will do so. They can generally turn an application around in about two weeks. But," he added, "they will not start until the Greek deregistration documents are sent over. And there are no guarantees, even if I submit the request."

I had been warned that a little extra cash could help clear up bureaucratic delays in Greece, but I hadn't expected this in the U.S. *A $300 gamble,* I thought darkly. *In most systems, bribery at least gets predictable results.*

I looked at the calendar. I imagined that somewhere in an office in Volos, Greece, the *Aldebaran's* paperwork was buried under a cluttered stack of unprocessed documents on a desk behind which sat a man shouting in Greek to a colleague about the Olympics, while chain smoking and drinking endless little cups of coffee. The calendar and my imagination told me that, best-case scenario, it would be early June before the Greek paperwork could possibly be completed, before we could even *begin* the documentation with the Coast Guard. We were, at a minimum, already at least three weeks behind schedule. My ticket to Greece was for May 6. Janet's was for 10 days later, May 16. We had planned, in our naivete, to sail about May 20, after working on the *Aldebaran* for two weeks. It became clear I should try the other option suggested by the man in Kentucky—documenting the boat in the Virgin Islands.

Back online, I found a boat documentation company in the Virgin Islands and called the number. "No problem," the jovial agent assured me in delightful English when I finished my tale of woe. "We can fix you up in a week after the deregistration papers are finished in Greece. We just set up an entirely legal offshore firm for $2,100, and then for an additional $1,100 we supply the entirely legal boat documentation."

Before he finished the last sentence, I already decided I'd go with Drew, the agent from the express boat documentation company in Kentucky. He sounded like he knew what he was doing, the time difference wouldn't be significant, and the cost was one-tenth of the fee in the Virgin Islands. I sent Drew the information he requested and the first installment of funds. I realized that I'd been transferring a lot of money to strangers lately, and sensed the unavoidable necessity of doing so. One cannot make this kind of voyage without taking risks.

This voyage is a lot like life, I thought, lying awake in bed one night. *The only difference is that in life we spend most of our time seeking to eliminate or forget the risks. In preparing for a journey into unknown territory, we know the journey itself, and even the preparations, are costly risks, and we have very little assurance about how things will turn out. We must trust complete strangers with our money and plans. We must let go of the security of the predictable. We have to live by faith on this kind of journey.*

Meanwhile, Captain Steve's e-mails had grown increasingly friendly and helpful. He offered to order sail covers and a new mizzen sail that was missing. He invited Janet and me out to dinner with his Belgian wife, Jenny, as soon as Janet arrived in Volos. He offered to let the *Aldebaran* stay in his berth along the wharf in Volos for as long as we needed while working on it and until all of the documentation was completed. I'd be able to live on the boat from the day I arrived. There were times during those hectic 10 days at home when I actually thought that the plans for the sabbatical, with a little creative flexibility, just might work.

Then on Thursday, April 29, a week before I was to fly to Greece, we received the shocking news that my brother-in-law,

Dewey Miller, had died. My sister, Sara, asked me to take part in the funeral service. I agreed immediately to fly out to Oregon as soon as I could. The sabbatical plans would just need to wait. I discovered I could fly to Oregon for the funeral and spend some time with my family there, then fly back again in time to connect with the flight to Athens. No tickets had to be changed.

But now the pressure was on. On Saturday Janet and I drove to Washington, D.C., to buy equipment from the West Marine store and easily spent $1,040 on a few items.

On our last Sunday for a long time at our church, Immanuel Mennonite, was highly emotional. We shared with the congregation our sabbatical plans and how we'd miss everyone. Pastor Basil invited anyone who wished to come to the front for a prayer of blessing. We were deeply moved and uplifted by the support. In the afternoon we met with our small group from the church and they gave us additional support, advice, and encouragement.

On Monday I took a non-stop flight from Washington, D.C., to Portland, Oregon, for three intense days of celebrating Dewey's life and grieving his death with my family and my 87-year-old mother. Somehow I made it through that week. On Wednesday night, I flew the "red-eye" from Portland to Washington, D.C., then drove the two-and-a-half hours home, with just enough time to pack up the clothes, supplies, equipment, books, charts, and everything else we thought we needed for the next 15 months on a sailboat. Janet drove me back to Dulles airport in Washington, D.C., and we said a quick goodbye. "See you in Athens in 10 days." Then we parted. Two hours later I boarded a plane for an all-night flight to Athens.

The plane touched down in London as the sun rose following a short night. I felt excitement triumph over fatigue as I changed planes for Athens. The man in the seat next to me asked, "Are you going to Greece on holiday or on business?"

I pondered the question. "I really don't know," I finally responded. I told him our plans and he listened with growing interest. "I'd give everything to be able to do what you are doing," he declared. *Thank you,* I thought. *You have just helped me see that even if I feel at times that I've given and risked everything for this voyage, this opportunity is really a privilege, a priceless gift.*

The plane landed. The luggage came through. The rental car was ready. By 6:00 in the afternoon, I was driving out of Athens and heading north toward Volos for the five-hour drive. It was dark for several hours before I saw the lights of Volos shimmering on the harbor water. Parking close to the restaurant where two months earlier I had shaken hands with Captain Steve, I walked along the waterfront, past the outdoor cafés full of people now that the weather was warm, toward the *Aldebaran*. She was rocking gently under the street lamps, looking exactly as I remembered her. I stood there for a long time in the darkness, thinking of the challenges and rewards of the next several months.

"Contact me when you arrive," Captain Steve had e-mailed me, "and I will meet you with the key to the *Aldebaran*." It was too late that night, so I got back into the rental car, drove out of Volos, and pulled into a dark parking lot. Sleep came easily after two nights on airplanes.

The next morning dawned bright and beautiful. I drove back into Volos and found an Internet café and a message from Captain Steve. "I am out of town until this evening," he wrote. "I gave the key to the *Aldebaran* to the owner of the coffee shop across the street from my shop." He included the name of the street and I set out to find the man with the key.

Thirty minutes later I found the coffee shop, a sleepy little hole-in-the-wall down a very narrow alley. Five elderly men were sitting silently at a chrome table. They all stared mutely as I entered. *I must be the youngest, palest person they have seen in here for a while,* I observed to myself. I discovered quickly that English was a useless language in that particular establishment, and began to act out "sailboat" then "key" while saying "Captain Steve" over and over. This might seem impossible and ridiculous to you; it did to me, too, after what seemed like a lengthy performance before the bewildered old men. I began to wonder if I had the right coffee shop, or if Captain Steve had really left the key to the *Aldebaran* anywhere. Suddenly the coffee-shop owner, perhaps recognizing that I wasn't going to entertain them any longer, handed over the key. Yes!

Captain Steve forgot to mention that there was a security alarm on the hatch door of the *Aldebaran*. The instant I touched it, I was startled by an electronic scream while passersby stared suspiciously as I fumbled frantically with the keys. Finally I got the hatch open and found a little key on the ring that shut off the alarm. I descended and sat in the *Aldebaran*. Our boat!

For the next 30 minutes, I sat alone in the *Aldebaran* for the first time, gazing at the boat that would be our home for the next 15 months. I've purchased vehicles and houses in my life. I've taken other long journeys with challenges and risks. I've lived abroad in four different countries for 16 of my 54 years of life. Yet this experience was different. This boat would take us for thousands of miles into countless unknown harbors in seven different countries. It would teach us lessons we needed to learn whether we were ready or not. At that moment I felt close to the tremendous, fascinating mystery of God.

In retrospect, this is understandable, for Abraham, Moses, and Paul, following God's call to leave on their journeys, also faced the unknown. After all, Paul had written, close to the end of his life after having sailed thousands of difficult miles in the Mediterranean, about "living by faith." Sitting in the cabin of the *Aldebaran* that first day, I understood a little more clearly what Paul meant, and perhaps a little how he felt when he set off from Antioch on the first missionary journey in 47 A.D. toward the island of Cyprus.

1 *The* Aldebaran *in Volos, Greece, as she appeared at the time of purchase.*

2 *Captain Steve, the owner of the* Aldebaran, *in his shop in Volos, Greece.*

3 *Applying the* SailingActs *decal.*

Preparing SailingActs *for voyage.*

5 *Old Corinth, Greece, with Acrocorinth in the background, site of the famous temple of Aphrodite. In the foreground is the temple of Apollo. Paul would have seen both.*

6 *At the ancient harbor of Cenchrea, Greece, the Aegean port of Corinth, mentioned in Acts.*

7 | *The reconstructed* stoa *in Athens, Greece. Paul would have preached in this kind of area.*

8 | *Leaving the harbor in Volos, Greece, in a threatening squall on June 18, 2004 for 14 months of sailing Acts.*

9 · *Our first anchorage on the tiny island of Palaio Trikeri, Greece, after a brief but eventful voyage.*

10 · *Janet (left) and Dorothy christening* SailingActs *in Panormou anchorage on the island of Skopolos, Greece.*

11 *The famous theater in Ephesus, Turkey.*

12 *On Harbor Road leading from the harbor to the center of Ephesus, Turkey.*

13 *On the road to Miletus, Turkey.*

14 *The Ionic* stoa *at Miletus, Turkey.*

15 *Sailing north from Ephesus, Turkey, with the auto helm, "Timothy," steering.*

16 *Checking out the new sails in Mytilini, Lesvos, Greece.*

17 *The little St. Paul's Church on the island of Lesvos, Greece.*

If only faith would fix boats! I found out, not surprisingly, in the next several days that it would take "works" as well. "She has never left the wharf for the past three years, except for the survey in March," Panos, the Greek man on the boat next to the *Aldebaran* told me the next morning.

So I plunged in, pumping the oily water that threatened to rise above the cabin's floorboards out of the bilge and into jerry cans for disposal. I dug through years of accumulated garbage crammed everywhere, half-filled bottles of detergent, corroded flashlight batteries, and arcane instruction manuals for obsolete, broken equipment. I made three trips to the dumpster with the rental car stuffed full of debris from the *Aldebaran*. I spent one day sorting through the maze of dangling wires, mislabeled switches, and non-functional buttons.

Captain Steve came by every morning with more obsolete equipment that was supposed to go with the boat and gave complex instructions on how to keep the electrical system from catching fire.

"Don't push this button until you flip this switch," he warned, "or the whole thing will go sccchhpfrshshh," which didn't sound good to me. I drew diagrams, listed the sequences on everything, and sweated every time I flipped a switch for the next several days.

I slowly located a number of shops which sold the needed supplies for cleaning and repairing. Traditional shops in Greece are specialized, archaic, cluttered, little spaces crammed to the ceiling with a bewildering display of the shop's specialty goods. But what you see is only a small portion of what they have in stock. You must ask for the items you want. This works just fine if you speak Greek fluently, which is what all the customers ahead of me did every time I went to buy something. I'd wait patiently in line while for 10 or 15 minutes the customer and the two or three shopkeepers all argued, discussed, debated, and dissected the merits of, for instance, a 10-amp versus a 12-amp fuse. Eventually I'd get to the counter with my pathetic, broken piece of equipment only to be told in Greek what I guessed was something like, "Sorry, we don't carry spare parts for Noah's Ark."

"Where can I find it?" I'd beg, and they'd motion out the elaborate directions I needed to follow. These directions never seemed to work, so I'd aimlessly wander the streets of Volos, carrying my little broken pieces of pumps, burned-out fuses, and worn washers, trying shops randomly until somehow I blundered across the right one. To complicate matters, all shops shut down in the afternoon and reopened only on certain evenings of the week. Therefore, all of my shopping for supplies that I needed for afternoon projects had to be concluded by 2:00, or the afternoon was wasted.

On the positive side, once I found the right shop and established a relationship with the owner, the personal service was outstanding. I visited one chandler so often that he'd ask me what was wrong if I missed a day. He had a replacement in stock for almost any part I needed, no matter how obscure or obsolete. If he didn't have it in stock he could get it in one or two days, or, failing that, he could make it. I installed a new head, a new hatch, and new water pumps. I bought a new dinghy and new bumpers, and replaced all of the ropes in the rigging with new ones.

Earlier that year, Janet and I read Frances Mayes's popular book, *Under the Tuscan Sun,* in which the author described the trials, misadventures, and rewards of buying and renovating an ancient house named "Bramasole" that she and her husband purchased in Italy. "The *Aldebaran* is a floating Bramasole," I commented to Janet in an e-mail on a day of net loss, when more problems emerged than were solved.

After a week of 14-hour days, cleaning, repairing, sorting, and testing, a good friend, Michael Hostettler, who was directing the Nazareth Village project in Israel, arrived to give me a hand for several days. What a boost! On the first day Mike was there, we worked with scrub brushes and removed at least three years of collected grime from the deck. Slowly, a boat emerged under the suds, and I felt I could board it in daylight without being afraid someone would see me and ask, "Did you actually pay money for that boat?"

With another four days of Mike's help, the *Aldebaran* was almost ready for Janet to see. Mike was worn out and limping after days of dedicated sanding, scrubbing, sweating, fixing, and cleaning the *Aldebaran*. On May 17, Janet was scheduled to arrive at the Athens airport at 4:30 in the afternoon. Mike and I got up before daybreak in order to drive the five hours to Athens and arrive before the government offices close at noon. I left a Greek document, required by the U.S. Coast Guard, at the government translation office to be translated into English and sent to Volos within the week. We then drove out to Piraeus where Mike caught a ferry for a short vacation on the Greek island of Hydra before returning to his work in Nazareth, Israel. Then I headed to the airport to deliver the rental car and meet Janet.

It was wonderful to see her, safe, smiling, and excited. We collected the two large bags labeled "heavy," full of all the books and equipment I couldn't bring with me, and staggered to the shuttle bus stop. It had begun to rain. We disembarked in the dusk in downtown Athens and walked the two blocks to the bus station. The rain began to pour, forming five-inch-deep puddles that we misjudged and dragged our luggage through, soaking the bottoms. At 8:00 in the evening, we caught the bus to Volos, driving north in the dark and pouring rain. Janet and I didn't mind; the trip gave us time to catch up on all the news of the last 10 days. The staff in Janet's department at EMU had planned a tremendous farewell celebration for her, and Janet told me with deep emotion about the wonderful acknowledgments she received for her 13 years as the parent and alumni director.

It was 12:30 in the morning by the time we arrived in Volos and took the short taxi ride to the wharf where the *Aldebaran* was tied. As we slogged our way toward our boat, which Janet had only seen from pictures, my heart was pounding. Would Janet say, "Oh what a beautiful boat!" or, "Do you expect me to live on this awful thing for the next 15 months?"

SailingActs

We walked up the slippery gangplank, opened the hatch with water running everywhere, and descended the three steps into the cabin. "Oh, what a beautiful boat!" Janet said, "I love it!"

Yes! I looked around again. All I saw for two weeks was the garbage, the broken water pump, the oily film over everything, and the neglected teak. Now I saw a boat with charm and character, full of possibility. The boat had undergone a conversion and I was too busy to even notice.

Crawling into the bunk that night, I thought about conversions, both Paul's and the *Aldebaran's*. Both were roughly the same age when their respective conversions occurred. Both were once full of junk and covered with grime. Both had hidden potential, but it required someone who took risks and invested a lot of love to bring about the change. Both had changed their names for their mission. Both came under command and were occupied by the one doing the converting. The itineraries of both changed dramatically after their conversions. Finally, while there were dramatic moments of change, in reality it was an ongoing process for both the Apostle Paul and for the *Aldebaran. Why does the word "conversion" have such negative connotations for modern people?* I wondered.

Our son, David, joined us a day after Janet arrived. It was wonderful to be together for the first time in many months. He helped with the restoration work, and we held lively discussions around the table about world events, his future, and the similarities of the Roman world in Paul's day and globalization today. We compared Paul's privileges as a Roman citizen with our own as American citizens and the dilemmas of being identified with a superpower that is admired and hated at the same time.

We discussed the problem of flying the U.S. flag in the Mediterranean during a time when American foreign policy in the Middle East has awakened resentment and hostility. Captain Steve, on one of his morning visits in which he casually would glance over our progress on the *Aldebaran*, was the first to alert us to the problem.

"You say you will be documenting the boat in the United States?" he asked.

"Yes."

"That means that you will be flying the American flag."

"Yes. I understand we are obligated to do so," I replied.

"That is like flying a red flag in a bull ring," said Captain Steve.

I feared he was right. The United States is the most powerful, feared, admired, hated, attractive, and scrutinized nation on earth. A boat flying the American flag symbolically represents the U.S. on the Mediterranean. I wanted to slip in and out of harbors without being feared, admired, hated, and scrutinized, but this wouldn't be possible flying the American flag. I noted that world sentiment toward the United States is similar to how people in the Mediterranean regarded Rome during the first century.

"What would you advise us to do?" I asked Captain Steve.

"Fly a very small flag when you enter and leave harbors," he recommended. "When you're at sea or in harbors, furl it up or take it down."

Paul's reluctance to be identified as a Roman citizen was becoming clearer. While citizenship had advantages, Paul didn't want to fly the Roman flag either. In Paul's day, only about 10 percent of the people that made up the Roman Empire were Roman citizens. These were the elite, the ambitious, the wealthy, or the fortunate. The privileges of Roman citizens were something the other 90 percent, the non-citizens, dreamed about and struggled to achieve. While citizens had more rights and could expect a higher level of protection from the military, they were also objects of resentment and violence, not unlike American travelers in the world today.

Sailing Acts

A few evenings later, Captain Steve and Jenny invited Janet, David, and me out for dinner. We drove out of Volos, up a winding road high in the mountains that surround the harbor, to a little village of Makrinitsa, where we sat on a terrace feasting on excellent food and enjoying Captain Steve's tales of sailing freighters all over the world.

"Why are there so many Greek merchant ships and so many Greek captains in the shipping industry?" I asked.

"We Greeks are adventurers, explorers," Captain Steve explained. "We like to explore the world, and the world of ideas as well. We're not afraid of new things, of change."

I wondered, *Does living on the edge of the sea affect how one looks at the world? Was the Apostle Paul, a Jew, affected by his years of close association with Greeks, who were so at home on the sea? Perhaps Paul met people like Captain Steve, whose stories of travel in far-off places fueled his curiosity about the world. Two words seemed to describe Paul in the book of Acts—"explorer" and "experimenter." Maybe Paul's efforts to include Greeks into the kingdom had something to do with these Greek traits he admired so much. Perhaps he saw these traits in himself and found so few of his fellow Jews, especially in Jerusalem even among those who followed Jesus, to whom he could relate.*

Captain Steve and Jenny wanted to know more about the project of sailing Acts and learning about Paul. I explained the goals. "We want a book from you when you finish," Jenny said.

"You will want to read it," I said, "because you will be in it." Everyone laughed.

Another guest from Germany arrived on May 5, Rebekka, David's friend. Now there were four people on board. Rebekka moved into the aft cabin, David claimed the main cabin, while Janet and I slept, as always, in the forward cabin. The next few days of work raced by amid discussions in German about the Apostle Paul and learning how to live together in very small spaces. Soon it was time for them both to fly back to Germany. While it wasn't particularly easy having guests on board in the cramped quarters, tiny head, and miniature galley, it was even harder to say goodbye. Janet and I felt very alone when they left, the boat strangely big and empty.

Paul often said goodbye during his journeys, leaving behind little groups of Jesus' followers in the pagan cities of the Empire. One of these departures is described in Acts 20:37-38: "They all wept as they embraced him and kissed him. What grieved them most was his statement that they would never see his face again. Then they accompanied him to the ship." I understood the pain of Paul's farewells just a little better after that morning saying goodbye on the dock to David and Rebekka.

With plenty of time to finish up the restoration tasks until the documentation process was completed, we decided to rent a car and drive south to explore Corinth near Athens. In looking at our schedule we realized that our original plans put us in the Athens area during the summer Olympics. It was already difficult to visit Athens and would be worse during the Olympics because of the numbers of visitors and the high security. So while we were waiting anyway, we decided to get a head start by working on some of the research in Corinth.

Corinth was one of the key centers of Paul's mission activity. He spent about 18 months during his second missionary journey, in the years 52-53 A.D., in this important, wealthy, hedonistic city. Corinth was located on the main trade route between Rome and the eastern Mediterranean, and from this position, exercised great influence throughout the Roman Empire. It was in Corinth that Paul's thought and vision matured.

In the early morning of June 2, Janet and I left Volos in our rental car, driving southward toward Athens and Corinth, following at times the route of the famous Egnatian Way. Several hours later we arrived in the modern city of Corinth, then drove the short distance inland to Old Corinth, a small village next to the ruins of the ancient site. We checked into a small, friendly pension along the narrow main street from the many available, then drove on to the entrance of the site. Because it was mid-afternoon and the site would be closing shortly, we decided to explore Acrocorinth where the famous temple to Aphrodite once stood directly above the city of Corinth (see Photo 5). This temple, we had read, reputedly was served by 1,000 male and female temple prostitutes and had attracted devotees of Aphrodite from all over the Empire.

We drove to the parking area part way up the mountain, then hiked up the trail to the summit. The view was magnificent. From our vantage point we could see the strategic location of Corinth, built on the narrow strip of land that connects the Peloponnesian Peninsula with the rest of Greece. On the eastern, Aegean side of this narrow land bridge was the port of Cenchrea (see Photo 6). On the western, Ionian side was the port of Lechaion. Transporting cargo overland between the two ports saved considerable shipping time and expense, and made Corinth an extremely wealthy city through its control of, and profit from, this major trading route. Corinth's wealth, beauty, and especially its famous temple to the goddess Aphrodite not only attracted worshippers, sightseers, and hedonists from all over the Empire, Corinth attracted Paul also.

Most of the ruins visible on Acrocorinth today are military fortifications built throughout the centuries following Paul's time in the city. We continued searching the top of the mountain, climbing over stones and through great patches of thistles, until we found the only visible vestiges of the temple of Aphrodite, a few half-buried, marble pillars of that once-magnificent structure.

The goddess of love and the god of war were both worshipped on top of this mountain, I thought looking at the temple ruins and military fortifications atop the craggy mountain. *Both deities promised so much and attracted so many throughout history. They still do.*

There was still enough daylight left for us to search for the ancient harbor of Cenchrea from which Paul sailed when he left

Corinth for Jerusalem in 53 A.D. (Acts 18:18). So we set off. Cenchrea, we discovered, was not on any of the maps we had, but we knew its general location and drove over narrow rural roads from Old Corinth toward the sea, then turned north and followed the coast, calculating where the old harbor would likely have been. Suddenly we saw the small brown sign used throughout Greece to indicate historic sites—"Ancient Harbor of Cenchrea."

We parked the car and hiked around the edge of the picturesque harbor. Beneath the sparkling, clear water we could see foundations of buildings. The harbor was once surrounded by warehouses, businesses, and temples. A passenger on a ship entering this harbor would have seen a temple to Aphrodite on the left entrance of the harbor, and a temple to Isis on the right. The grateful sailors and passengers could offer their sacrifices of thanksgiving immediately. Perfectly centered between the two harbor temples, the lofty temple of Aphrodite, glistening on the top of Acrocorinth, could be seen from the decks of approaching and departing ships.

The next day in the archeological site of Corinth did not start out very promising. The evening before, we checked the opening time—8:30 a.m., according to the sign on the gate. So, at 8:45 a.m., we were there, ready to visit the site before the heat of the day. The guard was *closing* the gate. A handwritten sign in English read: "Today site opens at 12:30 because of strike."

Janet, thinking she might be able to stop a national strike by staging a one-person protest, proclaimed, "My husband came all this way to do research and it is possible only today. We have to leave tomorrow."

"Come back at 12:30," the guard replied. "We will open then. We have not closed in six years. Today is the only time we are on strike." This was supposed to make us appreciate that it was only that day, when we were there, that the site of ancient Corinth was closed, instead of any time during the preceding six years when we were not there.

Sailing Acts

At 12:30 we returned and examined the ruins during the withering heat of the afternoon. We looked for clues to help us understand Paul's ministry in Corinth and the dramatic events of the riot; Paul's trial before the proconsul Gallio; and the mob attack on Sosthenos, the ruler of the synagogue, as described in Acts 18. The *agora* is where Paul would have worked with Priscilla and Acquilla in tent-making. Over there is the *bema* (the raised speakers' platform) where his enemies accused him of anti-religious activities before Gallio. Janet, hot and tired from clambering over dusty rocks, decided to go back to the hotel and rest. After she left I retreated under a shady tree and watched groups of tourists trudging doggedly in the shimmering heat behind their indefatigable, enthusiastic guides. Several of the more energetic tourists climbed up on the *bema*, striking a Paul-before-Gallio pose for a quick photo before catching up with the group.

I climbed the *bema* myself and found the inscription from Paul's letter to the church in Corinth, written several years after he left the city: "For our light and momentary troubles are achieving for us an eternal glory that far outweighs them all" (2 Cor. 4:17). I read the next words from the Bible I had in my backpack: "So we fix our eyes not on what is seen, but on what is unseen. For what is seen is temporary, but what is unseen is eternal" (2 Cor. 4:18).

Paul certainly saw plenty of impressive "temporary" in Corinth. Standing on the *bema* I imagined that I was Paul in 53 A.D. I looked south and saw Acrocorinth, where the temple of Aphrodite glittered. Facing north, the massive temple of Apollo loomed across the street. Looking right, the beautiful fountain and Roman temples, and to the left, a thriving market. The open area directly in front of me was filled with a screaming mob, and at my side was Gallio, the proconsul representing the mighty power of Rome. Paul saw all this, but he also saw far more. I looked again and saw an empty, ruined site. *Paul was right.*

I spent the rest of the day in ancient Corinth and the small museum with its splendid collection of artifacts found on the site—numerous statues of Aphrodite, Dionysus, Zeus, and other gods, statues of emperors, a stone inscription from the synagogue in Corinth, and many other pieces of evidence to the wealth and ethos of Corinth.

Leaving the archeological site of ancient Corinth, I stopped at a small Orthodox church in the center of the village, just outside the perimeter of the site. Paul's words about love from 1 Corinthians 13 were inscribed on a white block of marble in four languages in this church yard at the foot of the mountain where Aphrodite was worshipped. It occurred to me that Paul didn't spend any time in his letters to the Corinthian believers condemning the flourishing worship of Aphrodite on the mountain above. Instead he redefined love. "Love is even greater than faith and hope," Paul wrote to the Corinthian love-seekers.

Back in Volos a few days later, the last of the Greek documents finally arrived. I sent them immediately by special delivery to our agent, Drew, in the United States. Now we'd be waiting on the U.S. Coast Guard for the documents that would allow us to sail. We'd continue to work as we waited—however long it would take.

Paul didn't know how long he'd need to wait at any particular port. He didn't have a fixed schedule because, at least when he traveled by sea, he wasn't in control. Paul was at the mercy of the captains with whom he was sailing, and their schedule was contingent on the weather. To follow his journeys—in buying a boat and in sailing the Mediterranean—we were experiencing, and would continue to experience, the same conditions.

This was different from all other international travel Janet and I had done with public modes of transportation. The global travel industry is served by international infrastructures and multi-lingual staff-persons who are paid to treat travelers with deference, making them feel "at home." No such infrastructure or service industries exist for the foreigner fixing up his boat in a Greek port or sailing it in Greek waters. This experience requires complete reliance on strangers, port officials, local business persons, and boating neighbors from all over the world. We were acutely aware of being American. We feared becoming tiresome to others. We weren't sure who would give good advice and who would try to profit from our ignorance. We could only negotiate, develop trust, and rely on people who weren't paid to help us.

This is good, I began to realize, *our status as resident aliens. This is like Paul. We haven't left the wharf and already we are sailing Acts.*

By early June we settled into a comfortable routine of work and waiting, punctuated by the occasional small crisis. Such was the case on June 11. The day began with the usual shopping run to the suppliers and the familiar two-hour routine of waiting, discussing, and paying. Janet and I made some final purchases—a book of charts for the Aegean, battens for the sail, and six new fenders. By noon we were back on the boat with our supplies for the day. I finished up some of the small jobs while Janet made a foray to get supplies for the galley, bringing back a new kettle. Each new acquisition required a decision of where to stow it. The kettle, we decided, would fit on the floor under the galley sink.

When I opened the access door, I noticed water under the sink. This was not unusual, as I had repaired leaky hoses all over the *Aldebaran,* but the water this time seemed to come from somewhere else and was running steadily into the bilge. So with a flashlight I began searching, following the leak backwards, lifting up the floorboards, crawling into tiny, wet, oily spaces. With a sinking feeling, I found that the hot-water heater was leaking. This called for immediate action. I began to remove the hot-water heater to see if the leak could be fixed. The sun beat down as I sweated and strained, rigging up a rope to the mizzen mast and winching the half-filled tank out of the hold. The water heater was completely rusted through and needed to be replaced if we wanted to have hot water on board.

I plugged the hot-water hoses in order to get the cold water working again, then went to check the price of a new hot-water heater. Four hundred euros! That was a lot of money, but because we'd be living aboard the *Aldebaran* for the next 14 months, I resignedly ordered the new heater. Then I went to look for a connector to replace one that broke when taking out the old hot-water heater. I located a shop with the part and returned to the boat, only to discover that I bought the wrong size for the existing hoses. I walked the four blocks back to the shop, feeling helpless and pathetic. *Maybe I should write on a piece of cardboard, "Will trade information on the Apostle Paul in exchange for a plastic hose fitting the right size," and sit at a traffic light waiting for someone's pity,* I thought dismally.

I returned to the shop instead and waited 15 minutes, holding my wrong hose fitting, while two men in front of me were buying what seemed to be enough plumbing supplies to outfit the *Titanic* from the solitary man running the shop. Eventually another shopkeeper came in and I told him my sorrowful tale of woe. He handed me another fitting, the right one, and said, "You can just have it—no charge."

Back on the boat, the fitting snapped into place as the sun sank low in the west. I turned on the water; everything stayed dry. Life, with the prospects of hot water someday, seemed almost worth living again.

The man who pulled his sailboat into the berth next to us, I discovered, happened to be from Austria, and we began discussing how we sailing foreigners suffer. We laughed about what made us want to do this kind of thing. I noticed that even while commiserating, both of us seemed rather happy with suffering— the misunderstandings, the waiting, the humiliation of not being able to communicate, the uncertainties, the endless challenges, and the stupid mistakes we were prone to make.

I was reminded, after that conversation with the Austrian, that Paul talked about his suffering in a number of letters he wrote during and after his journeys. He seemed to use his suffering to establish his credibility, to demonstrate that he was genuine. To go through difficulties because of a choice, or a calling, and to emerge alive and happy, gave Paul credibility among those who sought to avoid suffering but suffered anyway. As I struggled with outfitting the *Aldebaran* while waiting for the documents that would allow us to set sail someday, I began to appreciate Paul's skill in redefining the status quo of the Roman system.

That evening after dinner, Janet and I went to the Internet café to check our e-mail as usual. An e-mail from Drew was waiting. We opened it with bated breath. The news was unbelievable. He had the completed documents for the *Aldebaran*! Had we read this right? Since April we'd been working on the documentation, haunted by the possibility that we'd wait in Volos all summer. We had taken a leap of faith that we'd be able to get the documents, without any guarantees. Now, after countless e-mails, frantic trips to offices, waiting on stamps and translations, the documentation was completed! Janet and I burst into celebration, then became subdued as we realized that our comfortable routines and familiar world of Volos wharf were over.

We decided to leave Volos the following Wednesday or Thursday. We needed to work quickly now, finish getting the obligatory insurance, and obtain the Transit Log and permission to sail from the Greek Port Authority. The *Aldebaran* was now officially *SailingActs*, and we needed to apply the decals on her stern and sides that Janet brought in her luggage a month earlier.

We'd been revising the sailing route each time our departure date was pushed back. Now, with the paperwork almost completed, we could finalize the revised sailing plans. As soon as we had in hand all of the documents and permission to sail, we'd sail to the island of Skiathos, about 36 miles from Volos, and from there begin our sea trials of sailing Acts. Dorothy Scheffel, Janet's sister and also a sailor, would join us and we'd work our way toward Samos and begin Paul's itinerary from there, with plans to sail the southern end of the Mediterranean in late summer and fall on our way toward Israel. At least that was the plan, but like Paul, we were beginning to accept that our plans could change drastically.

On Monday of the final week in Volos, a reporter from a local paper came by to interview Janet and me, take some photos, and discuss the world. He sat in our boat: Why did you buy your boat in Volos? What gave you the idea to follow Paul? How do you like Greece?

The next day, we were on the front page. Now all the neighboring boat owners, shopkeepers, and passersby knew where we were from and what we were up to. They smiled and nodded or stared, and sometimes shook their heads at the couple from the United States, working on their boat and trying to figure out Greek culture and Paul. Two days later, a journalist from an Athens newspaper called and conducted an interview by telephone.

The day after the Volos journalist interviewed us, he brought us a newspaper hot off the press. I met up with him again, later in Captain Steve's shop, where he and several customers were discussing the newspaper article.

"Why is Paul called an apostle, even though he was not a disciple of Jesus?" Captain Steve asked.

"What does the Greek word *apostolos* mean in English?" I inquired.

"Messenger," a customer explained.

A weather-beaten fisherman in the shop chimed in, "It also means someone who is sent out by someone else to deliver that message."

Greeks in a shop, discussing Paul's credentials, I noted. *These discussions must have happened almost the same way in this area some 2,000 years ago.*

SailingActs

Two days before we planned to sail, Captain Steve telephoned to inform us that our new spray hood, sunshade, and repaired genoa (sail) had arrived from Thessaloniki. Great news! I went over to pick them up and a few seconds before I got to the shop, the DHL package with our boat documents came! The timing was unbelievable. I ripped it open in Captain Steve's shop, and there it was: the official registration papers for *SailingActs* in a little plastic pouch. A handwritten note from Drew read: "Good luck on your voyage."

I read the simple document from the U.S. Coast Guard on which the whole sabbatical project hung. Vessel: *SailingActs*; Owners: Linford Stutzman and Janet Stutzman; Port of Call: Alexandria, VA; Length: 33 ft.; Beam: 11.5 ft.

This document would allow us to go over to the port police in the building several hundred yards from where we lived for the past six weeks and get the required Transit Log, then the last Greek stamp that would give us the permission to sail. Now we could hoist the Greek courtesy flag from the main mast. And we could finally re-christen the *Aldebaran* to *SailingActs*.

I returned to the boat, toting the sail, spray hood, and sunshade. The package seemed weightless. Janet was excited to see me coming with arms loaded, but her excitement shot up exponentially when I waved the envelope with the document at her. We celebrated briefly, then went back to work in earnest. I began installing the sunshade and soon everything was in place. The Greek sail company, DL Sails, had done a perfect job of fitting.

Using the dinghy, I removed the old lettering and eased the *SailingActs* decals into their places on the hull (see Photo 3). Incredibly, they fit perfectly. *Like the name Saul to Paul,* I thought. *Now the* Aldebaran's *conversion is complete.*

We had dinner under that beautiful new sunshade feeling like yachting royalty. Later, when John and Val, the British sailing couple we had invited over for a visit, were sitting in the cockpit, they were greatly impressed and kept telling us what a great boat we had. It occurred to me that we had truly transformed an old, decrepit boat into a thing of beauty, something that we could enjoy sharing with others. The boat had undergone its own Damascus experience, and its identity, itinerary, and image would never be the same. Love and sweat can change a boat, and in Paul's case, history and the world.

The next evening, Captain Steve and Jenny took us out for a final meal on the waterfront of a small village south of Volos. The Captain ordered the local fish dishes for all of us, then placed a small bag on the table. "A gift for you," he said. Inside the package was an icon of the Apostle Paul. Among the many icons in Greece of St. George and especially of St. Nicholas, the patron saint of seafarers, one very rarely sees the Apostle Paul. They searched all over Volos to find this one, a beautiful, traditional, Orthodox icon. We hung it in the main cabin the next morning. Paul, and memories of the good people of Volos, would be on board *SailingActs* for the entire journey.

The final day in Volos, June 17, was yet another lesson in flexibility. The day before, we decided to leave on Friday, June 18. But there was much to finish up, and without the final Greek paperwork in hand, it was impossible to make concrete plans for leaving. At 10:00 I received a call from Captain Steve. He had spoken with the customs officials, and I was to go to their office several blocks away and pick up the Transit Log.

Captain Steve gave me a name of a person and elaborate instructions on how to proceed. What followed next was a primer in Greek bureaucracy that I'd experience again and again in the following days: Two hours of waiting, answering questions, watching people painstakingly fill out the endless forms by hand, then enter all the handwritten information into a computer with one or two extra people watching and giving advice. Then, finally, when all the papers were stamped and signed, but just before actually holding them in my hand, "One-hundred-fifty euros, please."

"Really? The receipt here says 30 euros."

"Yes, that is for the Transit Log itself, and the rest is for fees and processing."

SailingActs

I paid the extra 120 euros. I wouldn't stay in Volos for the rest of my life demanding justice, and, of course, everyone in the customs office knew this. Besides, why should I complain? It had cost me $300 extra in the U.S. to "expedite" the application for SailingActs.

That evening we sat in the cockpit of SailingActs, aware that we had spent our last full day in Volos. Tomorrow we would sail! A mournful melody from an album of sailing songs we brought along for the voyage kept playing in my head, "Tis our sailing time." I always wondered, when I heard that song, why it was so melancholy, why it sounded like a funeral dirge. On the last evening in Volos, I understood why. Our time of departure was at hand and our feelings were mixed with both anticipation and anxiety. I thought, This must be a little what facing death is like—a frightful yet hopeful journey into unfamiliar territory, but with the promise of life.

I imagine Paul felt this way after being in places like Ephesus or Corinth for extended periods of time. He left, not knowing if he'd ever return, or what extreme difficulties and terrifying challenges he'd face on land and sea. He left the familiar for the unknown.

Tomorrow, we would, too.

CHAPTER 4

Backing Acts in Greece

Perhaps some voyages begin smoothly. When Jason and the Argonauts boarded the *Argos* in the Volos harbor thousands of years ago and sailed off toward the Black Sea in search of the Golden Fleece, it's likely their friends and families gathered on the shore and thought to themselves as they waved goodbye, "Those Argonauts sure know how to handle a boat." Or perhaps the Christians from Antioch, waving to Paul from the wharf in Selucia as his ship headed off toward Cyprus in 47 A.D., noticed that the captain looked sure and steady.

That is not the way it was for Janet and me in *SailingActs*.

On the morning of June 18, we woke early. I noticed, checking the barometer, as usual, the first thing in the morning, that the hand had fallen considerably overnight and was still dropping. Locals had been commenting on how unsettled the weather had been that spring, so this didn't surprise or discourage us from leaving that day as planned. Janet and I scurried around taking on fuel, checking our e-mail at the Internet café for the last time, buying last-minute supplies, and saying goodbye to our boating neighbors whom we had learned to know in the six weeks we were in Volos.

We had aimed for a noon departure, but at 1:00 the insurance agent still hadn't brought the necessary documents to the boat as promised. And besides, we were still stowing things and chatting with friends. Janet was on the shore talking to Jenny, who came to see us off, when the agent arrived and handed me the insurance documents. Suddenly we were ready. It was exactly 1:35 in the afternoon.

SailingActs

With so many people watching our every move, I was a little nervous about pulling out, even though it seemed like such an easy task. We'd been living aboard the *Aldebaran* since May 7, during which time I had started her engine, hoisted the sails, spun the wheel, and changed her name. But she'd been tied firmly to the wharf the whole time. We had no idea of how she would handle.

We began to unfasten the mooring lines. Somehow, it seemed, a growing and bemused crowd began to gather out of nowhere, anticipating some sort of "inept American" spectacle. With Jenny looking on apprehensively from the wharf, the Austrian boat neighbor on one side shouting encouragement in German, and the Dutch couple on the other side defending their immaculate boat from an assault they seemed to anticipate, I threw *SailingActs* into gear and moved smoothly away.

For a few feet all was well. Then suddenly a mooring line caught and we were almost rubbing against the fine Dutch boat— a boat you do not want to scratch, especially when the alarmed Dutch owners are standing on deck. This was a situation in which the famous Dutch tolerance perhaps would not apply! To avoid disaster within the first 10 seconds of voyaging, I hurled myself to the rear rail to free the line, then heroically lunged face down across the hatch of the rear cabin and grabbed the wheel in order to get back on course. From this undignified position— flat on my stomach, legs sticking straight out over the stern rail like a human wind-vane—I steered *SailingActs* away from the wharf. For some reason the Dutch woman found this amusing. I could hear her thunderous laughter above the throb of the 42-horse-power, diesel engine from 100 yards off shore. But who needs dignity if you have adrenaline? We looked back and everyone was waving and smiling and so were we. We were off!

We watched the disappearing shoreline where we lived for six weeks. How small it seemed compared to the open sea in front of us! Farewell, Volos, the Internet café down the street, the helpful shopkeepers, the international boating neighbors, Captain Steve and Jenny.

We rounded the harbor entrance, the motor throbbing. Janet and I were still congratulating each other when we noticed dark clouds rolling in from the north. Thirty minutes later, the sky turned black. We stared uneasily, then with alarm, at the dense sheets of rain pouring in the north, then around us, and finally directly on us from above. We continued to motor as the wind increased, whipping the water into whitecaps. I shut down the motor and just ran with the wind, doing three knots with no sails. Janet steered *SailingActs* as she pitched and heaved in the squall, while I went below to check our bearing and position on the chart. I'd never been seasick in my life, but on this day of many firsts, I got seasick instantly. This was not good.

We needed to get some sail up to steady the boat. I managed, in 45 minutes of nauseous struggle with the wind and the waves battering the front deck, to raise the storm jib, then the mizzen, and *SailingActs* settled down as we picked up speed. I pulled on the foul-weather gear Janet gave me for Christmas the year before and ploughed through the torrents of rain and great gusts of wind, peals of thunder and bolts of lightning (see Photo 8). I realized, with gratitude, that we had purchased an extremely sea-worthy boat.

Then the squall passed, the sun came out, and for the final hour that day, we followed the course we had plotted over waters we had never before crossed, on a boat we had never before sailed. We were heading for the island of Palaio Trikeri, some 16 miles from Volos. The charts made sense, the descriptions were accurate, and we found the harbor—full of charter boats. As in Volos, when we had pulled away from the wharf, everyone in the harbor seemed to be watching us as we drew near. Not wanting to demonstrate to the spectators that we had never dropped *SailingActs'* anchor before, we decided on a secluded anchorage just west of the harbor. Janet released the brake on the windlass, and the anchor dropped but did not seem to hold.

"Let's try over there," I suggested to Janet, pointing to a patch of sandy bottom we could see through the crystal-clear water.

"I'll push the button to run the windlass and raise the anchor. Then I'll move the boat and you release it when we get directly above that spot."

I went back to the cockpit and pushed the anchor-windlass button. Nothing happened. I tried again harder, jiggling then pounding the button. There was no movement or noise from the anchor windlass. *Did Captain Steve forget to tell me something?*

Although Palaio Trikeri is a very small and rather remote island, and even though the anchorage we chose was even more remote, there were a couple of houses on the cliffs overlooking the little bay in which we were struggling. One of the island's few inhabitants watched the whole nautical circus with binoculars from the porch of his house above the little bay. Others joined him. I ended up cranking endless yards of chain up with my hands, which I thought were quite tough by this time, but I had blisters before I finished the job. We finally got the anchor up, found another anchorage on our chart, and headed toward it with the hope that in this one there would be no spectators. *If it's this difficult to anchor smoothly,* I thought to myself, *what will it be like trying to back into a crowded berth? Tomorrow we're going to do some practice maneuvers,* I vowed.

We tried again in the isolated anchorage we spotted. Watching the depth sounder carefully, we crept into 12 feet of water and dropped the anchor, which set firmly, then backed the boat toward the shore. As our cruising guide recommended and is often done in the Mediterranean for extra protection, I took a line to shore with the dinghy and fastened it to a tree on the water's edge. Before boarding *SailingActs*, I checked the depth under her keel. There were only about six inches—too risky. Though very tired, we decided to reset the anchor a little farther out. I'm still not sure what happened next as Janet attempted to pay out the line tied to shore while I winched up the anchor by hand, then motored forward in order to drop the anchor in deeper water. Somehow the line became tangled, and as we moved ahead, the rope suddenly whipped through Janet's bare hands and she screamed with pain and fear. It was terrible. She sat in the cockpit sobbing with the pain and frustration.

We eventually got the anchor reset and the boat tied off properly, but Janet was still in shock and pain. That evening wasn't quite as idyllic as we imagined it would be in our first anchorage (see Photo 9). We had sailed only 16 miles that day but were physically and emotionally exhausted. *And we still have several thousand miles and 14 months to go,* I thought to myself.

Around 9:00 that evening we made something to eat, then climbed into our bunks. I lay awake, thinking and praying. *Please, God, help me make wise and safe decisions on this journey. Help me to stay calm, to be helpful and encouraging. Bless Janet tonight especially, and help this voyage be enjoyable for her.*

Sailing the Mediterranean hadn't changed a lot in 2,000 years, I realized that first evening on the water. We had already experienced the reality of sea travel on the same sea as Paul sailed. We faced some of the same kinds of perils that Paul experienced and were no more in control than he was. I thought about how my resolve to continue on had wavered that evening as we were overwhelmed and confused. *Did Paul ever waver during his "trials at sea" that he writes about?* I wondered. *Maybe, but he endured and triumphed. So will we,* I thought as I drifted off to sleep.

We woke the next morning in a peaceful, beautiful paradise. Only 18 hours on the sea and we were already learning about living with the dramatic and sudden shifts in weather on the Mediterranean, from chaos to tranquility and back again in a matter of minutes. No wonder the ancient Greeks perceived that their gods who controlled the winds and waves were somewhat emotionally unstable and completely unpredictable. Their gods resembled the sea.

That morning, and for a number of days following a second day of sailing, repairs had to be made. I tackled the windlass problem and was relieved to find a corroded connection in the wiring. I celebrated briefly when the windlass worked perfectly after replacing the connector. We weighed anchor after our first breakfast at sea. Janet's rope-burned hands looked bad, but the pain had subsided some during the night. We quickly discovered other problems during the sail the day before. The mainsail, which appeared to be in reasonably good condition, was almost non-functional, stretched completely out of shape. We had lost both battens in the new mizzen. The steering was so stiff that our arms ached from the day before. The electrical inverter, which we needed to run in order to keep food cool in the refrigerator, didn't seem to be working. But all of these repairs needed to wait. Before moving out of the bay that first morning, we practiced maneuvering *SailingActs* back and forth, getting ready for our next major challenge of backing her into a crowded berth in the next port.

I was surprised how challenging it was to back a sailboat. As a teenager, I spent years on power boats in Canada when my missionary parents lived on the shores of the immense Babine Lake in interior British Columbia, Canada. It was no problem back then to come flying at a dock, then, when only a few yards away, to cut the throttle, turn, and reverse the engine, coming to a dead stop alongside the dock, the hull of the boat precisely two inches away.

But backing *SailingActs*, with her fixed propeller, her rudder, her deep keel, and weighing six-and-one-half tons empty, was another matter entirely. Going forward in a sailboat under power, one has total control, for the water, pushed by the propeller, flows past the rudder. Turning the rudder directs this flow of water, instantly pushing the boat in the desired opposite direction. When in reverse, however, control of the boat occurs only after backward momentum builds up and water moves past the rudder. The position of the rudder is irrelevant until momentum builds.

This backing difficulty in itself would not be too serious if it weren't for the "Mediterranean style" berthing, invented by people born on sailboats and imposed—for their amusement, it seems—on the remaining members of the sailing world who were not. In most parts of the world, boats can tie up alongside a wharf or pier, whereas in the Mediterranean, only one end of the boat is tied up. The advantage of this berthing system is that many boats can be tied to crowded wharfs in tiny harbors, which describes most Greek harbors during the months of June to August.

This complicated berthing maneuver, I learned, separates the tourists on charter boats from the seasoned sailors of the Mediterranean. Here is how it must be done: You enter the harbor at low speed, and if there is enough space between two boats to squeeze into, you head toward it, praying that the owners of the boats are either not on board so they won't hear you bump and scrape their boats, or that they will come on deck in a sympathetic, encouraging, helpful, and, if necessary, forgiving mood. At exactly the right distance from the wharf, you must turn sharply away from the slot where you intend to back into. Now you are heading away from the wharf. At precisely the right moment and angle of the boat, to compensate for the sideways pull of "prop walk," you must reverse, remembering that you will not back straight for a while. When the boat begins its backward movement, you must drop the anchor and pay out the anchor chain at the same rate that the boat is backing. Building enough speed to control the boat, you must squeeze your way between the boats already tied up, without hitting them, and come to a complete standstill about three feet before hitting the wharf with the boat's stern. You then throw the stern lines to someone who is watching on the wharf, which will be the case if you've been performing poorly. If no one is there—the case if everything has gone perfectly—you leap off and tie the two stern lines to the wharf, then back on the boat, you tighten the anchor to hold the bow toward the open water and adjust the two ropes tied to the wharf. You are then ready to lay your gangplank across the chasm, hook up the electrical connection if there is one, and relax on the boat or explore the town.

If this goes well, it takes two minutes and wins approval from anyone who might be watching—which, of course, is rare. If it doesn't go well, it can take 20 minutes, enough time for the Greeks on the wharf—who can sense incompetence from great distances—to run home and invite their friends, extended families, and business associates to join them at the wharf for an evening of fun watching the northern Europeans or Americans sweat, yell, and fumble their way into humiliation.

It was Sunday when we faced this challenge for the first time. We weighed anchor where we had spent the night. The windlass was working well, which was heartening, but fear and trepidation were hanging like a Mediterranean cloud as we made our way around the point toward the harbor on Skiathos Island. The picturesque harbor came into view, appearing exactly like our cruising guide described it. I tried calling the harbor master on the VHF radio but got no answer. So, using our cell phone, I called the Port Authority.

"Just pick up an open berth and come on in," he instructed. "Someone will tell you if you have to move."

As we came closer, we saw a man on the wharf waving at us. There seemed to be adequate space for a wide margin of error, as it was still early on Sunday and many boats had left for the day. I noted with satisfaction that there were only a few spectators.

So here goes, I thought. We yelled to the man on the wharf, "This is our first time."

"No problem," the man yelled back, "take your time."

We did just that. I made five attempts to back into the slot but kept getting immediately off course. Finally, I hit it just right and moved with some accuracy toward the empty slot where the patient marina man was waiting. I kept up the momentum to maintain control, threw the boat in neutral—still on target—and stopped with a short burst of forward propulsion. There was a mooring line for the front, so Janet didn't have to drop the anchor. I tossed the man the two stern lines, then tied off the front. We made it—with no insurance claims to file! Somehow I managed to keep from giving high-fives to the remarkably disinterested tourists strolling along the wharf.

There were electrical hook-ups and water. We recognized some people we knew from Volos. Life looked good again. I found the marina office and paid the mooring fees. Everyone seemed so friendly and helpful. Janet and I realized that this is what we'd be doing the rest of the summer—sailing, anchoring, berthing, exploring, and relating to all kinds of people.

The man who helped us with such patience and understanding was from Bangladesh. *Who better to help us than someone who has had to back into a cultural berth, so to speak, someone who needed to find his place within another culture on that culture's terms?*

Backing into a berth in Greece is a cross-cultural learning experience. We were flying the American flag, a powerful symbol, but were personally incompetent. We needed to perform and demonstrate our weakness in public and admit that we were inexperienced and needed help from others. We needed to ask our hosts for help, patience, and maybe even forgiveness. This was the hardest part of the experience.

But we were making progress. We were not merely surviving, but we were learning from the endless challenges of the past couple of days: leaving the dock, sailing in a thunderstorm, selecting a harbor, navigating, anchoring, weighing anchor with a broken windlass, fixing problems on the sea, and communicating at sea. Then we passed the final exam of sailing in the Mediterranean— backing into a berth. Our grade was at best a C-minus, but I knew we would improve.

That afternoon I talked at length with Vlasios, the Greek sailor from Volos whose boat had been tied next to ours for the previous four weeks. He was extremely helpful and gave me a number of pointers on how to back in smoothly, as well as advice on what to do about the stiff steering-wheel problems and worn mainsail. I learned a vast amount that afternoon, and my confidence began to return.

I imagined that Paul had these intense moments of anxiety, despair, doubts, and fears as he faced challenges traveling the Mediterranean among the Greeks. These challenges also must have been punctuated by moments of joy, celebration, and a growing confidence. This is what a journey on the Mediterranean will do for you. Not only are the weather and seas out of control, and the equipment untested, but sailing is a reminder that life itself is an unpredictable voyage into the unknown. One must navigate among the extremes of comfort and suffering, fair weather and storm, people who give help and encouragement and those who do the opposite. And this is learned in public as you go.

The Mediterranean is a volatile and unpredictable environment, and the people who call it home share the characteristics of the sea. Paul learned to relate to these people of the Mediterranean, the Greeks. As we were doing, Paul, too, must have learned from the Greeks and likely grew to appreciate their competence while on the sea. Paul learned, in a manner of speaking, to back into Mediterranean berths, too. When he achieved this, he bonded with the people who were experts in berth-backing. When Paul went back to his landlocked Jerusalem brothers and tried to explain what he had learned, he was talking to people who had never backed into berths, and furthermore, never intended to do so. That was for Greeks to do. Backing boats into berths was not necessary in Jerusalem.

That afternoon Janet and I had a great time exploring the town before taking a taxi to the airport to meet Janet's sister, Dorothy, who would spend the next 10 days of her vacation with us on the boat, followed by a week on the island of Chios. Janet was especially excited. Dorothy has worked for World Vision out of

Washington, D.C., has lived abroad for years, and travels extensively. She understands the joys and sorrows of cross-cultural triumphs and defeats. To have Dorothy to talk to about what had happened in the previous six weeks would be excellent.

Dorothy came off the little plane from Athens, waving and excited. We collected the luggage, including one piece of luggage she brought from our house filled with more books and equipment for our journey. We got a taxi back to where *SailingActs* was tied. "Beautiful," Dorothy exclaimed as we gave her a quick tour. We had coffee, then went out for dinner in a waterfront café close by. As we waited for our *shashlik* (a form of *shish kebab*), Janet examined her hand and saw that the severe rope burn was beginning to heal. Over dinner Janet and I looked at each other. Maybe we can do this after all, we agreed. The journey so far had been hard, but today was very good, very good indeed.

We had been discussing our itinerary already in Volos when it became clear that we'd be starting almost a month behind the original schedule. Those first few days of sailing made us aware that we would not be able to sail all the way east to Tarsus, the birthplace of Paul, then to Antioch, where he began the first mission voyage. The distances were too vast. Now that Dorothy had joined us, we were able to coordinate our sailing plans with her vacation plans. We'd be sailing east/southeast from Volos toward the Turkish coast through the beautiful Sporades Islands, stopping every night at a different island as sailors did in the first century. We'd sail fairly quickly to the island of Samos, close to the Turkish coast on the east side of the Aegean. At Samos, we would begin following the actual routes of the Apostle Paul, visiting the sites mentioned in Acts. Dorothy would sail with us for the 211 sea miles to Samos, then take a ferry to the island of Chios, about 50 miles north of Samos, to spend her final week of vacation. Beginning from Skiathos, we'd sail between six islands of the Sporades in six days: Skopolos, Stena Valia, Skiros, Psara, Chios, and finally Samos.

On June 22 we left Skiathos for the short sail to the little bay of Panormous on Skopolos Island, which, according to the cruising guide, is one of the most beautiful anchorages in the Greek islands. We decided that this would be the ideal place to officially christen *SailingActs*. The tradition of christening boats by smashing a bottle of champagne against the hull has multiple obscure origins, both pagan and Christian. The pagan "sacrifice" of champagne to the gods when dedicating a ship to one of the deities, the Christian "baptizing" and giving a Christian name to the boat (christen), and the Polynesian tradition of blessing by "anointing" the boat with champagne, have all possibly contributed to the maritime tradition of boat christening.

We decided to go primarily with the Christian interpretation of the christening, along with the Polynesian mode of pouring, rather than the pagan smashing of the champagne bottle on *SailingActs*. The pagan backdrop was supplied by an Austrian couple aboard their sailboat anchored about 30 yards away, who stripped off all of their clothes during our little ceremony to swim, then showered stark naked on the deck of their yacht as we gathered on the deck of *SailingActs*.

I read Paul's own description of his dramatic conversion and subsequent change of life from Acts 22, and we reflected again on the parallels between Saul/Paul and *Aldebaran/SailingActs*. Both were about 25 years old when the course of their lives changed dramatically. Paul left Israel to journey toward Greece and *SailingActs* left Greece to journey toward Israel. We poured the champagne on the deck of *SailingActs* and committed her and the long voyage ahead to God (see Photo 10). Using our new gas barbecue for the first time, we enjoyed a fantastic meal of celebration, thanksgiving, and anticipation as quiet darkness crept into the bay.

Bringing *SailingActs* into the berth at Skopolos the following evening was a small triumph, as this was the first time we used the anchor instead of a mooring line when backing into the berth. We got into position and after failing in the first several attempts, Janet got the anchor set well but we ended up at a different place on the wharf than I was aiming at. *But who knew where I was aim-*

ing? I comforted myself. We were lucky. Because we were early, there were no other boats in the immediate vicinity. We fastened the lines and congratulated ourselves for having accomplished this feat without loss of life, limb, or dignity. There was no yelling. We were learning.

Within 30 minutes, three or four more yachts came in. The one next to us was the Austrian couple who had thoughtfully provided the pagan ambiance during the christening the night before, but it wasn't until they said "hello" and informed us that they had been next to us the night before that we recognized them. *I didn't recognize you with clothes on,* I thought. We had a friendly chat and enjoyed watching a British party on an expensive boat froth and thrash their way in and out, back and forth, trying to 1) get their anchor down, and 2) tie up to the wharf. They'd manage either one of these tasks, but not both simultaneously. The Austrian and I, out of sympathy, finally walked away. I recalled that only two days earlier, we had put on a similar performance and remembered how hard it was to get out of a botched berthing mess in broad daylight with strangers shouting instructions.

The routine for the trip to Samos was the same each day. We'd get up in the morning, buy fresh bread at a bakery if available, enjoy breakfast in the cockpit, sail all day, arrive in an anchorage or harbor just before dark, explore the town if time, then return to the boat and fix things. I'd fix the day's broken equipment— the list up to that point included torn sails, a boom failure, and persistent electrical problems—while Janet would fix an invariably delicious dinner. During the long days of June, it would be at least 9:00 by the time we ate our dinner in the cockpit. Then we'd clean up and, completely worn out, hit the bunks and fall asleep immediately. We gradually increased the distances we sailed each day, managing 58 miles between the islands of Skiros and Psara on June 26.

We sailed to the southern end of Chios on June 27, finding a small isolated anchorage early in the afternoon. This gave Janet and me time to do a little exploring. So we lowered the dinghy over the side and rowed across the bay to several fisherman's cottages on the shore, thinking we'd find a road leading to the next town, Mesta, which, according to our map, was about three miles away. We planned to hike into this town and try to find Despina, an extended family member of Dorothy's colleague from World Vision, whose house Dorothy was going to use several days later. From the information Dorothy had brought with her, Despina operated a restaurant in the town of Mesta.

Our guidebook described Mesta as a walled medieval town and one of the most attractive villages on the island of Chios. We began hiking up the steep road toward Mesta. As we climbed the road, I realized why Paul preferred ship travel to overland. Although ship travel was often uncomfortable, dangerous, and unpredictable, walking through the heat carrying your belongings was far worse.

After about 30 minutes of walking up the road through beautiful olive groves, a single car labored up the road behind us. We instinctively stuck out our thumbs as it approached and the driver kindly stopped and offered to take us to Mesta. Gratefully, we crawled into the back seat. Only after the driver dropped us off at the entrance of Mesta did Janet discover she had left her sun hat on the back seat of the car.

Inside the walled village, we discovered a maze of narrow, winding streets. We worked our way to the central square, shaded by massive plane trees, and found the restaurant and its owner with whom we were remotely connected through Dorothy's Greek colleague. The remoteness did not matter. As soon as we introduced ourselves through the tortured connections that explained why we were there, the woman, Despina, treated us like family, seating us in the shade and serving us mango juice from Chios.

"My father is a fisherman," she told us after we had sorted out her extended family tree. "The bay where you are anchored is ours, and one of the buildings where you left your dinghy belongs to my father. He'll be coming here soon, then driving over to go fishing tonight. You can get a ride back to your boat with him."

Moments later a weather-beaten old man appeared, instantly interested in our sailing plans the next day. "Big storm come," he warned, gesturing dramatically. "Beaufort-7. Bad. Bad. Don't go Samos. You stay here."

We had planned for a very early start in order to stay on schedule and make it to Samos. Should we take this scrap of information seriously? Fishermen are supposed to know, we were often told, but we were also warned before of winds that never came. Janet and I decided that when we returned to the boat, we'd discuss with Dorothy whether to stay on Chios an extra day or sail to Samos in the morning.

It was late afternoon by the time the fisherman and his wife led us through the winding streets and out through a small gate in the town wall to where their tiny, rusted car was parked. The back seat was missing and the space was piled full of fishing equipment, including a large, flat basket with perhaps 100 hooks lined neatly around its rim, each baited with a shrimp. We wedged ourselves into the mobile bait-and-tackle shop. The car roared to life and, with the fisherman's wife at the wheel, bounced back over the steep road to "our bay." We said goodbye, recovered our dinghy, and rowed back to *SailingActs*.

On board we discussed whether or not to sail in the morning. Should we wait a day, then leave Dorothy on Chios while Janet and I sailed on to Samos by ourselves? Should we risk it and try for Samos in spite of what the fisherman told us? Despina told us about a weather bulletin in English that we could hear on our VHF radio at 1:00 the next morning, so we decided to make the final decision after listening to that forecast.

At 1:00 I got up to listen to the forecast on our VHF, but in spite of groggily waiting for the broadcast for 30 minutes, nothing came on. I went back to my bunk to catch some additional sleep, setting the alarm for 5:30. When it went off, all was calm; the sky was cloudless. *Maybe the fisherman was being dramatic or overprotective*, I thought. The barometer had risen some, which indicated the possible build-up of the *meltimi*, the strong northerly winds of summer, but after a couple days of very light wind, that seemed a positive thing. I woke the crew and asked, "Should we go for it?"

Janet and Dorothy were both ready to take the risk of strong winds on the 50 miles of open waters between Chios and Samos. At 6:10 a.m., we weighed anchor and five minutes later were under way. Because the wind was so light, I started with the genoa, the largest of the three headsails, and put up the full main and the mizzen as well. The winds started to increase, and as they built further, I went forward and changed the headsail to the medium-sized working jib.

Changing headsails is one of the most physically demanding of the many sailing tasks. *SailingActs* didn't have roller furling, but used the old-fashioned (and more reliable, according to Captain Steve) system of headsails that must be clipped with a series of snaps to the front stay, the cable that holds the mast from falling backwards. So every time the wind picked up or lowered significantly, I needed to drag a sail of the size appropriate for the new wind conditions from out of the locker in the cockpit up onto the deck. I would then lower the existing sail onto the deck, unfasten the dozen or so clips from the front stay as well as the ropes holding the three corners of the sail, throw the sail down the hatch so it wouldn't blow overboard, then repeat the whole process in reverse with the smaller or larger sail replacing the one just removed.

In calm weather, this takes about five minutes. But this task becomes more difficult when the wind picks up and the waves begin to toss the boat violently, especially at the bow of the boat where the sail change occurs. In windy conditions, I need to use the safety harness and tether to avoid being lost if hurled into the sea. I crawl around on all fours, hanging on with one hand while trying to wrestle the sails up and down with the other. Fortunately, out at sea, there are no spectators to marvel at the propensity of humans to try outrageous stunts. Janet, steering from the cockpit, invariably yells, "Be careful, be careful, hang on!" assuming somehow that, without this reminder, I'd just allow myself to be washed overboard and lost at sea. Changing sails in rough conditions became the least favorite of all sailing activities for both of us.

On the sail to Samos that day, I changed the headsails from the genoa (large) to the working jib (medium) to the storm jib (small), working non-stop in a space of 20 minutes. We hit our top speeds of the entire voyage, over seven knots, within the first hour as we experienced exactly the kind of weather the fisherman on Chios had warned us about.

Another possibility for reducing the amount of sail in heavy weather is to reef the mainsail. *SailingActs* has a roller reefing system, which I used for the first time that day. By simply lowering the mainsail while cranking the foot of the sail around the boom, the sail becomes smaller, and the boat, in spite of the strength of the wind, becomes manageable. That day, I reefed several times until the mainsail was less than half its normal size.

SailingActs is equipped with an auto helm. This consists of a unit containing a gimbaled electromagnetic compass that's connected to a small motor that drives the steering wheel in the cockpit by a belt. To engage the auto helm once everything is connected, I just need to head *SailingActs* in the desired direction, and when she's tracking correctly, push the "engage" button, and the auto helm maintains the course, no matter how smooth or rough the seas.

This is the theory.

Before leaving Volos I hooked up the auto helm and tested it, and it seemed to function properly. Yet when I tried it out for the first time at sea, it held the course for a moment or two, then began emitting a series of beeps, like some kind of disgruntled robot, and steered us in erratic circles. This was roughly as effective as being steered by a demented, blind ape.

So we steered by hand the entire day under clear, sunny skies—12 hours of high winds, with waves between nine and 12 feet high. The howling wind, the discomfort of endless jarring, the tension

(What will break next? Will we be able to find a safe place in the harbor before dark?), and anxiety wore us down. It was comforting to observe that aside from the working jib disintegrating beyond use, everything else was holding up well. Our spirits rose a little as we at last approached the harbor.

I called the Port Authority on the cell phone and inquired whether the shelter was adequate. "Yes," the officer replied immediately, "it is completely safe, but you will find it a little uncomfortable. We're having Beaufort-7 (near gale) winds out there today."

At that point, "a little uncomfortable" sounded a lot more attractive than our current condition. I struggled one last time that day with the sails before pulling *SailingActs* alongside the wharf where the Port Authority officer was waiting to help us tie up. The wind wasn't nearly as strong in the harbor, and the waves seemed downright benign in comparison to the open sea. We had passed another test. We were safe.

Within 30 minutes we had everything shipshape—all the sails in bags and stowed, and five ropes holding *SailingActs*, jerking and bouncing, to the quay. We sat in the cockpit and chatted with several Greek-Americans about our project. All were extremely interested and positive. "I'd like to invite you for coffee in the next day or two and talk to you more about Paul," one particularly interested man offered. "He's my hero."

Later that evening I checked the week's progress on our little GPS. The accumulated mileage since Volos was 244 nautical miles. In favorable conditions, this is just about the speed that Paul would have sailed in the first century.

If 244 miles doesn't seem like a long distance to travel in a week, try sailing it in unfamiliar waters in a foreign country, in a boat you're just learning to understand, and in weather conditions you've never faced before. It is, to say the least, physically, emotionally, and relationally strenuous. Janet and I ached all over from stubbing our toes on the lurching deck, repeatedly ramming our heads on the mast or anything else above the bill of our caps, and crashing into solid objects in a heaving cabin. Our emotions swung from helplessness to elation, and fear and doubt to confidence. Janet and I worried for each other, blamed each other, yelled, reconciled, and forgave each other more in that first week than we had during the entire previous year, it seemed.

I kept thinking about Paul, traveling by land and sea some 10,000 miles during his mission journeys. Traveling at the speed of Paul for just 244 miles, I was beginning to realize that there was a whole lot more to Paul's missionary journeys than Luke describes in the book of Acts. Travel was slow and difficult by either land or sea. Paul's schedule by ship may have been preferable to land travel, but it was still fraught with hazards and perils—not to mention grueling. He was likely awakened, day after day, in the wee hours of the morning by the crew preparing to weigh anchor before dawn. And when Paul wasn't sailing, he was trudging along under the blazing sun, carrying his belongings, day after day, for thousands of miles in his journeys. Two hundred-forty-four miles in the Aegean and a couple of hikes in the heat had taught us to appreciate Paul in new ways. We were beginning to feel somehow personally acquainted with him.

When Paul hopped from island to island, as we had, crossing the Aegean, he was encountering different cultures, religions, landscapes, and customs every day. While these islands were all united under the Roman Empire, each island had its own histories, myths, and heroes and gods, to which were built temples that attracted visitors from all over the Roman Empire for worship. We learned, on the 244-mile voyage across the Aegean, that each island even today has its own culture that distinguishes it from the cultures of neighboring islands.

Our brief voyage in the Aegean resembled only a tiny fraction of the distance that Paul traveled during his 10 years of missionary endeavors, but 244 miles was an immeasurably long voyage in terms of our learning. Resting in Samos after that long, hard day, I found myself eager to explore the first of Paul's islands thoroughly, and to continue the remaining 1,600 miles of following Paul that summer.

CHAPTER 5

Learning at the Speed of Paul

The Greek islands of the Aegean are fantastic. Surrounded by sparkling blue waters, rugged peaks dropping into the sea, ancient harbors, picturesque villages, stunning scenery, and remains of some of the earliest civilizations in the world, these are islands of local legend and packaged tourism. Some of these islands were visited briefly by the Apostle Paul, and for countless generations since the first century, the islanders have remembered. Beginning in Samos, and for the remainder of the summer, we'd be exploring the islands and memories of Paul.

At the end of his third journey, Paul sailed from Philippi, an important Macedonian city in the north Aegean with its port of Neapolis (the modern Kavalla), to Jerusalem. The complete itinerary, including the places of overnight anchorages, are recorded in detail in Acts 20:15: "The next day we set sail from there and arrived in Kios. The day after we crossed to Samos, and on the following day arrived at Miletus."

Our plan was to begin in Samos and sail in the opposite direction toward Philippi, spending time in each of the places mentioned, ending in Philippi. According to our calculations, sailing these 10 verses in reverse order and exploring every one of the places mentioned would take us about a month.

We finally arrived in Samos and were eager to begin, but we'd been pushing ourselves and *SailingActs* for a week, "learning the ropes" of *SailingActs*, the Mediterranean, and ourselves. This had taken its toll. So we spent the first day in Samos recovering, leisurely enjoying meals in the cockpit, making small repairs, and catching up with correspondence on the Internet. On the cell phone we bought in Volos, we discussed the problem of our failing sails with Captain Steve, who also happened to be a dealer for DL Sails, a Greek sail-making company in Thessaloniki. "Please find out and let us know how much a new jib and mainsail would cost," I requested. Janet and I laid the sails on the wharf next to *SailingActs* and carefully took the measurements and phoned them to Captain Steve. He promised to get right back to us with the prices.

I also noticed with some concern that the water under the floorboards seemed to rise rather quickly now. I pumped out the bilge the day before but at least as much water had leaked back in during the night. "Just force some grease into the water seal around the propeller shaft," Captain Steve advised when I explained the water problem, "and that should take care of it."

I turned the screw-handle of the grease gun that forces grease into a seal, until the grease appeared around the shaft. The water slowed from a fast drip to a slow drip. Maybe this would do the trick, but water, any water at all, coming into *SailingActs* gave me an uneasy feeling.

Late that afternoon Captain Steve's wife, Jenny, called and urged me to find a TV to watch. "June 29 is a national holiday in Greece," she explained. "We celebrate the Apostles Peter and Paul."

Across the street from where *SailingActs* was tied, a café had a large-screen TV and I watched, astonished at the elaborate ceremony being broadcast from Athens. A large crowd of Greeks—church officials, political leaders, politicians, guests, and thousands of Athenians—were gathered at the Areopagus where Paul preached his famous sermon. Choirs sang, priests chanted scripture readings, and flags flew. The focus seemed to be on Paul.

Imagine a public celebration of Paul in the United States, I thought. *Greeks have such an awareness and pride in their historical connection with this great apostle. The national, religious, and cultural identity of*

Greece is shaped by Paul. Would Paul be surprised by these celebrations?

On our second morning in Samos, Dorothy left us. Janet and I decided to explore the rest of Samos Island that day, with the goal of discovering what still remains of the sights Paul might have seen during his brief stop there. I picked up a scooter from a rental office across the street from *SailingActs* and loaded water, guidebooks, maps, sunscreen, and hats into the little storage compartment on the back. Janet struggled on the back, and we wobbled off through the traffic, out of town and up the steep, winding road across the mountain to the town of Pythagorio, which is located where the ancient city of Samos, now listed as a World Heritage Site, once stood.

We parked the scooter along the harbor and admired the remains of the jetty that once extended some 450 yards into the sea to protect the harbor from the pounding waves. This immense jetty was built around 550 B.C. If Paul's ship had indeed anchored in this harbor overnight, I could imagine the impression it might have made on Paul as he gazed at this marvel of human labor.

But this wasn't the most spectacular feature of ancient Samos about which the sailors had likely boasted to Paul, visiting the island for the first time. A temple nearly the size of the famous temple of Artemis in Ephesus, and four times the size of the Parthenon in Athens, occupied a site about five miles outside the town, connected by a magnificent Sacred Way. The temple on Samos was to Hera, a goddess with roots going back to the Egyptian goddess, Mut. Paul certainly would have known of this temple, or at least would have heard about it when anchored in Samos, for the inhabitants of Samos had been worshipping Hera for more than 1,000 years before Paul arrived. Hera's famous temple attracted pilgrims from all over the Mediterranean.

Samos was also the island of Pythagoras. If Paul had never heard of the great Pythagoras before his visit to Samos, he most likely heard of him while on the island. Born on Samos about 500 years before Paul, Pythagoras's fame and influence in the Mediterranean was immense. Still remembered today by the mathematically informed for his theorem (the square of the hypotenuse of a right angle is always equal to the sum of the squares of the other two sides—a fact which likely did not impress Paul that much), he was far more popular in his day as a kind of spiritual guru. Physically attractive with his long, flowing hair and rugged, masculine looks, this mystical, charismatic figure, who taught his followers to practice self-restraint, adopt a vegetarian diet, and do good, eventually immigrated to Sicily and established a community of men and women who renounced their worldly possessions and lived under Pythagoras's rules. If someone decided to leave the community, they were considered to have died and a gravestone was erected.

We were so struck by Pythagoras at Samos that Janet bought me a special cup he had invented and gave it to me as a birthday present several weeks later. This cup, the story goes, was created in response to a problem among a group of laborers who were given a ration of one cupful of wine each day. Everyone wanted the cup filled as full as possible, so Pythagoras devised one that could hold the allotted amount safely, but would completely empty itself of the contents through a hole in the bottom if filled even slightly above the rationed amount. After several cupfuls of liquid down the front of my shirt, trying to outwit Pythagoras's invention, I, too, began to appreciate the man who could invent such an effective tool of instant, appropriate punishment for the greedy.

After viewing the remains of another temple to Aphrodite and Samos's other engineering achievement, the Evpalinos Tunnel built in 524 B.C. to divert water to the city, we climbed back on the scooter and with growing confidence sped along among the pine groves and olive trees over a twisty road that climbed steeply over the rugged mountains. I felt the cell phone vibrate on my belt so I whipped the scooter to the roadside and answered. Captain Steve had the price on the new the working jib and the mainsail—1,950 euros ($2,380). I gulped. We already spent all the money we had saved. I'd need to start borrowing. I stalled.

"How long will it take to get them?" I asked.

"Only several days," Captain Steve replied, "and we can ship them to any of the islands overnight."

"Let me call you back in a few minutes." Janet and I stood in the shade of a pine tree and weighed the options.

"We can't possibly sail for several thousand more miles with the sails we have," Janet declared, stating the obvious. "What other choice do we really have?"

I heard once that the definition of a boat is "a hole in the water, lined with fiberglass, into which you pour money." I was beginning to agree.

"We'd like to order the new sails," I telephoned back. Captain Steve generously agreed to pre-pay the sails while I arranged for a loan. I'd transfer the funds to him as soon as they were available. We arranged to have the new sails shipped to Lesvos (called Mytilini in Acts 20:14, and by many Greeks even today), an island we planned to reach in about two weeks. As we would be sailing in Turkish waters during most of the next two weeks, we decided to limp our way to Lesvos, Greece, rather than pay customs fees to import the sails to Turkey.

Luke, the author of Acts, doesn't mention any details of Paul's island-hopping, but Paul's commitment to including Greeks into the kingdom was likely impacted by this exposure to the diversity and unity of the Empire he observed everywhere on his journeys. If the Caesars could integrate these islands of diversity into their Empire, God could surely unite the peoples of the earth into his kingdom. If only Jewish believers in Jesus could also catch the vision of a kingdom far greater than the land of Israel and the Jewish people. Paul's mission, especially the immediate one to the believing Jews of Jerusalem whom he was about to meet again, must have been further developed as he sailed these islands of the Aegean.

SailingActs

We took a ferry to Chios Island the next morning to spend the day with Dorothy, who had arrived there from Samos several days earlier. Dorothy drove us north to where she was staying in the tiny village of Ano Kardamila. Although tiny, the roads, streets, and houses of that little village seemed so spacious and stable after being on *SailingActs* for six weeks. We spent an hour or so marveling at the comfort of chairs and sofas, showers, and toilets that flushed simply by pushing a lever.

I learned that Chios has been famous since ancient times as an island of seafarers. A local legend claims that Christopher Columbus visited Chios prior to his voyage to America, perhaps spending up to eight months on the island, famous then as now for its seafaring population. According to the island's inhabitants, it was on Chios where Columbus learned his navigational skills and caught the vision for exploring the world.

Paul and Columbus, I thought, *both great explorers. Both took such personal risks for what they were commissioned to do; both changed the history of the West; both visited Chios. Could Paul's brief stop on this island of seafarers, barely mentioned in the book of Acts, have affected Paul as Columbus's visit to Chios centuries later had? Could this brief visit have motivated Paul to push ever farther west to the "edge of the world" in the first century?*

The next morning Dorothy and Janet drove back down to the Chios airport to pick up one of Dorothy's colleagues from World Vision who was planning to spend a few days of vacation with Dorothy. After the luxury of eating breakfast sitting on a chair in front of a table, I set out to find the village priest in hopes that he would give me his opinion of Paul. After finding his house, I was met by his wife (marriage is allowed for priests in the Greek Orthodox Church), whose hand signals indicated I'd find him down in the village square drinking coffee.

In the square, under the shade of a huge plane tree, where the old men hang out and drink coffee all morning and *ouzo* all afternoon, I started asking for the priest. Everyone got involved in providing information about where I might find him. I showed them the Greek newspaper article from Volos; they were all impressed and the word spread.

However, the "Papa" was not there. Rumor had it that he was in the harbor village of Marmaro, several miles away. An old, retired sea captain offered to take me there. Once in Marmaro he started asking around, and soon everyone in the village except the Papa himself knew I was looking for him. I waited another hour at a café in the village while the grapevine did its work. Suddenly I saw the Papa drive by in his white pickup, and soon after the captain came back disgusted. He had talked to the Papa, who claimed he was too busy to talk to me about the Apostle Paul. "How can he be too busy?" he kept saying. "All he does is talk to people."

The captain stayed in Marmaro to eat lunch at a little restaurant, so I walked the two miles back to Ano Karamila. As I approached the shady square, I spotted the Papa eating lunch. He came over as soon as he saw me, looking slightly guilty, and explained in excellent English that he couldn't speak English very well.

"You really need to talk to the priest from Marmaro," he urged. "He would be happy to talk to you about *Apostolos Paulus.*"

I weighed my options, having just spent the morning in Marmaro looking for a Papa who might talk to me, and having just walked the two miles from there in the hot sun. I walked back to the house, hoping to find Dorothy and Janet back from the airport and willing to drive out to Marmaro for another attempt. They were there, so back to Marmaro we went.

We spotted the Papa, Tsapelas George, at a sidewalk café. I explained what I was doing and showed him the newspaper article. He'd be glad to talk to me about Paul, he explained, but he didn't have much time. The moment we started talking, however, he didn't seem in a rush at all.

"Is Paul well known in Chios?" I asked after we made ourselves comfortable at his table on the sidewalk.

"Everyone on Chios knows about Paul," Papa George replied with obvious pride. "We tell the story in our sermons, how he stopped here on his way between Lesvos and Samos. All the children on Chios learn about Paul in school. I teach religion classes to the children in the schools and always tell them about the Apostle Paul."

"Who is the most popular saint on Chios?"

"St. Nicholas, of course. He is the protector of seafarers. Every Greek ship anywhere in the world has an icon of St. Nicholas on the bridge."

That answer did not surprise me here on this island of seafarers. Papa George had been a sailor himself for 12 years prior to becoming a priest.

"But the Apostle Paul is very popular," Papa George continued. "On the islands of Lesvos, Chios, and Samos, there are many churches named 'St. Paul's Church,' which is different from the rest of Greece where there are hardly any churches named after Paul. The Apostle Paul is one of the greatest saints because he got his command to take the gospel to Greece directly from Christ."

"Why do you think Paul worked so hard to get the Jerusalem church to accept Greeks into the church?" I queried.

"I didn't know that he did. I don't know why there would be such a problem."

This answer surprised me. It was obvious that Papa George knew Greek history and the story of Paul on Chios much better than he knew the story of Paul in the book of Acts.

Papa George continued. "Jesus told Paul and Peter: 'You are the rock on which I will build my church.'"

"I've never heard that," I said. "According to the story in the Gospels, Paul was not with Peter when Jesus told him he was the rock." This seemed to surprise Papa George somewhat.

"But he meant it for both," he responded. "Our holiday celebrates both Peter and Paul equally."

A small crowd had gathered by this time, with a number of bystanders chiming in and adding to the story of Paul on Chios. I shook hands all around, took pictures of the beaming Papa and his flock, waved goodbye, and found Dorothy and Janet waiting near the harbor. Walking by the restaurant where I had left the captain hours before, I was surprised to see him still there, a number of small, empty *ouzo* bottles in front of him. With his English vocabulary now reduced by approximately one liter of *ouzo*, he insisted that Janet and I join him for coffee back in Ano Kardamila.

"Sure," I promised the man who helped me track down the Papa, "I'll buy the coffee."

But when we rejoined him later under the shade in the square where we met that morning, he ordered more *ouzo*. As the captain's English deteriorated further, Janet and I spent the next hour nodding and smiling, as clueless as the captain.

That evening we drove back to Chios town, ate dinner at a wonderful sidewalk café with Dorothy and her colleague, then said goodbye at about 7:30 p.m. so they could drive back over the narrow road to Ano Kardamila in the daylight. Janet and I waited on the waterfront until 11:00 for the ferry back to Samos. As soon as we boarded, we stretched out on seats in the lounge area and went to sleep, waking when the ferry pulled into Samos at 2:30 in the morning. We looked over where *SailingActs* still bobbed, and felt good. We were home once again. We decided that night to sail to Kuşadasi, Turkey, the next forenoon for our next important Paul destinations: Ephesus and Miletus.

The sun was high when we awoke after five hours of sleep. We were eager for our first experience of leaving Greece and sailing to Turkey. While the distance between Vathy on Samos Island, and Kuşadasi, Turkey, is a little less than 20 miles, the cultural distance is vast and with the tension and suspicion between the two countries, we would carefully follow the rules for exiting Greece and entering Turkey by sea.

First I went to the Port Authority office close by on the harbor and turned in our Transit Log and paid the amazingly low sum of

SailingActs

8 euros for the five days *SailingActs* had been tied at the wharf, including electricity and fresh water. Then it was a short walk to customs for the exit stamps in our passports, then back to the Port Authority for final clearance. Back on the boat, Janet and I went through the now familiar routines of getting the boat ready to sail, and by 10:00 we were off. *That was easy*, we thought.

A favorable wind pushed us toward the Turkish coastline, visible from Samos, and we made good time in spite of our ragged sails. How exciting, entering a new country by sailboat! It was time to take down the Greek courtesy flag that had been flying from the starboard spreader since Volos. I thought about how easy it was for the ships of Paul's day, sailing the Mediterranean without passports and transit logs or flying the different flags.

On that day, the Fourth of July, we flew four flags, sailing from Samos, Greece, to Kuşadasi, Turkey. In compliance with international conventions, we flew the American flag with the stars and stripes from the stern, and the Greek flag with the Christian cross up the main mast on the starboard side. Then, leaving Greek waters for Turkish, we exchanged the Greek flag for the "Q" flag, a plain yellow flag indicating that our boat had not been cleared through customs, and finally, when cleared, we flew the Turkish flag with the Muslim crescent.

So with flags flying, we approached Kuşadasi, called the marina on the VHF, and entered the harbor. Friendly, uniformed help was everywhere. A man in a launch led us to our berth and helped us tie up. Someone else appeared and connected us to electricity. Another man formally welcomed us and explained the check-in and customs procedures, and another helped us with the water. We were impressed by the clean toilets, warm showers, and swimming pool. Even though the price of $17 a day was hefty by our meager standards, we decided to stay for five days, not three, as originally planned. The marina even provided services to take care of customs and passport paperwork!

After tidying up the boat, we explored the marina and surrounding town, ate a celebratory meal in a restaurant, then went to the outdoor bar in the marina to watch the final game of the Europe Cup being played between Greece and Portugal. Most of the others in the bar were Germans and all seemed to be cheering for Greece. The Turks were not quite as enthusiastic as Greece pulled ahead, but everyone cheered when Greece, against all odds, won the championship that night.

The next day Janet did some shopping and arranged to rent a motor scooter to ride out to Ephesus the following morning. Bright and early we finished breakfast, and I went to the main gate of the marina to wait for the young man to deliver the motor scooter as he had promised. Fifteen minutes later he still hadn't shown up. A taxi driver, waiting patiently at the gate, asked what I was waiting for. I explained that Janet and I were going by scooter to Ephesus. "Big adventure," he said. It had already begun.

Janet decided to walk the 10 minutes to the rental office in the town center to check about the scooter. About 10 minutes after she left, a man on a decrepit scooter roared up to the gate. "Sorry, we slept late," he apologized. "Jump on."

We roared down the street, flying by a startled Janet, and screeched to a halt in front of the rental office where I signed some papers, collected the helmets, then roared off with a trail of smoke. I picked up Janet, still walking on the street, and soon we were on our way to Ephesus. The scooter was a two-cycle, a noisy, smelly, and uncomfortable little machine, but it performed amazingly well as we climbed up the mountain out of Kuşadasi and drove through the beautiful coastal countryside toward Ephesus less than 10 miles away.

We arrived at the entrance at the same time a number of tour groups were exiting. A mob of souvenir vendors surrounded us, each with creative schemes to get us to visit their rug shop or purchase their coins, statues of gods, postcards, or backscratchers. We successfully bantered, declined, and refused our way through the good-natured gaggle of peddlers, purchased our tickets at the gate, and entered one of the most famous archeological sites in Turkey. *This is the city where Paul spent two-and-a-half years, more time than in any other city during his mission travels. The church he founded here grew to become one of the most important in Asia Minor for hundreds of years,* I thought as we walked the tree-lined road toward the theater.

Though Paul wanted to come here since the beginning of his second journey, it wasn't until his last missionary journey that he finally was able to stay for a length of time. He never really explained what drew him to work in Ephesus. Was it because Paul recognized how strategic this wealthy, influential, regional sea power was to the rest of the area? Scholars believe that the famous cluster of important churches, the Seven Churches of Asia Minor listed in the book of Revelation, all resulted from the mission work of the church in Ephesus. This was one of the richest, most influential, and largest cities of the area, and with the famous temple to Artemis, it attracted huge numbers of tourist pilgrims. Like Corinth, it attracted Paul as well.

Walking down the magnificent marble street, past the theater, the *agora*, and the villas of the wealthy, it wasn't difficult to imagine why Paul would have wanted to come to Ephesus. The *agora* area was huge and successful. It's quite possible that Paul's antagonist, Demetrius, the silversmith whose primary income came from the silver statues of Artemis that he sold to pilgrims, had worked in the central *agora*. Perhaps Paul worked there, too, for a time, fabricating awnings, tents, and other woven goat-hair products. Demetrius could have observed and interacted with people in the *agora* to whom Paul had spoken.

The riot, described in Acts 19, made complete sense. This riot, instigated among the silversmiths by Demetrius, who maintained that Paul's preaching in Ephesus was wrecking their lucrative image-making trade, ended with an unruly mob looking for Paul. Failing to find him, the rioters seized two of Paul's team members and dragged them into the nearby theater, which is located in the center of the city at the main intersection of the Harbor Road and the Marble Way next to the *agora* (see Photos 11 and 12). As was common for theaters in the Roman Empire, the theater in

Ephesus was used for a number of public events, including gladiator battles in which the crowds could either acquit criminals or condemn innocent people without a trial. This time the mob was intent on the latter. Eventually, the city clerk was able to calm the crowd. And although it seemed that the danger had diminished, Paul left Ephesus quickly, probably taking the Marble Way north from the theater, heading toward Troas.

Why did Paul leave so quickly? I pondered as I walked the overgrown but still impressive Marble Way north of the theater. *He never returned to Ephesus again. It wasn't like Paul to be so intimidated by anyone. Had he been banished from Ephesus?*

Back at the *agora*, Demetrius and his fellow craftsmen returned to their profitable work. Even if Paul's activities threatened the silversmiths' trade, it was likely many years before the image business went into significant decline. With or without the silversmiths, the *agora* itself had thrived for another 700 years.

The exotic and the erotic, which once attracted thousands of pagan pilgrims to Ephesus, now attract equivalent numbers of Christian tourists. They pay $10 to see the ruins of a city which Paul made famous, but there is almost nothing for sale that has anything to do with Paul, whose influence eventually undermined the Ephesians' devotion to Artemis, whom they had worshipped for at least 1,000 years.

Today as in Paul's time, Ephesus is full of little statues for sale, especially of Artemis with her many breasts, and Bes, the tiny male god with his gigantic, perpetually erect penis. A thriving business still exists, selling these images to the many Christian tourists who daily visit the ruins. Demetrius would be delighted with the brisk image business today. I bought a statue of Artemis.

Janet and I climbed back on the scooter and roared to the nearby town of Selçuk to visit the splendid archeological museum, then turned back toward Ephesus after viewing what little remains of the once famous Temple to Artemis. Under the scorching afternoon sun, heat waves danced above the isolated stretch of road leading to the upper entrance of Ephesus. Suddenly the scooter began to cough and sputter, roar to life, then choke and die with a feeble gasp. It wouldn't start.

"It can't be out of gas," I asserted to Janet. "I've been watching the gauge all day. It's still full."

"Doesn't E stand for 'empty' in Turkey?" Janet inquired.

"Can't be empty," I said. "It was completely full when we started this morning."

But it was empty, and had been near empty from the beginning. Having never rented a vehicle with an empty tank before in my life, I'd been struck by a dumb, temporary dyslexia and realized I'd been reading the gauge backwards, the E as an F, all the while marveling at the excellent gas mileage we were getting. I even noted at one point with genuine gratitude that the gas tank was actually getting *fuller* as we drove along.

I began pushing the scooter toward an intersection on the main road about a mile behind us in the scorching heat. Janet kindly didn't ask me more than once how I could be so stupid as to read a gas gauge backwards. We passed three different groups of amused fruit vendors selling their produce under the shade trees along the road. No one had fuel but they all motioned that there was a petrol station two miles back out on the main road. This wasn't too bad, but though they *all* said 'two miles more,' we went at least one mile from the first fruit stand to the third. We pushed on.

At last we saw the gas station ahead. We pushed the scooter in and filled the tanks with gas and oil. We bought some water and ice cream to reward ourselves, then headed back to Ephesus, honking and waving to the fruit sellers who gave us directions. We spent the remainder of the day among the archaeological ruins of the once glittering city of Ephesus, rereading Act 20 and thinking of Paul's amazing experiences in that place.

Lying awake on the bunk in *SailingActs* that evening, I reflected on Paul's message in light of the special display on gladiators we viewed in the Ephesus museum that afternoon. The theater in Ephesus was the site of many gladiator contests. Paul may have actually witnessed such a contest while he was in Ephesus and most certainly knew all about them. The contests followed a general pattern. This was an all-day event, beginning with gladiators fighting wild animals in the forenoon, followed by executing criminals around noon. Both these events warmed up the crowd for the main event of the exciting day—gladiator contests. Up to 10 pairs of gladiators would fight in the afternoon.

Recent interpretations of the evidence have challenged the idea that gladiator contests were merely bloody entertainment for an increasingly jaded public satiated with brutality. These contests were about life, not death, some have speculated, and allowed the people to confront death and chaos personally and to overcome this vicariously. Watching wild animals being defeated by the power of the human gladiator was somehow satisfying to those living in a world where nature constantly threatened life. The execution of criminals reassured people that the evil in their midst was being addressed and held at bay. Finally, the victory of the gladiator was everyone's victory, for the gladiator had defeated death on behalf of everyone. The contests allowed the spectators to share in the triumph of life over death.

After visiting the gladiator exhibit that afternoon, I reread the letter Paul wrote to the Ephesians. Paul must have keenly understood the anxiety about death in the Roman Empire and recognized how inadequate, how evil, and how destructive the violence of the gladiator contests actually were. Life comes from God alone, Paul would write, and because of his "great love for us . . . made us alive through Christ even when we were dead . . ." (Ephesians 2:5).

I began to recognize a pattern of communication for Paul as he traveled throughout the pagan world. He spent very little time condemning the brutality and debauchery of paganism, or the oppression and injustices of the Roman system. Instead, recognizing the inadequacies of religion and empire, Paul offered an attractive alternative message of hope, morality, and life—the good news of the abundant and eternal life of the living Jesus. As the taxi man promised that morning, the day had been an adventure. I was already looking forward to exploring Miletus when I fell asleep to the gentle rocking of *SailingActs*.

"You just go to Miletus yourself," Janet suggested the next morning. "I'm not sure my behind can take 45 miles each way on that stinky scooter." We were planning our day and discussing the details of Paul's journey toward Jerusalem at the end of his third voyage.

Leaving Ephesus because of the riot in early 56 A.D., Paul walked north overland to Troas, a port city, and then took a ship to Macedonia, where he headed south to Corinth for a short visit. In the spring of 57 A.D., Paul began the return voyage to Jerusalem from Philippi in the northern Aegean. It was on that voyage, over a year after being run out of Ephesus, that Paul stopped in Miletus. Miletus is at least two days' journey by foot from Ephesus. With the ship Paul was traveling on docked in Miletus for several days, Paul sent some messengers to Ephesus to tell the leaders of the church there that he was in the region.

The scooter ride became pleasant after I turned off the main road and roared and smoked my way out through the flat, rich farmland of the Meander River delta (see Photo 13). This river was once navigable all the way to Miletus, but now, due to silting, had left the port of Miletus stranded a number of miles inland from the sea. I was beginning to wonder whether I missed the turn-off when I spied a mound that looked like a tell off to the left, with a very small brown sign, "Miletus." I pulled into the vast parking lot. In contrast to Ephesus filled with tour busses and hawkers, I was the lone visitor. My scooter was the only vehicle in a parking lot that could have parked 100 tour busses. A man approached me. "One dollar for parking," he said. I stared at him in disbelief, sensing I was dealing with a "freelance" parking attendant. "No," I said.

"Okay," he replied and sauntered off to sit under a shade tree and wait for more victims.

I purchased my entrance ticket for $1 from the three young attendants in the office, who were visibly happy for a customer. They spent 10 minutes giving me advice on what to look for. *All at one-tenth the price of a ticket to Ephesus,* I thought to myself.

I was delighted with the site, with its well-preserved theater from which I surveyed the remains of the whole town below that had once surrounded the busy harbor, now silted. I imagined what Paul observed while waiting at least five days for the Ephesus church leaders to arrive. Paul would have seen the Great Monument on the edge of Lion's Harbor even before disembarking from the ship. Because only the base of this monument is left, it's not certain what the monument commemorated, but the best evidence suggests it was erected following the victory of Pompey over the pirates in the Mediterranean in 67 B.C.

It was Pompey's military victory over piracy that made it possible for Paul to sail the Mediterranean in relative safety, I thought. *Did Paul think about the good news of the gospel of peace being spread because of the brutal military might of the Roman Empire? Did he appreciate military power? Do I, as a committed pacifist, appreciate the protection of the Greek and Turkish navies that makes it possible for us to sail the routes of Paul today without worrying about pirates?*

I walked the streets where Paul would have walked—along the Sacred Way leading from Miletus to Didyma with its huge temple to Apollo, in front of the Delphinium with the god in the form of a dolphin, through the *stoa,* impressive even today (see Photo 14), around the theater, and by the senate house that was constructed under the order of Antiochus Epiphanes in 164 B.C. This was a typical successful Greek/Roman city. We don't read that Paul preached here, but he certainly had a lot to observe and think about.

Hours later, I emerged from Miletus, feeling strangely connected to Paul in this hauntingly deserted specimen of past glory and wealth. "Did you know that the Apostle Paul spent several days in Miletus?" I asked the three young staffers in the ticket office who were eager to talk to their visitor of the day.

"We never heard of him," they replied.

One of the poignant differences between Greece and Turkey is the memory of Paul—or the lack thereof. In Greece Paul is hero, a national treasure. In Turkey very few people among the many I talked to had heard of Paul. Considering that Paul, a key figure in Christianity, is not mentioned in the Koran, and that Turkey is predominately Muslim, this is understandable. In spite of history, ruins, research, monuments, and museums, it takes a living community with an emotional attachment to their heroes to preserve their memory.

After two full days of exploring, it was time to stay "home" and prepare *SailingActs* for the three-day sail up the Turkish coast. I fixed a leak in the water system's pressure tank. Janet stocked up on food and drinks. We filled the water tank and settled the marina bill, preparing to leave on the morning of July 10. We planned to find an anchorage that would give us protection from the *meltimi*, the fierce north or northeast winds of July and August, then sail to Çesme, the last marina in Turkey in which we could take care of the exit documents.

From Kuşadasi the following morning, we began a long sail headed toward an anchorage that looked promising at the tip of a bay. After a fair sail with our deteriorating mainsail, we arrived in plenty of time to anchor before dark, but the wind gusts were tremendous as we dropped anchor. It seemed to hold well, but the wind buffeted and screamed, pushing the boat around. As we were coming in and I was taking the headsail down, the headsail halyard flew out of my hands and, before I could retrieve it, wrapped itself in the rotating blades of the wind generator. WHACK! I spent a restless night wondering if the anchor would hold and how I'd get the rope out of the wind generator without climbing up the mast.

The next morning I tried all the ideas that seemed completely feasible during the night but ridiculous in the light of day. In the end, I climbed the mast, untangled the rope, and tied it in such a way to prevent it from getting caught again. We left the anchorage in a light wind, which began to build immediately. The day before, in a last-ditch effort to get some performance out of the decrepit mainsail, I poked a hole in the foot of the mainsail, threaded a rope through, and tied it to the boom in a way that improved the shape. This improved performance—until the whole thing ripped and the destruction of the mainsail was complete. It was now worthless, so we tried to make progress with the genoa and mizzen only, shifting to the working jib, then the storm jib as the winds picked up.

We arrived at the "marina" in Çesme, Turkey, in late afternoon. The marina was dilapidated and dusty, surrounded by a rusty fence. A rickety shed across a dirt parking lot housed a men's toilet only. There were no showers or electricity. The relentless wind circulated the dust-laden, stifling air. No one spoke English. I don't know if ugly surroundings had anything to do with it, but Janet and I found our confidence and optimism replaced by anxiety and fears. Our spirits rose only as we eased out of the Çesme harbor two days later and headed *SailingActs* north.

CHAPTER 6
Sailing Acts to Macedonia

The passage to the little island of Oinousses was pleasant in spite of our tattered sails. In favorable winds, I put up the genoa and we barreled along on flat seas, so flat that I decided to take apart the dysfunctional auto helm. I discovered the problem—an adjustment screw mounted backwards—and when I put everything back together, it performed flawlessly for the first time of the journey. Suddenly Janet and I were freed from spending endless hours at the helm. It was like having another crew member that didn't take up a berth, drink water, or eat food. We called the auto helm "Timothy," figuring that Paul must have appreciated his young helper at least as much as we did our blessedly functioning auto helm (see Photo 15).

We were the only boat in the anchorage on the evening after leaving Çesme. We picked a promising spot, sheltered as much as possible from the violent gusts of wind. As we began to relax in the cockpit, a charter boat full of Germans we had spotted earlier that day pulled into the anchorage and attempted to set their anchor. We watched in bemused superiority as the Germans struggled for 30 minutes what had taken us, experienced in anchoring now, only five minutes to do. They'd drop the anchor but before it reached the bottom they'd begin backing into deeper water, so that by the time their anchor finally connected with the bottom, they were completely out of the anchorage. Back and forth they went until finally they figured it out, their anchor seemed to hold, and we went back to reading our books.

I glanced up from time to time and noticed with pity at one point that their boat had drifted again. They hadn't realized this yet, as they were all looking in our direction.

They are really pathetic, I thought. *They don't even know their anchor is dragging.* Wait! Their boat was in the anchorage close to shore. I sprang up and looked around, then leapt into chagrined action as I realized *SailingActs* was drifting backwards out to sea. We hauled up our heavy (45-pound) CRC anchor and motored back to our original anchorage and set it again, putting our second Danforth anchor down for good measure, letting out plenty of chain for both. Then we reversed with the motor, setting both anchors well. This time they held. We had just learned another lesson at sea—humility.

The next day, with a gentle tail wind, we limped 40 miles in a 10-hour sail into the harbor of Mytilini, Lesvos, with our tattered sails. Although we were arriving from Turkey and needed to get a new Greek Transit Log again, we had replaced the Turkish flag with a Greek flag instead of the yellow "Q" flag when we entered Greek waters. Without calling the Port Authority on our VHF, we motored into the harbor and found an empty place alongside the wharf. I tied up the boat and took the required papers into the Port Authority office. But when I reported in, I was told I was supposed to have gone to the customs area with the boat before coming in.

"How was I supposed to know that?" I asked.

"Didn't they call you on your VHF?"

"No, and I had it on the whole time."

I returned to *SailingActs* to get additional documents and was just getting off the boat to find the customs office when a uniformed customs officer approached. "Why didn't you stop at customs?" he asked.

"How was I supposed to know that I needed to stop there first?" I queried again.

"I was waving at you when you came in," he claimed.

But we were watching carefully and didn't see anyone waving. With his stark white uniform, he would have been easy to spot. He instructed us to untie *SailingActs* and follow him back to the customs area. When we re-tied *SailingActs*, he accompanied me to the customs office for passport control and a new Transit Log. But all the offices were closed, and as I tagged along behind, he wandered around, banging on doors and calling people on his cell phone, until finally an agent showed up. Two hours later we finally finished.

I walked back to the Port Authority for directions on where to tie up, and then moved *SailingActs* to a berth in the corner that they permitted us to use. We were appalled by the quality of the water; it seemed like we were floating on sewer. The sight and smell was so awful we couldn't even consider eating a meal on the boat. This was the first, and last, time we ever experienced these conditions in the Mediterranean. The relentless disco music blaring from the bars 50 feet away added to the ambiance. We decided to spend as little time as possible in Mytilini.

The current and wind shifted just enough the next morning, which enabled us to eat breakfast on board as usual. We slept well, in spite of the music blasting from the bars at such a high volume that I felt the solid hull of *SailingActs* vibrating against my leg during the night. Now we were ready to track down the new sails. We found a taxi driver who knew the location of the shipping agent where the sails were to have been delivered. He spoke excellent English and shared his extensive knowledge of Lesvos as he drove up the mountain out of Mytilini. The subject turned to Paul.

"Oh yes," he said, "Paul had to spend a night in a harbor on this island because of a storm. Everybody in Lesvos knows this story. There's a church on the shore that marks the spot."

"Do all the children learn about Paul in school?" I asked.

"They used to," he said, "but now religious education is not compulsory in Greece since it joined the EU. Since it's voluntary, not all children are learning the stories."

"This is too bad," I said.

"I think this is better," the taxi driver said. "A person's religion should not be part of the educational system."

He's right, of course, I thought. *But I wonder if future generations of Greeks will continue to remember the story of the Apostle Paul on their island. Will a taxi driver 20 years from now say "I never heard of him" when a passenger asks about Paul on the island? I'm sure that the story of Sapho, one of the greatest poets of ancient Greece, born on Lesvos around 630 B.C., will not be forgotten with the changes in religious education. What is lost when a culture forgets some of its stories and remembers others?*

We arrived at the warehouse, and within five minutes we had the sails in the taxi. This was one of the quickest transactions I made in Greece, which made me vaguely uneasy. Maybe there was only one sail inside. I opened the package. The two sails were indeed there, and we were on our way. Back on the boat we put up the new sails immediately and were pleased—or more accurately, ecstatic—that both brilliant white sails fit perfectly (see Photo 16). We were especially pleased that the mainsail held the boom exactly where it should. Now we could use the spray hood and mainsail at the same time. Captain Steve and DL Sails had delivered!

The next morning we rented a scooter and set off to find the church dedicated to St. Paul on the Gulf of Kalonis, about 25 miles from Mytilini that the taxi driver had told us about. While this story is not in the book of Acts, it's entirely possible that it occurred. Violent weather often develops with little warning between Assos, where Paul's ship left, and Mytilini, where, according to Acts, they anchored that night. The Gulf of Kalonis would have certainly been a good location to seek shelter from a storm.

The morning was pleasant and the scenery stunning as we climbed the mountains outside Mytilini, then descended the other side. We stopped briefly at the ancient site of Pira to look at the submerged foundations of magnificent buildings under the crystal-clear water. At a small *taverna* we asked the woman where to find the church of the Apostle Paul. She motioned that it was farther in the direction we were going, so we continued on. We were intrigued by the unusual mixture of beaches, lush olive groves, tractors, goats, and sunbathers as we drove along the road that skirted the bay.

SailingActs

Suddenly we spotted a little white church just yards from the water, the church of the Apostle Paul, exactly as the taxi driver described (see Photo 17). Inside, it was a thing of simple beauty. The twittering birds in the plane trees and the waves gently lapping on the shore a few yards away created an aura of peace. Judging from the number of icons, Paul held a position of primary importance in this church. There were at least three large and quite unusual icons of Paul, all of him holding a scroll or book, representing the authoring of scriptures. On one icon, Paul held both a book and a sword.

Back outside several old people had gathered. An old man without a shirt had been sitting in a chair by the water's edge when we arrived, and an old woman and another old man came up and sat on the white plastic garden chairs on the front porch of the church. The man in the chair by the sea asked where we were from, and we asked him about Paul. Then they all began, in very limited English, to talk with obvious pride about Paul's visit in that very gulf on their island.

Why are so many Greeks, especially the islanders, so proud of Paul? I wondered. *Why do so many Western Christians fail to appreciate him? Maybe the Greeks recognize the huge effort Paul made on their behalf to get the early Jewish Christians to accept them as equals. Western Christians are just too far removed from the dynamics of Mediterranean culture to appreciate this extraordinary accomplishment. All non-Jews, especially Western Christians, owe a debt to Paul and the historical achievements he accomplished by his relentless, personal efforts to include the Greeks in the kingdom.*

We left Mytilini the next morning, a morning in which I recorded in our log book as "the worst checkout through customs yet." Because we were sailing back to Turkey, having picked up our sails and explored Paul's legacy on Lesvos, we needed an exit stamp in our passports and were required to turn in our Transit Log which we had worked so hard to purchase two days earlier. We were planning to leave at 8:00 and by 7:15 a.m., I was at the customs office for the passport stamp. I arrived to find a number of people gathering in front of the locked building. The offices would open at 8:00. I decided to go back to the boat, eat breakfast, and prepare for sailing, then come back for the paperwork.

Back at the customs office at 8:30, I was dismayed to see hundreds of ferry passengers waiting in front of the building. The line slowly inched forward. Forty minutes later I stood at the counter with both Janet's and my passports.

"Where is your wife?" the officer snapped.

"On our boat, according to Greek regulations," I replied. I wasn't certain these were the regulations, but previously in Samos, Greece customs officials had assured me that only the captain needs to appear with the passports.

"No," he snarled, "I have to see her face."

It was now one-and-a-half hours since I started this process. We were more than an hour behind schedule, and my response, which I shouldn't have made, instantly caused his face to turn a deep red. He immediately dispatched a police officer to escort me into a back room, away from the crowds waiting in line, who were clearly delighted with the exchange.

Am I actually going to be arrested? I thought with alarm. I found some comfort in remembering that Paul had often been arrested for what he said, but I knew in my heart that there was a big difference here.

"You will have to go back to the boat, untie it, and bring it back to the customs area. Then come with your wife back to this office."

"Sure, no problem," I hastily replied, suddenly compliant. I couldn't bear to think of floating on the sewer of Mytilini any longer. I did take the time on the way back to *SailingActs* to stop at the Port Authority office and lodge a complaint. They were sympathetic and explained that the man was likely uptight because the Olympic torch was going to arrive later that day and security was high.

I don't know if a Port Authority official called the customs officer or not, but by the time Janet and I arrived 15 minutes later, he was completely cooperative, stamped our passports without delay, shook my hand, and wished us a pleasant journey.

We left Mytilini at 10:30, thinking about the use and misuse of authority in Paul's day and in the present. Paul wrote to the Christians in Rome: "Everyone must submit himself to the governing authorities, for there is no authority except that which God has established. The authorities that exist have been established by God" (17:1). I thought about both Paul's teaching and his examples of "submission," how he once escaped from the authorities in Damascus over the wall in a basket, and how he argued with Roman officials on some occasions and cooperated with them on others. In Paul's practice, submission to authority was not just meekly accepting whatever an irate official demanded. While Janet and I didn't reach a conclusion about what Paul meant exactly by "submission," I began to wonder if emulating his pattern in Damascus might be the best way to leave Greek islands.

With her new sails, *SailingActs* seemed to fly over the water as we sailed toward Ayvalik, Turkey. In contrast to Mytilini, in Ayvalik we were helped into a berth by the friendly marina staff, the water was sparkling clean, and all the paperwork was done in a matter of minutes. In an inexpensive restaurant that evening, a vacationing Turkish couple from Germany, sitting at the table next to us, saw Janet and me discussing the white liquid they were drinking. They bought us a glass of the popular buttermilk to try, then we chatted about many things—except Paul, who neither had ever heard of.

After a day of routine maintenance on *SailingActs*, we planned to rent a car and drive to Assos and Troas, two ports on the Turkish coast through which Paul passed but which can no longer accommodate a boat the size of *SailingActs*. A British man on the

18 *The temple of Athena high above the Assos harbor in Turkey.*

19 *Some of the remains of the Baths of Herodes Atticus among the ruins of Troas, Turkey, a once huge and bustling city with an immensely important harbor.*

20 *The ancient harbor of Troas (in modern Turkey) with the Roman columns still visible in the water.*

21 *In the farmers' fields we found the columns that once lined the road from the harbor of Troas, Turkey.*

22 *St. Paul's Bay on the island of Limnos, Greece, where we thought* SailingActs *was sinking.*

23 *On the hill above the harbor in Mirina, Limnos Island, Greece.* SailingActs *is on the wharf on the far right.*

24 | *Janet inspects the ancient temple complex at the Sanctuary of the Great Gods on the island of Samothraki, Greece.*

25 | *Janet with the family of the non-practicing Greek Orthodox priest that we met on Samothraki, Greece.*

26 | *Admiring the mosaic in Kavalla (Neapolis), Greece, depicting Paul's vision to come to Macedonia and his first step on European soil.*

27 | *The Egnatian Way at Philippi, Greece, that runs through the center of the town.*

28 *Janet in the river near Philippi, Greece, at the traditional site where Paul baptized Lydia.*

29 *Janet admires the Lion Monument near Amphipolis, Greece. Built in the fourth century B.C., Paul would have seen this.*

30 *Aram, the seminary student who sailed briefly with us, reading Acts at sea.*

31 *Walking on a marvelous example of Roman road on the island of Kos, Greece.*

32 *Janet among the columns of the temple to Apollo at the Asklipion, Hippocrates's medical center on the island of Kos, Greece.*

33 *Janet hanging out the bed sheets after a freak wave dumped gallons of seawater on our bunks just before arriving in Rhodes, Greece.*

34 *Hauling out SailingActs on Rhodes, Greece, in order to replace the damaged propeller.*

boat next to us in the marina gave me advice on how to repair one of the mast spreaders. I needed a small part and went to the local ship chandler. I found the chandler easily. The door was open but no one seemed to be tending the shop, so I poked and rummaged through the supplies on display until I found the small clamp I needed. *When would the shopkeeper return?* I wondered. Then I heard a light snoring sound and realized he had been there all the time, sound asleep in a chair behind a stack of supplies. I banged and coughed until he woke up and took my payment.

Back on the boat, I had just finished fixing the spreader, when a marina workman came by in an inflatable launch. "Come with me," he requested, "you need to go to the passport police."

Oh no, I thought, remembering Mytilini, *here we go again.* The British sailor from the boat next to us also climbed aboard and with the 50-horsepower outboard at full throttle, we shot out of the marina and across the harbor at what seemed, after weeks of five miles-per-hour on *SailingActs,* like an incredible rate of speed. "We were not made to go this fast on water," the British man yelled above the roar of the motor as he gripped a handhold with white knuckles.

We whisked to a sudden stop in front of the police station and followed our launch driver into the building. The woman behind the desk looked at us and our passports. "Okay," she said and stamped them. Sixty seconds after arriving, we left the office to the launch and roared back to the marina. "This is the way bureaucracy should be done," I yelled to the Brit.

"Right you are," he yelled back.

The drive to Assos and Troas the next morning in our rental car took us two hours through beautiful countryside as we followed the rugged coastal route. We rolled across flat plains, rolling hills, and over steep mountain passes, through forests of pine trees and then along mile after mile of camping areas, cheap pensions, signs advertising *Zimmer frei,* and ragged lines of sunburned northern Europeans trudging toward the pebbly beaches with their enormous burdens of colorful equipment needed for a day of fun.

We turned inland and ascended to the village of Behramkale with its steep, cobblestone streets, then parked the car and hiked to the entrance of the hilltop ruins of the ancient Assos. Along the way, old men and ladies tried to get us to buy knit socks; gooey, edible stuff on sticks; and a variety of pagan religious images. Janet decided to skip the site, so I went in and was immediately impressed by the former grandeur of this seaport, with its imposing temple of Athena dominating the city (see Photo 18). Back outside the gate, Janet joined me and we spent several hours exploring the lower ruins of the *agora, stoa*, small temples, gymnasium, and theater, all built on the steep slopes of the mountain. Below us lay the ancient harbor from which Paul left on his southward journey to Jerusalem.

We searched for clues to the mystery of why Paul chose to come to Assos by foot from Troas while his companions sailed. Could it be he came earlier because he had time on his hands and wanted to use it exploring and preaching?

Tradition claims that Paul did, indeed, preach in Assos, and that this was one of the first cities in the whole region to accept Christianity. There does seem to be some knowledge of Paul's visit and even some pride among the writers of history. But when I tried to ask people in the harbor area about Paul, I discovered that the people who could speak English there were not prepared to answer such unusual questions as, "Do you know anything about the Apostle Paul?"

"Would you like a room? Something to eat?" they responded.

"No, just wondering whether you have heard of Paul."

"Who? Wasn't he a saint, maybe? We have really good fish for lunch. You can look at a room."

The spectacular ruins, the region, the harbor, all provided information about Paul. As we drove on to Alexandria Troas, another hour north following the coast, we were again impressed by the rugged terrain and the incredible distance Paul traveled.

"Paul was one tough traveler," Janet and I remarked to each other as we navigated our rental car toward Troas. And then, out of the fields, the famous arches of the Baths of Herodes loomed (see Photo 19). We had arrived in Troas. We stopped the car. The place was completely deserted, an overgrown cluster of ruins, with fields cultivated right up to the base of ancient walls, columns, and arches. We pushed our way through the tangle of bushes and were amazed at the size of Troas, the distance to the harbor, and the way it had sprawled toward the distant sea.

Covered with scratches from the briars, we returned to the car and set out to find the ancient harbor. With nothing to go on but a sense of where the harbor might have been, we arrived at a small village near the town of Daylan. I pulled out my copy of William Ramsey's updated classic, *St. Paul: The Traveler and Roman Citizen*, that contained a photograph of Troas's ancient harbor. I showed the photographs to an old stonemason and his young assistant working near the waterfront. Their English was limited, but they made it clear that they had never seen such a place and thought maybe we'd find it about 25 miles south. "No this way, no that way," the old man said, which we took to mean that the old harbor of Troas was not in the immediate vicinity.

Somehow this didn't fit the evidence. The ancient harbor for Troas had to be nearby. I walked down the beach around a small point and, sure enough, there were the ruins of the ancient harbor which Paul had sailed into and out of on two missionary journeys. The location, the lagoon, and the huge columns at the waterfront all clearly indicated that this was the site of Troas's important, artificial harbor (see Photo 20).

Up through the fields, leading away from the harbor toward the city of Troas, was a line of Roman columns. We drove the car back toward Troas, then found the line of columns and followed them through the fields (see Photo 21). Along the route we found the ruins of a theater and a temple to Dionysus.

We drove back to the harbor where the stonemasons were still working and showed them the photos again, explaining that the ruins were just around the corner. They grinned and apologized that they had never been around that particular corner, and we all laughed. Janet and I marveled that no matter where people live, they tend to explore everywhere except in their own back-yards. The two workmen most likely marveled that we would come one-third of the distance around the planet in order to find some old rocks on their beach.

Over the next few days we rested and caught up with boat maintenance work. The wind had been literally screaming in the marina for several days. Our wind generator, which has no shut-off possibilities, had produced so much electricity that we had charged all four of our batteries to capacity. We then needed to run lights in the middle of the day to keep the batteries from over-charging.

The night before we left Ayvalik, I made elaborate plans for how to get out of the crowded marina without banging other boats in the wind, but as we were preparing to leave, the marina work-er appeared in a dinghy, fastened a line to the bow of *SailingActs,* and helped guide us out. We had given up our Turkish Transit Log as we were now heading back into Greek waters. We planned to anchor along the Turkish coast, then sail to the Greek island of Limnos on our way to Samothraki and on to Kavalla.

The *meltimi* that had whipped up the waters most of the day dropped off in the afternoon, until the precise moment we entered the anchorage toward evening and tried to get our anchor to hold on the weedy bottom. There were fishermen everywhere preparing to depart later that night, and they watched with appreciation as Janet and I ploughed their harbor bottom with our anchor. Eventually, after almost winding up on a reef, we retreated to another spot up the beach, got the anchor to hold, and settled in for the night.

At 4:50 the next morning, the alarm went off. We wanted to make 64 miles that day, and so, in the pitch-dark, we switched on the navigation lights for the first time of the voyage, weighed anchor, and eased out of the harbor with a sense of satisfaction, knowing this was how Paul would have experienced sailing in the first century. I put up the genoa in light winds, then when the wind picked up, I put up the working jib, followed by the storm jib and reefed mainsail as the wind grew in strength. We set the auto helm and braced ourselves in the cockpit. The steady wind pushed us between five and six knots for hours, with no need to adjust the sails. Once we got used to the huge waves, we began to enjoy the sail, out of sight of land for the first time on the voyage. When the wind subsided slightly, I put the working jib back up and took out the reefs in the mainsail, and our speed climbed to above seven knots.

By 4:30 we were approaching the mouth of St. Paul's Bay on the island of Limnos. The wind was dropping and I was just ready to reduce sail to motor to the anchorage when Janet went down in the cabin and said something like, "Why is all this water on the cabin floor?"

"Probably just spray," I replied, "nothing to worry about." But when I poked my head into the cabin, I saw that it *was* something to worry about. The floorboards literally floated as the boat rocked. "Take the wheel," I yelled in dismay.

I hit the switch on the bilge pump, then grabbed the handle of the manual bilge pump and began pumping furiously, but no water came out. Broken! I had never actually tested it because the water in the bilge had never been high enough. The water didn't seem to be going down with the electric bilge pump alone, so I grabbed a bucket and began bailing the water from the cabin out into the cockpit as Janet calmly hove-to. "We're taking on water," I panted, and Janet began wondering whether she might end up driving *SailingActs* on St. Paul's Bay beach, which seemed almost like a biblical thing to do.

In the meantime, I managed to bail the water level down far enough, with the bilge pump still going, to try to find the leak. I checked the shaft for leakage. Normal. Then all the sea cocks. Dry. How about the fresh-water tank? Maybe it had sprung a leak.

Couldn't be—that was saltwater in the bilge (yes, I tasted it). Yet water still seemed to be coming in. So I got one of the two replacement bilge pumps we had on board, cut a piece of water hose to make an emergency discharge into the cockpit, connected the wires to the battery and, with two pumps going, finally succeeded in lowering the water in the bilge. Water still seemed to be running in, but it finally became apparent that the water was simply draining from under the floor into the lower part of the bilge. Where had all that water come from and why did it stop suddenly?

That would need to be solved later as we were now hove-to in the bay, all the sails still up. I began taking them all down quickly. Janet started the engine and we headed toward the anchorage, found the perfect spot, dropped the anchor, and then got to work.

Instead of a relaxing evening, enjoying the solitude and beauty of the surroundings (see Photo 22), we began checking the damage and cleaning up. Our tools, everything under the chart table, and all of the contents of the port settee lockers needed to be taken out to dry. We mopped out the greasy water, then stowed all of the stuff back again. Three hours later we finished. We made dinner then sat in the cockpit, eating and figuring out where the water came from, thanking God that we were safe, and, for some reason, laughing hilariously. I suppose there is nothing so fun to celebrate on a boat as not sinking.

We set aside the next day to find the problem. We did. The electric bilge pump on *SailingActs* exits into the water on the port side only inches above the water line. As I traced the hose back, I was startled to see that there was neither a safety loop nor a check valve to prevent the water from running into the boat when heeled over on a starboard tack. The pump, which is supposed to pump water out, was actually letting water in! Being heeled over for 10 hours put this outlet below the water line and allowed the water to siphon in, which stopped the moment we quit sailing. I resolved to fix the problem at the next port.

Janet and I discussed that night how Paul had experienced these kinds of moments a number of times while at sea. We realized that in spite of the momentary terror we felt, this had actually been a memorable way to understand Paul better. We thanked God for the timing, location, and other features of this near disaster, for if this were going to happen, St. Paul's Bay was the perfect place. If it had occurred in the middle of the white-capped Aegean, it would have been extremely difficult to cope with. I understood a little better why Paul wrote that his experiences at sea demonstrate his commitment, faithfulness, and suffering for the sake of the gospel.

Janet took this opportunity to remind me—again—that we needed to think more about safety equipment and backup plans. Her arguments suddenly made new sense, so I decided to have an emergency tiller made at the next port, to repair the manual bilge pump, to get additional man-overboard equipment, and to devise jacklines to attach myself to the boat when sailing in rough seas.

The following day we left the anchorage and had a leisurely sail into Mirina, the main harbor of Limnos, a port of entry into Greece (see Photo 23). When entering the harbor we discovered that we had lost our U.S. flag in the high winds several days earlier. I radioed in to explain. "Don't worry about it," the officer said.

We dropped the anchor and came in stern-to, feeling triumphant that we were getting good at the Mediterranean-style berthing. When I took my papers into the Port Authority office, a navy officer advised me not to fly the U.S. flag while at sea.

"Isn't it required by law?" I asked.

"Yes," he said, "but no patrol boat is going to stop you. With the way things are, it's better not to be identified as an American boat."

When we purchased a replacement flag several days later, I devised a quick-release system for flying it only when entering or leaving harbors. The flag would remain hidden most of the time.

With its rugged rocks and ruined castle dominating the skyline, we liked Mirina immediately. There were few tourists, and a relaxed atmosphere pervaded the picturesque waterfront. My 54th birthday was approaching, and I couldn't think of a better place to celebrate it. On my birthday I wrote in my journal:

"Today is my birthday. I have a feeling I will not forget this one for a while. Paul had a number of birthdays in the Aegean. Who knows, maybe even his 54th."

On one of the last evenings on Limnos, after spending several days catching up on writing and boat maintenance, we were sitting in the cockpit drinking coffee after dinner. A Greek man, Bill, with his son, Alexander, stopped by the boat and began talking about Limnos, then about Paul, Christianity, and the world. Bill explained that he was Greek Orthodox, a history teacher, and was born and raised in New York, where he currently lives, but has close connections to Limnos, the home of his extended family. Like most Greeks, he was proud of St. Paul.

"Why does Limnos have so many places named after St. Paul if he never came to this island?" I asked.

Bill explained that Greek geographical names like "St. Paul's Bay" are everywhere because of the respect Greeks have for him. "It is like Washington state," he clarified. "George Washington never went there, but his influence is part of the history of that part of America."

"Come to think of it, I don't think St. Paul ever made it to Minnesota either," I added. "What do you think of Paul?" I asked Bill.

"Paul is being disparaged and attacked by people who do not understand the world he lived in or the brilliant way that he connected the gospel to the Greek world," Bill replied. "No one runs down Paul or attacks the Church in Greece," he continued. "Greeks are Christians; the Church is powerful."

In his view, the strength of the Greek Orthodox Church is its ability to preserve tradition and to resist cultural pressure to make theological changes. Bill reaffirmed the idea that Paul connected the message of the gospel to the pagan Greeks, not by denouncing all of the evil that he encountered, but by focusing on that which was missing within the pagan religion, particularly the resurrection. While pagan religion was obsessed with life, the concept of eternal life remained vague and uncertain.

Among the Greeks Paul preached to, the resurrection story became the most compelling and attractive feature of the gospel, and it became the central focus of Paul's message. Anyone celebrating Easter in Greece, especially in Athens, recognizes the legacy of Paul's emphasis on the resurrection in contemporary Greek culture.

On July 28 we left Limnos for the harbor town of Kamariotissa, on the island of Samothraki (Samothrace). We were picking up the route of Paul's second journey, described in Acts 16:8-11. As Paul, we were on our way to Macedonia. As we approached Samothraki, we admired its rugged and barren beauty. I was looking forward to exploring this island where Paul had stopped on his voyage from Troas to Philippi. I had read that Samothraki was once the center of intense worship of pagan gods, both indigenous and imported. The people of Samothraki had worshipped the Great Mother Earth from earliest history, and the island had been considered her sanctuary. As such, it attracted initiates from great distances to join this and other unique religious cults on the island. Paul was likely aware of all of this, but there is no record of his activities on the island during his layover. I hoped to find some local opinions on the matter.

Samothraki has only one viable harbor on the entire island. "What will we do if there is no room in the harbor?" Janet worried as we neared Samothraki. We were relieved to see plenty of room as we entered the large harbor. All the boats were alongside the quay, so I yelled to a man on a yacht flying a Swiss flag to ask if I could come in behind him, and to some fishermen if I could go in front of their fishing boat.

"Yes, fine, no problem," everyone shouted back, so I eased *SailingActs* gently into place, stepped off, and tied up. Five minutes after entering the harbor we were done.

SailingActs

The following morning before breakfast, I found a scooter-rental agency on the waterfront which rented small, 50-cc scooters for 15 euros a day, made the deal, and rode the little yellow scooter back to the boat. After a leisurely breakfast, we packed the equipment into the scooter and rode out of town toward the Sanctuary of the Great Gods, our primary site for the day. The man who rented me the scooter was from Cyprus and was surprised that morning when I had asked him if he was aware that St. Paul had stopped in Samothraki. No, he hadn't heard that. But it piqued his interest so he made a telephone call to someone and discovered that near the Sanctuary of the Great Gods was something related to Paul. "Ask the man at the museum about it," he suggested.

We found the site easily, purchased entrance tickets, and started through the small museum, which displayed a fascinating collection of ancient, unusual religious objects from the Sanctuary area. Stone ox heads, signs forbidding the uninitiated from entering the holy of holies in the temple, and many other unique artifacts filled the simple building. I asked the museum curator about the Apostle Paul.

"We know he came to Samothraki," he explained, happy to talk, "but I have never heard any other details." He gave us directions to the ruins of a very early Christian basilica close by that had been built in honor of Paul. "It's right here, down by the ancient harbor," he showed us on the map.

"Not many Americans come here. What brings you to Samothraki?" he wanted to know. When we told him about our project, he seemed very pleased. "This is the best way to see Greece," he said, "just like Paul himself saw Greece."

Surrounded by deep shadows, lush vegetation, and mist hovering over the craggy peaks of Samothraki's highest mountain, Mt. Fengari, we felt a sense of awe as we entered the Sanctuary. It was filled with the stunning, gigantic remains of temples and associated religious structures (see Photo 24). I felt the same sense of wonder as when Janet and I visited Stonehenge years before. I imagined the scene on this site 2,000 years earlier—throngs of people from around the Mediterranean gathering for festivals and religious ceremonies in honor of the powerful, ancient gods, especially of the Great Mother, goddess of fertility. I imagined Paul walking up the path from the harbor below, observing these fervent activities with interest and concern.

The remains of the cultic buildings and other evidence uncovered over the years by researchers indicate that the cult of the Great Mother was a mystery religion. Initiates swore, on punishment of death, not to reveal the secrets of what went on within the inner sanctuary. On the other hand, the religion was not exclusive; initiation was open to all who desired to join. There were two levels of initiation: the lower and the higher. In the lower, the gods were invoked to bring about a spiritual rebirth. In the second, higher level of initiation, the initiates were promised forgiveness for any transgressions they committed. *Justification and sanctification,* I thought as I read the descriptions. *Paul would certainly have observed and listened with great interest to the beliefs and practices of this religion while at Samothraki.*

We continued out of the main site to some peripheral ruins, trying to find the basilica which the museum curator had described. From the top of a hill we could see ruins below at the water's edge, so we started down the path. Janet walked on ahead while I lagged behind taking photos. As I started down the path, I met a man with a wild beard and bushy pony tail climbing toward me. Ahead of me Janet had just met two women who turned out to be the man's wife and daughter. The man was an Orthodox priest. "I tried to resign," he explained, "but once you are a priest, you are a priest for life. So I'm a non-active priest."

"Why did you resign?" I asked.

"I wanted to work with the homeless and drug addicts," he explained, "but the Church said my duties were spiritual, not physical. So we argued and discussed and in the end I quit. The Church has to share the good news to people outside of its own walls." *A modern Paul,* I thought (see Photo 25).

After a delightful conversation, they assured us that we would find the basilica below and we parted ways. We climbed down the hill, and sure enough, there were the ruins of the basilica. When I examined the site carefully, it became obvious that the basilica had been built on the edge of the ancient harbor. The remains of an ancient breakwater and the contour of the ground were proof of this. Why is this important? Samothraki has no natural harbors. This was the harbor for the town of Paleopolis, and Paul's ship would have anchored there, below the famous Sanctuary only a short walk up the hill. Paul would have had adequate time to look around, observe the throngs of the faithful and the seekers, and even to talk to the initiates.

Later we continued by scooter along the beaches, stopping for lunch at a waterfront café under the trees. An old man, a native of Samothraki, asked us what we were doing on the island. We explained our project and he affirmed my conclusions about Paul's ship at the harbor of Paleopolis. "Everyone knows this is where he stopped," he declared, and described submerged remains of the harbor he had discovered when diving there.

We left Samothraki for the island of Thasos the next morning. No one from the Port Authority seemed interested in us, so we didn't pay any fees. Immediately we had good winds coming from the starboard side. I started with the working jib and a reefed mainsail, and we made good time in heavy seas. Around 11:00 the wind eased a little and I took the reefs out of the mainsail and we cruised between five- and six-and-a-half knots until the wind began to die in the early afternoon. I put up the genoa and we managed four knots, then three. Finally, when we were below two knots, we took down all the sails and motored into Thasos. The harbor came into sight, and we eased in. It was large and virtually empty, with five yachts in an area with room for 40, so we pulled alongside the wharf and fastened our mooring lines.

We spent the following day on Thasos, working on boat maintenance and catching up with the laundry. A man came by as

Janet was washing the clothes in the cockpit. "This is a great boat," he said.

I was working on something in the cabin and listened with interest. No one had called *SailingActs* "great" up to that point, and I wanted to make sure I heard right—or that we didn't have a dangerous lunatic on the loose. So I wiped the grease off my hands and joined Janet in the cockpit.

The man introduced himself as Cornelius from Luxembourg. "I sailed a Westerly 33 exactly like this one across the Atlantic by myself once." *So the man does know what he is talking about,* I thought. "A beautiful boat," he repeated again and again as we invited him aboard. After weeks of maintenance work, spending thousands of dollars on *SailingActs*, and sailing the Mediterranean among flashy yachts, this well-informed compliment was both rare and priceless, and we wanted to keep hearing his praise for as long as possible. So for the next hour, we plied Cornelius with snacks and drinks while we discussed sailing, Paul, and religion.

The following morning we sailed for Kavalla, the biblical Neapolis mentioned in Acts 16:11. A gentle breeze pushed us toward our destination, and we arrived early in the afternoon. As we came into the harbor, we weren't sure where to berth. We saw plenty of room to dock at the Yacht Club, but our guidebook had warned us not to tie up there—we would be unceremoniously thrown out. What appeared to be a place for visiting yachts was almost full of a motley assortment of local boats.

"Come on in. There is plenty of room," the Port Authority instructed when I called. Indeed, I noticed some empty space between the two "Visiting Yachts Only" signs along the wharf, but when we got close, it seemed all the available spaces were filled with homemade mooring lines that might get tangled in the propeller or anchor if we ventured too close. We searched until we found a relatively open spot, then dropped the anchor and backed in cautiously.

We noted that our guidebook's description of the quay in Kavalla as "extremely high" was certainly accurate, as it loomed above our heads. Rickety ladders hung down toward the water, and we needed to place our gangplank between the boat and the ladder, making each venture to shore a thrilling circus act without a safety net. I was beginning to understand why *SailingActs* appeared to be the only visiting yacht in the whole harbor. We planned to spend about a week in this harbor and hoped to connect with electricity and water, but I noticed with a little concern that there were no utility hookups on the wharf.

After we finally secured *SailingActs* to the concrete wall, I checked in with the Port Authority office. The woman who inspected our documents asked, with what appeared to be a note of concern or pity, why were we planning to stay there for six days. "We're visiting all the places the Apostle Paul visited on his mission journeys," I explained.

"Then you must go to my home town," she said. She wrote down "Methini" on a small scrap of paper and handed it to me. "Paul went there." Knowing that Methini is not mentioned in the book of Acts, I was a little skeptical, but decided to try and visit if we had the chance.

Exploring Kavalla later that afternoon, we were pleased to find a beautiful mosaic mural outside one of the churches. Only recently completed, the mosaic depicted two scenes, one showing Paul's call to Macedonia while he was in Troas and another of Paul stepping out of a boat in Neapolis, now "Kavalla" (see Photo 26). His first steps in Europe were likely only yards from the mural. We admired that magnificent mural sparkling in the late afternoon sun and thought about those first steps. *The rim of the Mediterranean is drenched in blood,* I thought, *from centuries of invasions from the sea. The temporary conquerors of those endless, violent invasions established their cultures, their products, and their religions around the Mediterranean. But Paul, the peaceful invader from the sea, carrying the good news of the gospel, did more to change the course of Mediterranean history in the long run than most of the heroes of war whose memorials, ancient and modern, we've been seeing in the public squares of towns and cities all around the Mediterranean.*

During the next days in Kavalla, we planned to explore nearby Philippi, then rent a car to visit Thessaloniki and Veria before picking up Aram DiGennaro, a student from Eastern Mennonite Seminary who would be joining the voyage for three weeks of independent study, which I had arranged to direct for him. Before beginning this phase of the journey inland, we needed to prepare *SailingActs* for the voyage south, so we spent the day after arriving in Kavalla on the now familiar tasks of boat maintenance. Right after breakfast, a man came by to hook up our electricity. I doubted it was going to work; there was no outlet in sight. But he led me far down the wharf to a solitary outlet. I stepped off the distance on the way back to the boat—100 yards! *SailingActs* carried a lot of extension cords but I never had to reach shore power from that distance. I connected all the cords we had on board and they easily reached. The electricity problem was solved.

At one point during the afternoon, while tracking down parts for *SailingActs'* diesel motor, I stopped in at the Church of St. Paul which I had seen earlier. Inside several priests were sitting in the church office in the back, and I inquired if I could interview one of them about Paul. A man who appeared to be the head priest arranged to meet me at the church at 8:00 that evening. Back on the boat I showered on the deck and, for the first time since May, got all dressed up in Dockers, a shirt, and even shoes and socks. Janet unloaded her writing folder so that I would look professional, carrying my materials to the interview. Then I set off to the church to meet the priest.

When I arrived, the church was dark and the priest was not in the office. I queried the lone human in the church building, assuming from his dangling keys that he was the custodian. He was in the process of closing up. "No Papa," he said, once he interpreted my gestures. "Tomorrow *morgan* at . . . ." He held up nine fingers. I stood around, refusing to believe the Papa would not show up. But then the custodian started slamming gates and rattling keys and soon had the whole place locked down. Feeling like a well-dressed, professional, excommunicated heretic, I waited outside the locked gates of the church until he left, but no Papa showed up.

I walked back to the boat, discouraged, until I realized that I had not experienced the feeling of excommunication as a heretic at all. I was, in that moment of disappointment, a Greek "God-fearer" in the first century, attracted to Judaism, all dressed up and eager to be included in the Jewish synagogue but brushed aside with no good explanation, waiting outside the locked gates. Paul had risked his reputation, even his life, to open the gates of the Jewish Church for the Greeks. The risks he took in Philippi, 10 miles inland from Kavalla, got him thrown in prison there.

Tomorrow we would visit Philippi and the prison.

CHAPTER 7

Macedonia

Over breakfast in the cockpit of *SailingActs*, moored to the high wall of the Kavalla harbor, Janet and I realized that we had come to the northernmost part of Paul's journeys and our own as well. For the remainder of the summer, we'd be sailing south and east toward Israel. According to our log, we sailed a total of 629 sea miles since leaving Volos in June.

How far is it to Israel from here? I wondered. I entered the coordinates of Ashkelon, Israel, into our GPS and "Dist. 740 miles" popped up on the screen almost immediately. After sailing for six weeks, we had covered less than one-half of the planned voyage for the summer. While the distances are not great in the Aegean, the history is vast. The cultures and their durable remains are everywhere. Neither Paul's journeys through this region, nor our own following him, could be measured by the distance sailed but rather by the significant events that occurred along the way.

Philippi was a city where several significant events occurred for Paul, and Luke, the writer of the book of Acts who was traveling with Paul in Macedonia. Luke describes in detail some of the drama (Acts 16). When Paul arrived in Neapolis, he traveled directly to Philippi, "the leading city of the district," 10 miles inland from the harbor. For the first time in history, the gospel was introduced in Europe.

We took the local bus the 10 miles to Philippi. The modern road, which follows the ancient route from Neapolis to Philippi, runs right through the ruins of the city. As we climbed down from the bus, entered the site, and began wandering through the ruins, the former glory of the city was immediately apparent. On the Egnatian Way, the important Roman road that linked the administrative city of Philippi to the primary Macedonian city of Thessalonica to the south and eventually to Rome itself, we clearly understood why Paul chose this city to begin his work in Europe. Janet and I found a shady spot that provided a measure of relief from the blazing August sun, and reread the story of Paul's imprisonment. Then we spent the next several hours searching for clues that would explain the events.

Philippi was a typical Roman city with its large *agora*, temples, and administrative buildings which housed the prison, all clustered near the city center. While the theater in Philippi lay a short distance from the center of the city, Paul's ministry in Philippi, as described in Acts, seemed more like improvisational street theater performed in the center of town. Paul, as usual, probably preached in the *agora*, attracting not only the throngs of people doing business, but also a slave girl who apparently had the ability to tell the future through the power of Apollo, the Greek god associated with giving oracles. Working in the *agora* for fees, the slave girl was very profitable for her owners. When the slave girl saw Paul and his companions, she began screaming incessantly: "These men are servants of the Most High God, who are telling you the way to be saved." The meaning of this was not immediately clear to those listening in Philippi, for the expression "Most High God" was used by both pagans and Jews.

Neither the slave girl's owners nor Paul seemed to appreciate this free publicity. The owners received no fees for this sustained outburst, and Paul found it hard to cope with the distraction. He turned suddenly and commanded the spirit "in the name of Jesus" to leave the girl, which it promptly did. The girl no longer prophesied. The owners no longer profited. They immediately stirred up a riot, accusing the visiting Jews of disturbing the peace. The magistrates, whose primary job was to keep the peace, intervened immediately. They had Paul and Silas beaten and thrown into the prison directly across the street from the *agora*. For some reason, Paul did not reveal that he was a Roman citizen, which would have spared him the beating and imprisonment without first a trial. At midnight, while Paul and Silas were singing, an earthquake shook the area, damaging the prison and allowing all of the prisoners a chance to escape.

Standing on the site of the prison, Janet and I carefully reviewed the details of this story, especially of the jailor who came to believe and accept baptism. We noted that the earthquake would also have damaged all of the surrounding buildings, which included official residences, administrative buildings, and—most importantly—the sacred precinct of the temple complex next to the prison. The earthquake and its effects brought about a dramatic change in the jailor and the magistrates, and completely reversed their attitudes toward Paul and Silas. But more than that, the earthquake shook their understanding of the world, and the religious and political foundations on which their authority rested.

With Paul and Silas's dramatic release from prison and the jailor's baptism, Paul began to perform a little drama of his own. When the magistrates apologized to the Roman citizen for illegally punishing him, then asked him to leave Philippi quietly, he responded: "They beat us publicly without a trial, even though we are Roman citizens, and threw us into prison. And now they want to get rid of us quietly? No! Let them come themselves and escort us out."

Paul had been silent about his citizenship, but now he took advantage of it. So on the Egnatian Way that runs right through the center of Philippi, between the prison and the *agora*, in full view of everyone who had rioted earlier, Paul left Philippi with the magistrates meekly escorting him (see Photo 27). Paul was forced to leave, but his short piece of street theater challenged the authority of the Roman Empire. And his audience, who knew and appreciated drama, understood the plot.

Janet and I left Philippi and walked the short distance to Lydia, the traditional site of Paul's first baptism in Europe. In spite of the intense heat, we were refreshed by the beauty of the simple, shady baptismal site, with gentle, running water, full of lively fish, surrounded by sweet-smelling fields of hay (see Photo 28). Janet and I sat in that peaceful place and read about Lydia, a successful businesswoman, the first convert in Europe, who was baptized with her whole household. She then insisted that Paul and his companions make her home their headquarters while in Philippi. Janet, moved by this amazing woman of faith, asked me to baptize her in the place where Paul baptized Lydia. We returned to Kavalla that evening refreshed in soul and spirit.

The following day we rented a car and drove south toward Thessaloniki on the modern road that runs beside, and in some places directly on top of, the Egnatian Way that Paul took when traveling overland to the south of Macedonia. This route covers almost 100 miles over mountains and plains, a long hike for someone who had just been severely beaten, Janet and I agreed as we sped along in air-conditioned comfort. We searched for traces of the Roman pavement along the route and found Amphipolis with the magnificent statue of an enormous lion that would have dwarfed Paul as he walked by (see Photo 29). Then we drove on to Thessaloniki, where Paul's memory is covered with modern city buildings. We found all of the important sites that were remotely connected with Paul's ministry in the city: the *agora* and the forum where he may have preached; the Arch of Galerius, named for the emperor preceding Constantine; the Church of Agios Dimitrios, the largest church in Greece; and the Rotunda, Thessaloniki's oldest church.

Paul likely spent about six months of successful ministry in Thessalonica before the next riot occurred (Acts 17:5-9). The Jewish leaders—obviously concerned about their own status in the capitol of Macedonia, where anti-Semitism always lurked below the surface—incited the mob with this accusation: "'These men who have caused trouble all over the world have now come here, and Jason has welcomed them into his house. They are all defying Caesar's decrees, saying that there is another king, one called Jesus. When they heard this, the crowd and the city officials were thrown into turmoil. Then they made Jason and the others post bond and let them go." When it was dark, the believers in Thessalonica sent Paul and Silas west to Berea, 45 miles away.

While in Thessaloniki, we needed to buy a few items for *SailingActs* that were unavailable in Kavalla. In the afternoon we found four or five tiny shops crammed with sailing equipment, typical Greek chandlers, within 100 yards of each other. Among them they had what we needed: safety equipment, a U.S. flag to replace the one we lost, and new mooring lines. We then drove out of Thessaloniki, heading south, crossing the flat coastal plain and into the hilly region of Veria.

In contrast to Thessaloniki, a bustling port city where memory of Paul is obscured by modern buildings and traffic-jammed streets, Veria is an inland town at the edge of a manufacturing and farming area, nestled against the mountains. A huge traffic sign above the main street in the town's center indicates the main route out of the town in one direction, and "Paul's Altar" in the other. Following the signs, we found the little grotto with beautiful mosaics on the spot where Paul supposedly preached. There we read the story of Paul's short ministry in Berea. The Bereans, according to Luke, "were of more noble character than the Thessalonians, for they received the message with great eagerness and examined the Scriptures every day to see if what Paul said was true. Many of the Jews believed, as did also a number of prominent Greek women and many Greek men" (Acts 17:11-12).

We sat in front of the mosaic depicting the scene. A balding Paul holds a document in one hand, and with the other, gives the sign of blessing to a group of serious, studious, and meek seekers. The seekers are seated around him, holding open scrolls on their laps, with a medieval-looking Berea in the background. Janet and I marveled at the disgruntled band of Paul's enemies from Thessalonica, who heard of the Bereans' positive response to Paul's message and trudged the same 45 miles from

Thessalonica to incite a riot in Berea against him there. Paul was-
n't the only highly motivated religious person in 51 A.D. The
Roman roads made possible the movement of motivated people all
throughout the Empire.

Toward evening we drove out to the nearby town of Vegina in
hopes of finding a low-priced hotel for the night. We found Vegina
to be a restful, rural village with a charming little pension and
decided to stay. We enjoyed the rare luxury of showers, then set
out to look for an Internet café in order to check when we needed
to pick up Aram, the seminary student, at the Thessaloniki airport
the next afternoon. In the evening we walked the deserted street
to a nearby *taverna* for a delicious Greek meal and watched the
young people from the village hang out and eat gyros.

The next morning we drove toward the coast on the route
toward Methini, as the Port Authority woman in Kavalla had urged
us to do. "Look for the monument to the *Apostolos Paulus*," she
advised with pride. Although there is a tradition that Paul boarded
the ship to Athens at the port town of Dion, the Methini tradition
seemed to make equal sense as we drove toward the sea coast and
explored the region. While Luke normally records the precise harbor names, he was evidently not with Paul at this point, and no
place names are mentioned in Acts 17:14. *Did Paul forget where he
boarded the ship?* we wondered. We found the harbor of Methini,
but nothing in our guidebook or in the town itself gave any indication of Paul having been there.

We began asking shopkeepers, people in their gardens, and
waiters in restaurants where the memorial was. "Oh yes," they all
said in limited English or creative body language. "This way."

We drove not only "this way" but "that way" and "out of the
way" and "back a ways" and finally, hidden in a grove of trees, we
discovered a beautiful little shrine commemorating Paul's brief
stay and departure by a ship bound for Athens. After 2,000 years,
Paul, the Jew, is still a Greek hero in Macedonia.

We hurried back to Thessaloniki, a mere one hour late, to pick
up Aram at the Macedonia airport. We couldn't blame Paul for

making Aram wait after he had traveled for two days from Ohio to Thessaloniki. We could, however, blame the mapmakers or the road-builders. What appeared on the map to be a four-lane bypass breezing around the city turned into an unmarked, traffic-jammed nightmare. Walking through Thessalonica on the Egnatian Way would have been faster.

Aram was waiting on the curb in front of the airport. Having traveled for two days non-stop in order to save $50—a large sum of money for the typical seminary student—Aram was simultaneously semi-conscious from jetlag and fatigue, and hyperactive from adrenaline.

We headed straight toward Kavalla, chatting non-stop about our voyage thus far, discussing news from the United States, and getting updates from friends and colleagues at the university. In mid-afternoon we detoured through Apollonia for a bite to eat in an outdoor *taverna* and looked for anything related to Paul, who had passed through on his way to Thessalonica from Philippi (Acts 17:1). The food was superb and the friendly Greek woman who spoke some German explained where we could see a *"Kirche mit einem grossen Stein"* (church with a large stone). We drove right to it. A plaque on a large rock close to an ancient, abandoned church marked the very spot that Paul preached while traveling through Apollonia. We arrived back in Kavalla by late afternoon, introduced Aram to life on the boat, and discussed the details of the voyage south that would begin two days later.

With three crew members, we planned to do some serious sailing. From Kavalla, we'd hop from island to island down the Aegean, swing over to Kuşadasi, Turkey, then sail back into Greek waters to Rhodes, a distance of 360 sea miles. We planned to make this journey in less than two weeks, taking time for Aram to explore each of the significant sites related to Paul.

In the two days before the journey south, Aram explored Philippi and Kavalla, and Janet and I prepared *SailingActs* for the voyage. We installed two new jacklines to fasten ourselves to the boat in rough weather, finished fabricating the new emergency tiller, and fastened the floating man-overboard light and ropes to the stern. We should have had these from the beginning, but with a guest on board, we had to be prepared for the worst. It just wouldn't do to lose a seminary student at sea.

Now all we needed to do was to take care of the paperwork with the Port Authority. Through my experiences up to that time, I observed a direct relationship between the quality of the harbor and the difficulty of the paperwork: the worse the harbor, the higher the fees and the more difficult the bureaucracy. As Kavalla ranked about two on a scale of one to 10, I prepared myself for the worst. Upon arrival a week earlier, I had asked about the procedure for leaving. "Just come in the day before," the woman in the office said. "Then we will take care of the paperwork and you can leave early on Saturday morning."

On Friday afternoon I walked the 200 yards from the wharf to the Port Authority office, but it seemed to be closed. After checking a couple of times during the next hour, it occurred to me I probably needed to push the intercom button. I saw several buttons, all unmarked, so I pushed all of them. Several Greek voices crackled back on the intercom.

"I need to come to the Port Authority," I said.

"What do you need?" the voice of the Port Authority crackled back.

"I am leaving in the morning," I said.

"Do you have a boat?"

Why would I bother to check with the Port Authority if I were traveling by bus? "Yes," I answered.

"Come back in one hour," the voice instructed.

I returned an hour later. The office seemed deserted, except for a young woman behind the desk who told me to wait in a chair. I sat in the chair studying the Greek maps, Greek weather charts, and the icons of St. Nicholas on the wall. Finally a serious, important-looking, uniformed man came in.

"Where is your boat?" he asked.

For the past week, ours was the only visiting yacht in the whole harbor. It was tied up in the middle of the wharf, plainly visible to everyone in Kavalla except, it seemed, to the Port Authority. I was getting a little edgy by this time, having spent two hours attempting to comply with their regulations. A number of people came and went, asking me questions, but none seemed to have the authority to sign the papers.

"Why did you wait to come now?" a man in civilian clothes asked.

"I was told to come on Friday if I wanted to leave Saturday."

"You should have come earlier."

"I did, and the woman on the intercom said to come back in one hour."

"That was already in the afternoon," the man said. "You needed to come in the morning. Friday afternoon is like coming on Saturday. No one is here."

This wasn't obvious to me, as there were now four people sitting idly behind desks at that point. He made a telephone call. "In five minutes the officer will come," he promised.

I knew "five minutes" could realistically turn into 30 or more, so I asked if I could come back in five minutes.

"Do you have something to do?" the man asked.

You mean other than spending my sabbatical in the Port Authority waiting rooms inhaling second-hand smoke? I thought. "I sail," I replied. "I always have something to do."

"Okay, come back in five minutes."

When I returned 15 minutes later, all four officials, plus one new man, were there to finalize my papers. At least that is what I hoped they were there to do, but it wasn't clear as they were all shouting at each other. One waved me to a chair and returned to shouting with the others, who were pounding tables, waving their arms, and stalking around. This went on for approximately

20 minutes as I watched, with growing concern, as they glanced occasionally in my direction. This didn't look good. *Are they planning to shoot me, or are some of them defending me?* I wondered uneasily.

Finally everyone left the room except for one young woman and the new official, who kept arguing. The official had my papers in front of him and a pen in his hand. At times he lowered the pen as if to write, then something else would occur to him to reinforce his argument with the young woman, and he would pull the pen away. I watched his hand intently as a polite, hungry dog eagerly watches every movement of his master eating. The young woman seemed to be on my side, though clearly outranked, and her counter-attacks became increasingly feeble. At last she, too, left the room, muttering under her breath. I was alone with the man, who continued to shout at her. I couldn't tell if she was in the next room, the next building, or a nearby city, because she didn't respond. The man behind the desk continued shouting, undeterred, as he consulted charts, jotted down numbers, and punched formulas into a calculator.

"Forty-eight euros," he demanded at last.

I thought I didn't hear him correctly. *Maybe he means 4.80 euros, or .48 euros.* Only one other place in Greece had I paid more than 3 euros per night. We had stayed seven nights in Kavalla, which amounted to 7 euros per night. This wasn't excessive, but it had been one of the worst wharfs in Greece, without any services except an electrical outlet 100 yards from the boat. I protested the rate.

"We are not a shop," the officer said. (I took this to mean, "We do not bargain.") He explained, "This comes from the Greek Port Authority. These are not our prices."

I still couldn't grasp the system. "Why do most ports in Greece charge so much less, or nothing at all? Why do the worst ports charge the most money?" I was getting fired up. Thinking of Paul in Philippi besting the Roman authorities, and just having watched the Greek officials yell at each other for 20 minutes, I somehow felt that yelling was an entirely appropriate form of communication. "You can see for yourselves that ours was the only sailboat in your harbor during the entire week. No wonder all the sailors I've met say, 'Stay away from Kavalla!'"

By this time all the office staff had congregated back in the office, thoroughly enjoying the argument. Finally, knowing I had no other recourse, I relented, paid the fee, and quickly received the necessary stamps and signatures. Everyone smiled and wished me a pleasant voyage.

How can the Greek government afford to hire whole battalions who take care of the port when there is so little to do? I wondered as I walked back to *SailingActs*. *Maybe this explains why, when a boat actually does come into their port, they seek to recover a full year's salary for their maritime shouting society from that single, unfortunate boat. Stay away from ports with no visiting yachts,* I concluded. That evening we ate a delicious Greek meal—agreeing that the perfect antidote for Greek bureaucracy is Greek food.

Aram, Janet, and I discussed the experience. We agreed that governments need to charge fees for services, and that complying with a country's maritime laws and paying those fees sure beats dealing with piracy. However, because governments solely control who enters their waters, their fees can become a form of legal, legitimized piracy. In Greece, yachts from the European Union are charged fees 50 percent less than yachts from outside the European Union. I suppose the United States does the same thing. And while visitors can argue and complain, they hold no sway, except to choose not to come. The Greeks, with ruins, history, islands, and beaches are not too worried. They know that visitors will continue to come with their money, as they have for thousands of years, and they will leave part of their money behind, voluntarily or otherwise.

The Roman Empire, in uniting the nations around the Mediterranean, was able to monopolize the exploitation of those living within the Empire, especially of the non-citizens, who were, in the first century, about 90 percent of the population.

Sailing Acts

What we experienced as foreigners sailing in Greek waters is what all non-citizens have experienced throughout the history of travel.

Paul was a Roman citizen. As he sailed the Aegean, we concluded that night before hitting the bunks, Paul became increasingly aware of the privileges he had as a citizen. He must have recognized that the rights and privileges he enjoyed were highly desirable to non-citizens. No wonder he began to use language like "citizenship in the kingdom," "heirs," and "household of faith" when he preached to the non-citizen population of the Roman Empire. According to Paul, everyone who belonged to the kingdom of God, in contrast to the inhabitants of the Roman Empire, was equally valuable.

I went to sleep that night, thankful for the opportunity to learn the disadvantages of being a non-citizen, a pilgrim and a stranger, in Kavalla. And thankful to finally be heading south.

CHAPTER 8
South to Rhodes

We left Kavalla the next morning feeling that we were going toward, not away from, our destination for the winter. As predicted, there was almost no wind so we motored. By 4:30 in the afternoon we approached the sheltered area on the island of Thasos and dropped the anchor in crystal-clear water in front of a beach full of swimmers. For nearly half an hour we tried unsuccessfully to find a place where the anchor would hold. Finally a Bulgarian vacationer snorkeling around *SailingActs* kindly offered to dive down in about 20 feet of water and set the anchor by hand.

The following morning I awoke at 6:30, weighed anchor, and left the little bay just as the others were waking up. A gentle breeze pushed *SailingActs* out of the anchorage. The morning light on the water created a majestic beauty as we set out for one of our favorite harbors of the voyage so far, Mirina, on the island of Limnos. For the first time since beginning the voyage, we'd return to a harbor we entered earlier. It was a relaxing day. We set the auto helm when leaving Thasos, and it kept us on course for the entire day. By 6:00 in the evening, we found a good spot on the wharf in Mirina, dropped the anchor, and backed in on the first try, which was especially satisfying due to a small gaggle of onlookers in yachts. We threw them the stern lines, reported in to the friendly Port Authority, plugged the electrical cord into the shore power, then went to a small restaurant that we enjoyed several weeks earlier. We always felt at home on *SailingActs*, no matter where we spent the night. But to be back in a place that we enjoyed so much earlier, it seemed to us that

SailingActs

SailingActs felt at home as well. Like Paul, we were beginning to feel at home everywhere on the Mediterranean.

The next morning after breakfast, we sent Aram on some research assignments. I tackled the one safety-related task on SailingActs that I wanted to finish before the longer legs of the voyage to Israel—fixing the manual bilge pump that I discovered was broken the day water flooded the SailingActs cockpit. So after breakfast I removed the water pump from its place in the cockpit, disassembled it, and was not surprised to discover that the 25-year-old rubber diaphragm was ruined. Now, where could I find a replacement diaphragm for an obsolete pump on the island?

Taking the worthless diaphragm, about the size of a saucer, I began with the chandler. He had no replacement parts so we "discussed" other options, such as making a new diaphragm from an old car-tire inner tube. Without a common spoken language, the conversation for that particular option involved walking out to a parked car, pointing at the tire, making scissor-cutting motions with two fingers, and using appropriate hissing noises one might associate with a damaged inner tube. The owner pointed down the street toward what I assumed would be a tire store.

I didn't find a tire store after a half-mile walk, but I did come to a shop that had all kinds of unusual materials: coils of screen, netting, plastic, and a variety of products that seemed most fitting for being displayed on rolls. I hopefully showed the young man in the store my torn piece of rubber. For several minutes he rummaged among piles of plastic, rubber, nylon, and canvas before triumphantly producing a sheet of rubber about twice as thick as the diaphragm. It seemed too stiff, and I wasn't sure it would work.

"My ankle maybe has some," the young man offered.

I glanced down at his ankle, half expecting that he had sprained it and had wrapped it in rubber sheeting precisely the thickness of a 25-year-old bilge pump bellows, which he would willingly take off and sell to me. Or perhaps he had snagged a truck-tire inner tube walking to work that morning and was still dragging it around his ankle, now happy to get rid of it. But no rubber was visible.

"What do you mean?" I asked.

"My ankle has a shop, too," he explained. "Maybe has rubber."
He gave me the directions. I found his "ankle's" shop. The old
man running it had the same type of shop with identical rubber
as his nephew, and because it was near noon, I bought a piece.
Back on the boat that afternoon, I spent several hours fitting the
thick rubber into the bilge pump, reassembling and reinstalling
everything. It looked great but did not pump a drop of bilge water
when I tried it out.

Somewhat discouraged for accomplishing nothing that day, I
began to feel a little better as I grilled chicken for dinner on our
marine barbecue. We had purchased an expensive stainless-steel
unit in Athens before leaving Volos. We used it occasionally on
the voyage and those times were always special. I would take the
grill out of its place in the cockpit locker, assemble it in about one
minute, then attach it to one of the life-line holders by its special
bracket that held the barbecue unit suspended over the water for
safety. That evening we enjoyed our dinner as we exchanged stories of the day's adventures.

It was late and very dark when we began putting things away
to prepare for an early start the next morning. As I removed the
grill from its bracket, I heard a little splash and realized in dismay that the special tube that fed the gas into the burner had fall-
en into the 12-foot-deep water. Making a recovery dive in the
dark would be difficult. We'd either need to delay leaving in the
morning till after sunrise, or leave as planned, with the grill piece
on the bottom of the harbor. With a long day of sailing ahead of
us, we decided to leave before daylight in the morning. "We can
pick up a replacement in a good chandler," I promised Janet.

The following morning we were up at 5:30 and eased out of
the harbor 15 minutes later, hoping to reach Lesvos, a distance of
56 miles, before dark. In spite of light winds, we cruised into the
Lesvos harbor before 8:00. During the night, the wind rose and I
slept lightly, checking the anchor several times. But we had
anchored well with a generous amount of chain on the bottom.

SailingActs

In the wee hours of the morning, before daylight, we weighed anchor again and set course to the island of Chios, 52 miles to the south.

Since leaving Lesvos (Mytilini), we were not only sailing the precise route of the Apostle Paul at the end of his second mission journey (Acts 20:14-15), we were also sailing in a way typical of first-century passage-making in the Aegean. We weighed anchor before daybreak, sailed the maximum distance before nightfall, anchored in a protected harbor on an island, then repeated the procedure day after day until we reached the destination. First-century sailors avoided sailing at night if at all possible.

Aram was adjusting well to the sailing routine. Long days of sailing, broken only by minor sailing tasks, snacks, and extended conversations about the sea, Paul, and life in general kept things interesting (Aram is pictured in Photo 30).

"The Hebrew word *ruach* means both 'wind' and 'spirit,'" I observed to Aram as the wind filled the sails on our way to Chios. We had been discussing the physics of sailing, how it's possible to sail to a chosen destination by adjusting the sails to utilize the wind coming from any direction.

We discussed the first appearance of the word *ruach* in scripture—in the very first verse of the Bible. In the story of creation, in Genesis 1:1, the "Spirit of God hovered over the waters." The word translated "Spirit" is *ruach* and could just as well read, "the wind of God moved across the waters."

"That's really interesting," Aram commented. "The description of God's Spirit and the experience of the wind at sea are so similar. You cannot see either Spirit or wind, but you can see what happens when they are present. Both are powerful, even frightening at times. Both are unpredictable and totally out of human control."

"Both can be dangerous," Janet added, thinking of the gale we had survived a month earlier and which the fisherman on Samos Island had warned us about.

"But only if you don't adjust your plans, your sails, or your direction," I added, thinking how we had not heeded the fisherman's warning, and how I had waited too long to reef the fragile, old sails when the wind had risen—a delay that destroyed them.

We tried to think of other references to "wind" in scripture. "Pentecost," Aram said. "At Pentecost when the Spirit of God was given to the church, the story in Acts 2 describes the noise as 'like the blowing of a violent wind.'"

"And look what that 'wind' did," I reflected. "It blew the people right out of Jerusalem. They left the shore and put out to sea, and took the Church all over the Mediterranean. When they left the security of the room in Jerusalem, life became unpredictable and dangerous. And look what happened to Paul after the Spirit of God filled his life. He went in entirely new directions, sailed the Mediterranean on this very route, and ended up in Rome. Paul's life caught God's wind, and he became God's seafarer. His travels and his ministry were full of storms. He never knew where the wind would take him."

"The life of living by faith in God is a lot like this voyage," Janet observed. "It's wonderful, rewarding, and frightening all at once, but I wouldn't trade this experience for anything."

We likely would have had other profound insights about Spirit, wind, Paul, and life if *SailingActs* had not started behaving somewhat strangely. We looked up at the sails and around at the wind and waves. Everything was normal. Yet *SailingActs* was responding sluggishly to the wind, and the rudder seemed stiff and unresponsive when I turned off the auto helm and tried to steer manually.

Suddenly I noticed a thin, yellow, nylon rope trailing in the water from under the stern. I tried to retrieve the rope with the boat hook, but discovered that the rope was stretched extremely taut. We had snagged a fishing net and were dragging some poor fisherman's catch behind us. When I cut the rope, *SailingActs* immediately leaped to her normal sailing position, but the rope was still snagged under the boat. Aram and I tried everything we could think of to free it, without success.

We were getting close to Chios by this time, and it occurred to us that we might have a problem. If the rope had snagged the propeller, we would not be able to motor into the harbor at Chios. This wasn't good. Even if the rope was not around the propeller now, starting the motor in the harbor might pull the rope into the propeller. This could stop the motor and cause us to instantly lose control of the boat. This also wasn't good. Even if we could use the motor and successfully tie up on the Chios wharf, the thought of diving under the boat in a busy harbor in dirty water to cut the rope away did not appeal either.

From the first day of sailing, Janet had assumed responsibility for diligently studying the charts, and she knew every hazard and harbor at any given point. She suggested we anchor on a little island around one mile from Chios, so we quickly decided to deviate to the anchorage and drop the anchor without using the motor. Then in clearer water, we'd dive below and cut the rope free. Twenty minutes later we were in the little bay, Aram had the snorkel on, and after much splashing and gasping, cut the rope away, a feat that earned him a free dinner in a restaurant later that evening in Chios.

After leaving Chios at dawn the next morning, we enjoyed steaming cups of fresh coffee in the cockpit while watching the sun rise over the rugged Turkish coastline to the east. Then, as the wind rose, we set the sails and, for the rest of the day, skimmed across the waves toward Samos, the auto helm doing the steering. The day passed quickly.

"God is like the sea," I said to Aram later that day. "Both are awesome, beautiful, powerful, and vast."

"I'm not sure that is a good comparison," Aram reasoned. "The metaphors for God in the Hebrew scriptures are not from the sea, but from the land."

"You have a good point," I reflected. "The Hebrews were people of the land. They got their commandments from Moses on a mountain in the Sinai desert." Having climbed to the top of that mountain a number of times in recent years, I knew of no greater geographical contrast than the rugged wilderness of Sinai and the Mediterranean Sea.

But there were also some similarities. Life for the people of the land, who journeyed through the rugged and dangerous Sinai Desert, and for the people of the sea, who voyaged across the stormy unpredictability of the Mediterranean Sea, was equally insecure. Both the land and sea people sought to establish themselves in safe, secure, and productive areas. Both relied on their gods to protect them from the inhospitable, empty, and harsh surroundings.

However, the contrasts between the God of the Sinai and the gods of the Mediterranean are profound. We thought of the metaphors for God in the Hebrew scriptures: God is a rock, changeless and unmovable. God's temple is on a mountain. God is a river. God has power over the seas but is never compared to the sea. Of all the geographical metaphors for God, we could think of none from the sea.

"Think about the gods of the people of the sea, the Greek gods for instance," I remarked to Aram. "They resemble the sea. They are unpredictable, make no covenants, and are capricious." We thought about Poseidon, the god of the sea, and once the primary god in the Greek pantheon. We recalled that Aphrodite, one of the most popular Greek gods, emerged from the sea on the crest of waves.

"And isn't it remarkable that all of the monotheistic religions originate from people of the land, or of the desert and the mountains?" Aram noted.

"The sea people are *all* polytheists," I added. Both observations are logical, we concluded.

How did this affect Paul? we wondered. Paul was a monotheist, but was born in Tarsus, a port city in present-day Turkey. As a Jew, he came from a tradition of the monotheistic people of the land, yet he explored the world of the sea people who were polytheists.

"Do you think Paul's concept of God might have changed by experiencing the sea on ships with pagan crews, who after surviving stormy voyages offered sacrifices to the gods for protecting them?" Aram pondered.

This was an interesting thought. Paul's life when sailing was in the hands of pagans. These pagans knew how to sail, and Paul must have been grateful for them and their skills that brought him safely across the Mediterranean. Their ships were dedicated to the protecting gods of seafarers, and the ships carried images of the gods on their bows. The port cities into which they sailed almost always had pagan temples dominating the harbor. Whether Paul's concept of God changed through the experience is debatable, we concluded, but Paul's attitude toward the pagans most certainly changed from one of pharisaical superiority to admiration and appreciation for these people so familiar with the seas.

We were not finished. "Think of how Abraham and Paul were similar," I suggested to Aram. "Both were explorers of the future, of God's promises. Both lived by faith and let go of the security of their homes and status. Both lived the remainder of their lives among people who worshipped many gods, polytheists. Both tried to get along with their polytheistic hosts and succeeded much of the time. Abraham's descendants, however, 'possessed the land' and became extremely wary of outsiders who threatened them, including the Phoenicians and Philistines who were sea people. But it is much harder to possess the sea. Maybe Paul discovered, as he sailed the Mediterranean, how limiting it is to think of the kingdom of God as being confined to a specific geographical location, a particular land, something the descendants of Abraham tended to forget."

"The people who came after Paul tried to 'possess the Empire' in the name of Jesus," Aram noted.

We were still discussing land and sea people, the differences in their gods, and their shared propensity for building empires when we reached Samos in the late afternoon.

The next morning Aram rented a motor scooter and set off to explore Samos, including the monument of Pythagoras, the ruins of the temples to Hera and Aphrodite, and the scenic grandeur of the outlying areas. Janet and I spent the time catching up on maintenance, shopping, writing, and plotting our course for the next week.

We had discussed our course for some time. Ideally, we would leave Samos, sail the several miles to Kuşadasi, Turkey, so Aram could visit Ephesus and Miletus, then sail back into Greek waters to the island of Kos, then again into Turkish waters to Cnidus, an anchorage of Paul, then back yet once more into Greek waters to Rhodes. Because of the short distances between Greek and Turkish destinations, this made perfect sense in terms of sailing, but not in terms of the fees and time it would take to purchase and relinquish Transit Logs every time we left one country's waters for the next. The regulations would slow us down by a number of days, and would cost an additional $30 to $50 every time we reentered.

We discussed this problem with a number of other yachting people we met along the way. Almost everyone we met was either sailing exclusively in Greek or Turkish waters, or was crossing only once during the sailing season. If we wanted to follow Paul, we would need to go in and out of Greece and Turkey four times in one week, an almost impossible task. "Just don't turn in your Transit Logs to the authorities when you leave the country," several seasoned sailors recommended. "Don't tell either Turkish or Greek officials that you are leaving. The only way they will know is if they look carefully at your passports, because you will not have the exit stamp."

Janet and I debated the ethical and practical arguments for and against sneaking in and out of international waters. "Paul obeyed God rather than man," I pontificated to Janet, "so let's do what he would have done. We're trying to learn from his example."

"But God isn't commanding us to sneak in and out of Greek and Turkish waters," countered Janet.

"That's because it wasn't necessary. The Roman Empire controlled the whole Mediterranean," I reasoned. "Otherwise God would surely have told Paul to save the time and money."

Still, I wrote in my journal:

> I am a little uncomfortable with the whole thing, but am willing to try it. I am convinced it is an arcane set of laws from the Ottoman Empire, exacerbated by the tensions between Turkey and Greece, that keep reform from occurring. Hopefully we will not get caught, but if we do, we will try to plead for amnesty on the basis that we have been complying faithfully up until now, but have been repeatedly disadvantaged by trying to play by their impractical rules. We will tell them that we decided to do what the sailing veterans advised in order to accomplish our sabbatical plans.
>
> It seems like Paul played this kind of game occasionally with the authorities when he suffered under unfair and harmful restrictions, at least the ones that hindered him in his work. Now, of course, we cannot claim the moral high ground like Paul, in that this is not mission work that is being hindered and that God has called us to do, rather this is just sabbatical research. But, in order to understand Paul, I think this kind of experience will help. Authority needs to be exercised, we need to respect the laws, but there are bad laws that help no one at all and need changing. Everyone, including all Greeks I have talked to, agree that the yachting laws in Greece and, to a lesser extent Turkey, are stupid and keep people away.

The next morning I went into the Port Authority to pick up my Transit Log and passport that they had been holding since we arrived. They asked me a number of times where we were headed when leaving Samos. "Kos," I replied each time. This was indeed the case, but I didn't mention that we would spend several days in Kuşadasi, Turkey, on the way to Kos. That morning, experiencing a typical Greek Port Authority checkout, I was convinced we had made the right choice. The official working on my papers was rigorously engaged in a debate with his colleagues as I stood and fidgeted, coughing occasionally to remind him of my presence so I could get five minutes of his focused attention and we could be on our way.

Just as the conversation ebbed and the official turned to my paperwork, someone turned on a TV in the office and the excitement of an Olympic women's badminton match offered a second source of distraction. Eventually, during pauses in the badminton game, the officer punched complex formulas into a desk calculator and finally produced a figure of 15.50 euros. Earlier I had stayed for six days in the exact same port and paid a fee of 11 euros. This time we had been in Samos for two days and four hours—which they calculated as three days—and were charged much more per day. I politely commented, "Last time I believe it was much cheaper."

"Let's see your receipt," the women's badminton fan demanded.

I just happened to have it—1.90 euros per day versus 5 euros per day this time. The office people all gathered anxiously around the evidence and there was noticeable triumph when a woman in a smart, white Port Authority uniform discovered that the last time they charged me the rate for EU boats. "You are not EU," she explained. "They made a mistake last time."

Two wrongs would definitely make a right, I thought to myself as I paid the bill.

We motored slowly out of Vathy harbor, heading straight toward Kuşadasi, Turkey, only 18 miles away, hoping no one was watching. We exchanged the Greek flag for the Turkish flag halfway between Samos and Kuşadasi then, as we approached, called the marina on our VHF. We were greeted with the friendliness and efficiency of the marinas in Turkey that we had experienced earlier. There were no surprises that day.

The next day was Sunday. Aram had rented a scooter and was out exploring Ephesus and Miletus. Janet and I kept our Sunday morning ritual of playing Vivaldi's *Four Seasons* as soon as we woke up, as we do at home in Harrisonburg. As we read the *Herald Tribune* and sipped coffee to the strains of the music, it seemed that life couldn't get any better. "Is the sailing life really better," Janet and I would ask each other during such moments, "or are the challenges, frustrations, and fears so much more intense and frequent when sailing that the moments of peaceful relaxation seem so wonderful in contrast?"

As usual when in harbor on Sunday, we spent the day catching up on reading and relaxing. The previous Saturday afternoon I had talked to one of the workmen in the boatyard at the marina about my broken bilge pump. He was sure he had a diaphragm somewhere that might fit. Later we met him in the marina, carrying a promising-looking piece of rubber. I took it back to the boat, disassembled the pump for the second time, modified the rubber to fit, then reassembled and mounted the pump. When I tried it out, water from the bilge gushed from the outlet on the side of *SailingActs*. By 3:00 in the afternoon, everything was ready for the next leg of the voyage, and Janet and I went for a swim in the marina pool. Aram returned exhausted from riding the motor scooter nearly 100 miles, visiting Ephesus, the archeological museum at Selçuk, and Miletus all in the same day.

We left the marina at 7:00 on a gorgeous morning. Heading south along the Turkish coast from Kuşadasi, we needed to pass between the eastern end of Samos Island on our right and the Turkish coastline on our left. The distance between Turkey and Greece through Steno Samou (Greek) or Sisam Boğazi (Turkish), the Samos Straights, is only about one-half mile wide at the narrowest point. We were somewhat paranoid sailing through these heavily patrolled waters and flying the Turkish flag without having checked out of Greece. As we approached the narrowest point of the straights, we noticed with some concern that a large motor boat was rapidly overtaking us.

"Is that a navy patrol?" Janet asked.

We took turns watching the boat's progress through the binoculars and rehearsing explanations to either the Turkish or Greek naval officers who were pursuing us. We felt hugely relieved to recognize the boat, when it was close enough, as one of the motor yachts we had seen in the Kuşadasi marina, flying a Canadian flag. We waved and smiled back with unusual delight as they passed by.

Kos, the next main island we were visiting, was too distant to reach in one day from Kuşadasi. We had decided to follow the Turkish coastline south and to briefly pull into St. Paul's Bay or Trogyllium, mentioned only in Acts 20:15 of the King James Version. It's quite understandable that the ship on which Paul was sailing intended to arrive in Miletus by nightfall, but having rounded the promontory, the wind had likely fallen as it did for us, and they had to spend the night at anchor in Trogyllium.

We motored as closely as we dared into the ancient anchorage and reflected on the activities Paul may have observed. During Paul's time, one of the chief altars to Poseidon, god of the sea, was located on the slopes of the mountain above the anchorage. Ships sailing from Samos to Miletus would often stop in Trogyllium so that sailors could go ashore and sacrifice to Poseidon. Paul would have seen it all.

After visiting the deserted anchorage with its forgotten shrine, we set our course toward the lonely and almost uninhabited island of Agathonissi, about halfway between Kuşadasi and Kos. Arriving well before nightfall, we gladly discovered adequate room in the small anchorage. The only other boat in the anchorage was a French charter boat with five people aboard, who seemed to delight in being stark naked most of the time. Aram took the dinghy ashore after we secured *SailingActs*, waving nonchalantly to the naked French group as he passed unnecessarily close to their boat. Ashore, Aram noticed a hand-lettered sign in Greek facing the anchorage. Using his biblical Greek skills from seminary, he carefully translated the message: NO NUDE BATHING! Back on board we laughed that the only people who would likely not be bathing nude in that particular anchorage would be seminary students and Greeks.

By this time, in mid-August, we had grown accustomed to seeing our sailing neighbors from northern Europe cavorting stark naked on their boats in secluded anchorages. "Paul would have seen this and a whole lot more during his travels through the pagan world in the first century," we often remarked.

Indeed, Paul explored a pagan culture that celebrated and flaunted a startling variety of religious and social eroticism, a culture increasingly obsessed with pornography and licentious behavior. The pagan gods offered no moral direction in the area of sexual behavior; rather, they modeled endless, incredible promiscuity. The good news of the gospel that Paul introduced into this world, with its clear moral definitions and guidelines, was understandably attractive to those whose lives were empty and distorted by their own, or other's, hedonistic quest of happiness and pleasure.

By 6:15 the next morning, we weighed anchor and immediately a favorable wind whisked us toward the island of Kos, the island on which Paul's ship had anchored. By 3:00 in the afternoon we were securely moored in what we were told was "the best marina in Greece." I was just a little tense as I went to the marina office to pay the mooring fees and present our Transit Log to the Port Authority. We now had both a Turkish and a Greek Transit Log. A close examination of our passports would show that we had entered Turkey after leaving Greece, without having an exit stamp from either Greece or Turkey. The young woman behind the counter barely glanced at our papers and, for once, the photocopying and stamping were finished in a few minutes. What a relief!

Janet and I strolled down to the old harbor and ancient town of Kos which, in mid-August, was full of sunburned vacationers on holiday. Seeing them, we suddenly felt like being tourists for just a little and treated ourselves to a rare, expensive iced coffee and watched the crowds swarm off the ferries across the street. Later, we met Aram and enjoyed an inexpensive meal of gyros as we planned the activities for the next day.

We decided to explore the Roman sites in the town of Kos, and then visit the famous Asklipion, where Hippocrates, the father of modern medicine, practiced and taught in his famous medical school. We marveled at Kos's distinct culture and discussed the amazing geographical and cultural diversity among the succession of islands Paul had encountered, as we had, within a matter of days on his journey toward Caesarea in 57 A.D. Ferdnand Braudel, in his excellent history *Memory and the Mediterranean*, described the islands of the Aegean as "extreme micro-universes, wide open to the outside world, vulnerable to the invasions of people, technology, and fashion." Yet, "every foreign borrowing develops in an island as if in a laboratory, exaggerating features which become very different from the original model" (127).

The next morning we discovered that the signs of Roman success that Paul would have observed are still everywhere (see Photo 31). The *agora* with remains of an impressive *stoa*, forerunner of the modern shopping mall; temples to Aphrodite and Hercules; the Decumanus Maximus, the main Roman thoroughfare, flanked by an impressive *nymphaeum*, a large gymnasium; and an elaborate public latrine are all visible near the harbor.

If Paul explored the city, he may have visited the *agora*, but Luke, being a doctor, would likely have been most interested in visiting the Asklipion where the most famous medical doctor of antiquity, Hippocrates, had practiced and taught his rational approach to medicine some 400 years earlier. Before taking the tourist train to the Asklipion, we stopped to look at Hippocrates's plane tree near the harbor in Kos, the massive old tree under which Hippocrates supposedly taught his pupils. This plane tree, propped up with scaffolding and clearly on life-support, certainly looked ancient, but knowing that plane trees rarely live more than 200 years, we could hardly believe that this was the very tree under which Hippocrates's students swore to the god Asclepius not to harm or take advantage of their patients in any way.

Feeling like tourists, we clambered aboard the tourist train and chugged our way two-and-a-half miles out of Kos into the charming countryside to the Asklipion. For at least 900 years, from the fourth century B.C. until the sixth century A.D., this healing facility attracted people from all over the ancient world. This medical center had it all—temples to a variety of gods, including Asclepius, the god of healing; public baths and guest rooms; a healing center; and a school of medicine where the training followed the teachings of Hippocrates (see Photo 32).

That evening I called my mother in Oregon from the marina on our cell phone. It was her 87th birthday. We chatted for a few minutes as she tried to imagine just where we were. "Read Acts 21 and look in the back of your Bible," I told her. *Isn't life amazing,* I thought as our conversation ended. *Fifty years ago Mom gave me her Bible in church to keep me quiet and I tried to follow Paul's route in the back. Now, I am actually on that route and she can find me by looking at that same map.* I walked around on the wharf for a while, looking up at the starlit sky above Kos, filled with gratitude for Mom, the Bible, and Paul.

We planned to sail toward Rhodes the next morning, going as far as possible before dark, then anchor in some protected bay before continuing on to Rhodes the following day. The wind had been howling all day, and when we returned from the Asklipion that afternoon, we noticed the people on the sailboats that entered the marina had a beaten, shaken look about them. We knew that look from our own experience of hours on a heaving sea and went to sleep that night feeling somewhat uneasy, aware that the weather forecast called for more of the same the next day.

We had plotted our course to allow a brief stop at the ancient ruins of Cnidus on the Turkish coast, which is mentioned in the Acts account of Paul's journey from Caesarea to Rome in 59 A.D. While it is not clear from the story in Acts 27:7 whether Paul's ship actually anchored there or not, we thought Cnidus might make a good lunch stop on the way, especially if the seas were high, as predicted.

At 7:00 the next morning, we untied *SailingActs* and prepared to slip out of the marina. Grimly noting the wind whipping through the marina, we carefully edged out of our slip and eased into open water. Soon we were cautiously sailing with the working jib and reefed mainsail. Before long we realized that the conditions were not difficult as predicted, and I put up the genoa and full mainsails. Sailing briskly, we reached Cnidus around noon. It was crowded with Turkish *gullets*, the large, wooden coastal cruisers that specialize in taking crowds of noisy vacationers out for a day of swimming and drinking in peaceful and idyllic anchorages—or more accurately, in anchorages that are peaceful and idyllic until the *gullets* arrive.

Our cruising guide described the bottom of Cnidus anchorage as "poor holding." We tried unsuccessfully to get our anchor to hold in the crowded harbor amid idle spectators and fierce gusts of wind. The attractive ruins on the slopes around the harbor beckoned us to explore them, but time after time we dropped the anchor only to drift backwards, dangerously close to the anchored *gullets*. After six or seven attempts, I promised the frustrated anchor crew, Janet and Aram, "Just one more try. If we cannot get the anchor to hold, we're out of here." It didn't hold, and we left the harbor reassuring ourselves that this might have happened to Paul's ship as well.

We decided to sail for the island of Simi, 24 miles farther. This would require a full day of sailing but would put us in a much better position to reach Rhodes early Friday instead of in the afternoon. Our cruising guide repeatedly warned of the difficulty of finding room in the ancient Mandraki harbor of

Rhodes town, "especially on weekends, when fistfights can break out among visiting yachtsmen and local charter boat owners." Since we were arriving on the dreaded weekend, we figured we might have a better chance of avoiding a fistfight by arriving early.

We set the genoa in steady, strong breezes in order to make the 24 miles before dark. This would have been a brilliant decision with a much younger genoa. Even so, we still made excellent time, but the genoa developed a huge rip within the final hour of sailing that afternoon. We changed sails, proceeded around the island of Simi until we found the protected anchorage, then attempted to anchor. The conditions were roughly what we had endured in Cnidus, but this time we had no option of leaving. It was getting dark and the wind was still fierce. After a number of unsuccessful attempts at getting the anchor to hold, Aram took a long line ashore with the dinghy, to which we fastened *SailingActs*, then we dropped our anchor and backed down so that we were being held from two points at right angles. For good measure we dropped our auxiliary anchor from the stern and finally felt secure. Just before dark, I repaired the torn genoa with great patches of sail repair material.

"This should hold until we get to Israel," I said to myself after completing the job. We went to sleep, confident that all would be well.

We were under way again the following morning by 7:00. With only 20 miles to go to Rhodes, we were in high spirits. The pleasantness lasted until the rip in the genoa not only reappeared but extended across the whole width of the sail, rendering it worthless. In the middle of the crossing between Simi and Rhodes, I called Captain Steve. "What will a new genoa cost?" I asked after explaining what happened.

"Give me the measurements of the old genoa and I'll call you right back with the price," Captain Steve promised.

Aram and I stretched out the genoa on the deck and measured the three dimensions of the large headsail, then called back

Captain Steve. A short time later we had the answer—1,100 euros. It was time for a conference with the crew.

"Why invest all that money in a new genoa?" Janet reasoned. "Wouldn't this be a good time to get roller furling?"

This made some sense. I was getting worn out changing headsails in wildly fluctuating winds on the wave-drenched and heaving bow of *SailingActs*. Two of our headsails were destroyed. Our working jib was new, but we reasoned we could sell it somewhere and recover our investment. I called Captain Steve again.

"What would a new roller-furling system cost, complete and installed?"

The cell phone rang 30 minutes later. "I can get a new roller-furling system and a new state-of-the-art headsail installed on Rhodes for you from DL Sails for 3,150 euros," Captain Steve promised. "If you want it, I can order it today. I will put down 2,000 euros for deposit and it will arrive by Wednesday."

"Hold on," I said. Janet and I consulted quickly. It was a lot of money, but with thousands of miles still to go, we knew we needed to make the investment.

"We'll take it," I told Captain Steve.

During this conversation, at precisely the moment I was making the deal with Captain Steve, a high-speed ferry passed in front of us. Janet and I were in the cockpit and watched with idle interest, then sudden alarm, as the boat's gigantic wake combined with the high sea waves and engulfed the bow of *SailingActs*, burying it in water and foam. *SailingActs* proved her seaworthiness and merely pitched and bounced a little, then settled down. But the front hatch, directly above our cabin, had been open about an inch. During the one second of time it took for the wake to roll across the deck, gallons of water gushed directly on top of our bunks through the crack. We spent the next hour wringing out mattresses and other absorbent materials, and hanging everything out to dry (see Photo 33).

It was a short but demanding day, and Rhodes harbor was finally before us. Remembering the cruising guide's warnings about the Mandraki harbor, we were delighted to see an empty space next to a flashy multi-million-dollar yacht. A suave, movie-star type came up on deck and watched our water-logged and frayed *SailingActs* approach. The wind was gusting from the side, and I was not in the right position to drop anchor and back into the empty space for the now-familiar Mediterranean-style berthing. But the James Bond look-alike on the multimillion-dollar yacht commanded dramatically in Queen's English, "Drop your anchor, man, you're okay!"

I knew I was not okay and tried to explain otherwise in apprehensive American English, but he waved me off with a gesture that said, "I am not on deck to help you, only to make sure you won't damage my beautiful yacht with your incompetence. Make this quick so I can go back down below in the air conditioning and finish my cocktail."

Out of intimidation, an inferiority complex, tiredness, or the desire to impress, I did what the man said. Against my better judgment and against Janet's pleading advice from the bow, we dropped the anchor. I began to back, the wind gusted, and in front of everyone I drifted backwards, right into James Bond's long anchor chain. The propeller made an awful grinding sound that stopped the 42-horse-power diesel engine cold. I quickly started it again, but immediately knew the damage was done. When I engaged the gears, the whole boat shook as if *SailingActs* shared my feelings of the moment.

Eventually we vibrated and shook our way into the berth and tied up, but there was little celebration. We realized we'd need to stay in Rhodes, not only to get a new headsail, but to fix or replace the propeller as well.

It had been a challenging and eventful day of loss at the end of a long, hard week of sailing. Between the luxurious marina in Kos two days earlier, and the charming medieval, walled city of Rhodes where we just arrived, I had learned some lessons about defeat, humility, and weakness. As Paul wrote to his friends in Philippi, "I know both how to be abased, and I know how to abound" (Phil. 4:12). I think Paul and I learned some hard lessons, especially about ourselves, on the Mediterranean

There was a lot of diving and expense in the days that followed. I dove below and inspected the damage. I tried and failed at devising a homemade under-water breathing apparatus that would allow me to work longer than a minute at a time under the boat or to remove the damaged propeller. So we hired professional divers. They splashed, pounded, puffed, and debated for parts of two days but couldn't get the old propeller off the shaft. We would need to take *SailingActs* to a boatyard and have her hauled out of the water. Once out of water, our options would be clearer. How long would all this take? And at what cost?

It occurred to me in Rhodes that there is only one letter difference between "sailing acts" and "failing acts." For the first time since leaving Volos, we wondered whether we would be able to complete the voyage to Israel, either before winter or, for that matter, ever.

CHAPTER 9

Rough Rhodes and East Along the Turkish Coast

Mandraki Harbor on the island of Rhodes is crowded for some very good reasons. It must be one of the most picturesque medieval harbors in the world. For about 500 years, ancient travelers arriving by sea would have seen the legendary Colossus of Rhodes, a gigantic statue of Helios, the sun god, while still far out at sea. The Colossus, one of the Seven Wonders of the Ancient World, is thought to have been located somewhere near the Mandraki harbor, perhaps straddling the harbor entrance. Reputedly built over a period of 12 years (294-282 B.C.) and standing about 105 feet tall—tall enough for sailing ships to enter the harbor between its legs—the Colossus was destroyed by an earthquake in 225 or 226 A.D.

Rhodes is mentioned only twice in the Bible, once in the book of the Ezekiel (27:15) where Rhodes is listed among the major maritime trading partners of Tyre in Lebanon, and once in the book of Acts (21:1). According to the itinerary in Acts, the ship on which Paul was traveling, bound for Jerusalem in the spring of 57 A.D., spent one night in Rhodes. Paul would certainly have viewed the Colossus with interest. It's debatable that his ship sailed between the Colossus's legs, as there is no remaining archeological evidence that the Colossus actually straddled the harbor, but there is plenty of "solid" evidence filling souvenir shops in Rhodes: plastic replicas of the gigantic sun god and its picture on T-shirts with ships passing underneath with room to spare. Two 20th-century concrete blocks, one on each side of the harbor entrance, allows visitors today to imagine the Colossus.

Except for tradition and legend, no evidence exists as to where on the island Paul's ship anchored that night. One of the gates in the medieval wall that surrounds Rhodes is called St. Paul's Gate, and a small sign claims Paul entered the town of Rhodes there while his ship spent the night in the harbor. According to our guidebook, the local community of Lindos some distance down the coast of the island claims that Paul's ship anchored in their harbor. We would check out the evidence later.

A short walk from the Mandraki Harbor through the large gate in the wall of the city took us inside the World-Heritage-listed Old Town of Rhodes, the largest inhabited medieval town in Europe. Rhodes, with its rich history, quaint medieval charm, pristine beaches, 300 days of sunshine a year, and its ancient harbor—even without the Colossus—continues to attract tourists. They arrive by cruise ship, ferry, charter airplane, and yacht. Tourists love Rhodes.

Our second day in Rhodes was a Sunday, but instead of playing Vivaldi's *Four Seasons* while enjoying the ambience of that dream location, we sat on our crippled boat worrying that we might be delayed in Rhodes for the remainder of the sailing season.

Aram left by ferry to Athens that Sunday afternoon, his time with us complete. The emptiness aboard *SailingActs* added to our dejection. I tried to make plans and plot the passages for the remainder of the voyage to Israel, but found it too difficult to think beyond the task of repairing *SailingActs*.

Is uncertainty and apprehension really a necessary part of learning about Paul? I pondered. Sitting in a library and poring over piles of books seemed to be, for the first time on the sabbatical, far more appealing than sitting in the cockpit of *SailingActs* with a bent propeller and a damaged ego. *Maybe in situations of prolonged uncertainty, with events completely out of control, self-confidence turns into faith,* I reasoned. *Paul was not a person used to*

*being out of control or failing, and yet it was during the mission jour-
neys that he learned humility, weakness, and trust in God's power.*

That long Sunday slowly passed. We found an Internet café and
caught up with correspondence, walked to the beaches filled with
inert, prone, roasting vacationers, then returned to the boat. I took
a rare nap and awoke feeling slightly better. Toward evening the
boat from Turkey that had been moored next to us left, and its
place was immediately occupied by a sailboat with the hailing
port of Nevada, U.S.A. on its stern. We were intrigued at seeing a
boat from the landlocked, desert state of Nevada with Americans
actually on board. We chatted with the friendly owner about
where we had been and the *SailingActs* project.

"Where are you planning to winter?" he asked.

"Ashkelon, Israel."

"Are you crazy?" he snarled, his friendliness evaporating
instantly. "Israel is a horrible place. No one except religious
extremist nut cases would even think of going there."

"Have you ever been to Israel?" I asked, trying to demonstrate
my sanity and religious balance by explaining that we had just
spent two wonderful months in both Israel and the West Bank
that spring, and were reasonably certain that if hundreds of other
sailors could safely winter in Israel, so could we.

But for the next five minutes, like a man possessed, he spun out
a tirade of fear and loathing as Janet and I sat silently. Finally he
finished, the temporary insanity left, and he once more became a
friendly sailor. Later in the cabin, we began to feel better as our
own problems seemed to pale following the confrontation.

Monday morning, right after breakfast, I called the Nereus
Boatyard, the only boatyard in Rhodes. A helpful man with a
British accent answered. "Sure, bring your boat right over. We
aren't busy now and can lift your boat out and relaunch it for 200
euros, plus 5 euros per day while it is in the yard."

This didn't sound too bad. We immediately prepared to leave
Mandraki Harbor for the boatyard about one mile distant. The
cruising guide's description of the harbor again proved accurate as

we discovered that the anchor chain of the Swiss boat was on top of our anchor chain, so we heaved and strained to free ourselves, and by noon we were slowly motoring toward the boatyard. This was our first haul-out and we were a little nervous as we entered the slip and watched the huge mobile crane straddle *SailingActs*, place heavy straps under her, and smoothly hoist her dripping hull out of the water (see Photo 34). Within 30 minutes the competent crew in the boatyard had washed off all of the accumulated growth on the hull with a pressure washer, propped *SailingActs* securely on the concrete lot, and removed the old propeller.

Gilles, the boatyard owner, recommended that we get a new propeller from Athens and began making telephone calls to locate a shop that was open during the Olympics and the August holidays. Janet and I resigned ourselves to spending at least a week in Rhodes, living aboard *SailingActs* sitting solidly on land, surrounded by boats in various stages of dereliction, uptight territorial stray dogs, piles of nautical junk, and shouting Greek fishermen working on the hulls of their colorful wooden boats. In several days we would learn the names of the stray dogs from Gilles's son, find the trails to the boatyard's exit through piles of junk, and get used to climbing up a 10-foot ladder to board *SailingActs*.

During the days that followed, while we waited on both the parts and installation of the roller furler we had ordered through Captain Steve, and on the new propeller being made in Athens, Janet and I cleaned *SailingActs'* hull and applied a fresh coat of anti-fouling paint to the bottom. We painted the faded red stripes on the hull and the area above the water line a deep beautiful blue (see Photo 36). *SailingActs* may not have been able to sail, but she was getting a facelift in our hope that she someday would.

The old town of Rhodes is full of sidewalk cafés, restaurants, and *tavernas*, most of which had large TVs set up for watching the Olympics. So each evening we watched the Olympics along with Greek spectators whose ancestors had established the games—it was an extraordinary privilege. The cafés in Rhodes exploded with celebration whenever a Greek athlete won gold. Merchants were doing a thriving business selling Olympic souvenirs, ranging from the cheap, pagan, and bawdy to the expensive, pagan, and useless.

Thomas Cahill in his splendid book, *Sailing the Wine-Dark Sea: Why the Greeks Matter,* describes the Olympic games as "religious holidays" that were held in honor of particular gods. These games, like modern fairs, attracted a variety of merchants who displayed their wares in their booths around the edges. Paul, Priscilla, and Aquila very likely set up shop at these games, repairing or selling their awnings to the other merchants (Cahill pp. 85-86).

I had never thought about Paul practicing his tent-making trade at settings such as the Olympic Games, but while watching the Olympics in Rhodes, I was reminded every evening that Paul's immersion in Greek culture unavoidably included the spectacle of their games. These games, with their explicit pagan themes, nude athletes, and glorification of human achievement, must have contradicted Paul's pharisaic sensitivities at every point. Yet, he used the image of athletes as a model from which Christians could learn. Paul "became as a Greek," and the good news of Jesus the Jew connected to the imagination and ideals of competition and glory in Greek culture.

On the fifth day of waiting, I received a call from Captain Steve. "The sail has been delivered," he said. "You can pick it up at ACS Courier Service."

The woman in the boatyard office marked their location of 35 Amerikis Street on the map. Following the directions, I carried our little folding cart for a 25-minute walk to pick up the sails. It was midday and very hot. I found Amerikis Street, and eventually found number 35. *This is kind of odd,* I thought to myself as I stood among boutiques and trendy cafés. *Why is there no sign for the shipping company?*

After walking up and down the street for several minutes, checking and re-checking numbers and street names, I called the ACS number on my cell phone. The woman who answered was very helpful. "Yes, we have your sail. Yes, you are at the right place. Do you see the sign in front of you?"

"No," I said, wondering if bending the propeller had affected my vision. I described the surroundings from where I was standing, but they didn't make any sense to her.

"You must be at the wrong place," she said.

"I am at 35 Amerikis Street."

In the background I heard a quick consultation. "Wait, I'll come out the door and look for you."

Ten minutes later, I could see no one looking for me, so I approached a couple of women who seemed to be looking for someone, but they returned blank stares when I asked them. I am not, I decided, what the average Greek woman on the streets in Rhodes is looking for.

A kind Greek man tried to help solve the mystery. "This is the only Amerikis Street in Rhodes," he explained, "but I don't think there is an ACS courier here." Looking around at the upscale surroundings along the shady street, I thought it did seem a strange place for sweaty people like me to pick up heavy, industrial-strength shipments.

I called ACS again. "You aren't at the right place," she said in exasperation at this invisible, dense American.

"Yes I am," I replied to the woman in the invisible Greek place of business. "Something is wrong here."

"Give your phone to a Greek," the woman ordered.

I accosted a Greek-looking man. "Only French," he said. The next one spoke only Italian. *Can't anyone in Rhodes speak Greek?* I began to wonder.

The woman on the phone from ACS heard everything, and I imagined her rolling her eyes in her invisible office. Finally I went into a music store on the corner. The man inside listened and talked for a long time, while the customers in the store listened with bemused expressions. *This is strange,* I thought. *Aren't we just getting directions here?* The man handed back the phone. "You are talking to someone on the island of Kos, not Rhodes," he explained.

The sail was shipped to the wrong island! I had the correct address, but the wrong town! I called Captain Steve, who was also incredulous. "We'll get it sent to Rhodes right away," he promised.

Returning to the boatyard empty-handed, I stopped to buy a phone card for the cell phone. Inside the shop were some Americans from a cruise ship, happily buying a plastic Colossus of Rhodes lamp. One woman asked what I was doing in Rhodes. When I explained we were following the routes of the Apostle Paul, one woman commented, "You look like a famous sailor. Are you famous?"

"Not yet," I said. *But I will be one day if we spend the rest of our lives trying to get off the island of Rhodes.*

On the following day, the sail arrived in Rhodes. Now we were only waiting for the furler-system hardware and the new propeller.

Having finished with the painting and maintenance on *SailingActs,* we decided to visit Lindos, 21 miles down the southern coast of the island. We took a local bus to Lindos, full of questions. Did Paul's ship anchor in Lindos instead of in Rhodes? Did Paul visit the island again, or stay longer than the story in Acts indicates?

We alighted from the bus and walked into the town of Lindos, stopping by a bustling donkey station to watch the lines of tourists eagerly waiting their turn for a donkey to take them on a 10-minute ride up the hill to the entrance of the ancient acropolis for 5 euros. We hiked to the entrance in eight minutes and entered the acropolis where the Doric invaders 4,000 years earlier had established a temple to Athena. We admired the fine remains of a later temple to Athena, built in the fourth century B.C., and an impressive *stoa* from the second century B.C. At the base of the cliff lay a snug harbor where, the story goes, a ship carrying the Apostle Paul sought refuge from a storm, and where Paul preached on the shore (see Photo 35).

We hiked down to the harbor. Hot and tired, we went into a little market along the street to purchase a snack and a drink. The name of the market was "St. Paul's Supermarket" (see Photo 37). Guessing that the owner would likely have an opinion on Paul, we asked, "Do you think Paul really visited Lindos?"

"Yes, most certainly," George, the owner, declared. "Paul stopped at Rhodes—did you see St. Paul's Gate there? Then he sailed south to Lindos. The harbor is called St. Paul's Bay to this very day. Did you see the little chapel on the shore? That is where Paul preached. Every year on June 28 we celebrate Paul's visit with an all-night celebration at the harbor."

"But the book of Acts doesn't include that story."

"Yes, I know," George of St. Paul's Supermarket explained. "A lot of people are skeptical, especially about the chapel as being the spot where Paul preached. But let me tell you what happened. In 1954, I was only a boy of seven, but I remember this well. An old woman in Lindos had a dream in which she was shown an outcropping along the shore of the bay and instructed to dig at the spot; there she would find something important related to St. Paul. The mayor of Lindos at that time ridiculed the idea, but because the woman insisted and pestered him constantly, he instructed some men to dig at the spot where the woman told them to. With my own eyes, I saw my father and a few other men uncover some stones with very old inscriptions that proved Paul was here. These stones are in the chapel today."

We bought some ice cream from St. Paul's Supermarket and thought about the pride the people of Lindos have for Paul's visit. George and his supermarket confirmed Paul's claim when he said, "To the Greeks I became as a Greek."

The more we learned about Greek culture, with our background knowledge of first-century Judaism, the more impressed we became with Paul's ability to share the gospel of Jesus the Jew without alienating the Greeks. Something about the message of

SailingActs

Jesus the Jew, communicated by Paul the Jew, attracted at least some Greeks. Were these average Greeks? Were these people who experienced, or otherwise recognized, the shortcomings of the pagan promises for happiness and life? Were they dissatisfied with the pervasive religious pluralism and moral laxity? For the first-century Greeks, perhaps there was no moral or intellectual compass to assure people they were on the right path. Maybe Paul's message of the truth of the gospel was a welcome alternative to moral and intellectual ambiguity.

Paul was not content that his message was tolerated or that he was accepted within the religiously plural Roman Empire. He wanted the good news of Jesus to be recognized as truth and accepted by both Jews and Greeks. So he became both Jew and Greek, and he challenged both Jews and Greeks. He was a bridge across the ethnic, religious, and cultural chasm separating the two, and he paid for this personally every time he suffered misunderstanding, resentment, and abuse from either pagans or Jews.

Back at the boatyard that Thursday evening, we learned that the earliest we could find out about getting a new propeller was the following Monday. In addition, the roller furler still hadn't been delivered, nor had we received further word about when it would arrive. We would need to wait several more days as the wind howled, the stray dogs barked, and the dust blew in the boatyard.

On Saturday I took apart the saltwater pump on the engine cooling system. I didn't have spare impellers and was worried that one day the 25-year-old pump would suddenly need one while we were out at sea. After disassembling and cleaning the pump, it was clear I needed to replace the rubber impeller and find some spares. I finally found a shop where I could purchase new impellers and was delighted when the old man rummaged around in the back of the shop and found exactly the right replacements. "Are you from France?" he asked as I paid for the impellers.

"No," I said, "from America."

Usually this produced an awkward silence, but this time the old man's face lit up. He said something about being in the war with Americans, then shuffled off and soon returned with a faded, tattered, black-and-white photo of himself in a navy uniform as a young man, posing with a number of other young men. He beamed as he explained the photograph. "These three are American, these two are Italian, and these are Greek. We were all friends."

What a difference today, I thought sadly as I examined the photo. *Back then the Americans were liberators, allies, and friends to so many in Europe. Today, America is seen to be using its power in completely different ways,* I thought to myself. But meeting the very old man with his old, positive memories of Americans and getting an impeller for a very old pump was uplifting.

On Monday morning we received news of the propeller from Athens. One shop could make one for 240 euros, but it would take at least another week. Another shop could supply us with a new propeller for 120 euros, and it would be done in several days. Some decisions are easy to make.

In the afternoon I had a long telephone conversation with Captain Steve about the roller furler. He gave me the name of a technician in Rhodes, Fotis, and instructed me to call him directly. The name "Fotis" sounded like "fetus" when Captain Steve pronounced it, and I fleetingly considered asking him if maybe the cause for the delay was that we were waiting for "Fetus" to become a viable human being before he could begin the installation. Captain Steve explained that Fotis claimed he still had not gotten word from the shipping company that the parts were in. I was beginning to suspect something else was going on.

On the afternoon of September 1, a Wednesday, after having waited 10 days in Rhodes, we received a call from a certain Pierre that he, not Fotis, would be installing the furler as soon as it arrived. He dropped by later to look at the rigging of *SailingActs*. "Just as soon as we get the furler," he promised, "I'll install it."

The next morning Pierre called and informed me that the furler system was at Fotis's office at Mandraki Harbor. "Go and bring it to your boat," he instructed, "then I'll start working on it." I carried our folding cart the one mile from the boatyard to Fotis's office at Mandraki harbor. The office was closed, but on the sidewalk in front of the door was a furling system in several long boxes. My name was not visible on the box, but the furler had to be ours. I loaded everything onto the cart, then trundled the whole contraption through crowds of tourists disembarking from several cruise ships, and finally "home" to the boatyard. Pierre showed up and we began the installation. I climbed up the mast to take the forestay down. Fotis called while I was dangling from the bosun's chair at the top of the mast. "I will be able to start installing your furler soon," he promised.

"It's being installed right now," I answered.

"No problem," Fotis replied.

Wrong! Big problem! An hour later, as Pierre and I continued to assemble the furler, a group of men on motorcycles roared up in a cloud of dust. All were large men, wearing very dark sunglasses. Fotis, their leader, strode directly toward me as his "colleagues" lit cigarettes and stood close by in the shade. *This looks an awful lot like a scene from a low-budget gangster movie,* I thought.

"I'm here to take the furler back," Fotis greeted me.

"What?" I asked stupidly.

"The company called me. They said if you do not want the furler, then fine. I am supposed to take it back."

"I want the furler," I explained. "Otherwise I wouldn't have laid out over 2,000 euros for the down payment, waited for 10 days in a dusty boatyard, and be installing it at this very moment."

"If you want to keep it," Fotis said, "you have to pay 1,000 euros plus 400 more to Pierre for installing it." This was not part of the deal. On the telephone with Captain Steve, I had been instructed to pay the final 1,000 euros after the installation was completed, 600 to Fotis, and 400 to the installer.

By this time Fotis and his "colleagues" had moved into position to begin dismantling the partially assembled furler while hurling insults in my direction. Pierre had disappeared. Suddenly everything became clear. Fotis was trying to get an extra cut, and had stalled and lied for a week instead of installing the furler as soon as it had arrived in Rhodes. The tactic would make me desperate and I would, he likely reasoned, be willing to pay extra to finally get *SailingActs* back on the water. Things were tense, but I was not about to back down or pay Fotis.

"You can't take this from me," I challenged, standing over the furler. "I've paid for it." I was drawing inspiration from Paul.

"Show me your name on the box," Fotis challenged back. "It has my name on it." He was right.

It was getting ugly. The large men in sunglasses moved and began lifting the partially assemble furler off the ground. I needed to think of something quickly or the furler would be forever gone. I hurriedly dialed Captain Steve's number and described the situation with the gangsters watching. He agreed to talk to Fotis.

"Captain Steve wants to talk to you," I said, handing the telephone to Fotis.

"Who is Captain Steve? I don't know him. I don't want to talk to him."

"Captain Steve happens to be the dealer from whom I bought these sails. If you ever want to install another furler, you'd better talk to him," I retorted, sensing a slight advantage in the power struggle.

Reluctantly Fotis took the phone. What Captain Steve told him, I'll never know, but Fotis became very quiet, then subdued. From 20 feet away I could hear Captain Steve's voice from the cell phone, yelling as only a Greek sea captain can. Fotis wilted. The men, reading Fotis's body language, moved back under the shade, extinguished their cigarettes, then walked toward their motorcycles as Fotis handed the phone back to me.

"Okay, you can come to my office and pay me the 600 euros as agreed."

"I'll pay you now if you can give me a receipt." I was learning fast.

"Sorry," Fotis said. "The receipts are in the office. You will have to come by the office."

"No," I decided. Fotis had caused enough problems—stalling, threatening, delaying, and angling for extra payoffs. "You will have to go back to the office, bring back a receipt, and then I will give you the money here."

Fotis agreed and the greedy gang roared off on their motorcycles, defeated and deflated. Fotis returned 30 minutes later, all friendliness and cooperation. We shook hands, joked, and parted friends. *But if I am ever stranded on Rhodes in the future, I won't give my business to Fotis,* I thought as he left.

That afternoon Pierre and I not only finished installing the furler and the new sail, but the propeller arrived from Athens, a thing of gleaming, bronze beauty. The mechanic fitted it onto the shaft in a matter of minutes. We were ready to sail! That night Janet and I celebrated in a tourist restaurant and laughed about the excellent adventure of sailing Acts and the trials and triumphs on Rhodes, eager for the next leg.

The boatyard had scheduled our launch at noon the next day, a Saturday. I filled the water tanks and disconnected the electricity, while Janet made a last shopping trip to the grocery store. At 12:30 the crane lifted *SailingActs* and trundled her slowly to the water, gently lowered her, and suddenly *SailingActs* was floating again. She looked far better than we had ever seen her, with her fresh paint and a roller-furling headsail. We took her out to try the new propeller and headsail and noticed with satisfaction that the propeller turned smoothly now. But it was the new roller furler that made sailing a pleasure. Now, instead of going to the deck on the bow and struggling with repeated sail changes on rough seas, I could remain in the safety and comfort of the cockpit, opening, adjusting, and furling the headsail with ease.

We arranged to stay in the boatyard's slip, and then leave for the Turkish coast early the next morning. We slept that night, reveling in the gentle rocking of *SailingActs* and eager to begin the last leg of the voyage to the spectacular southern coast of Turkey, then on to Cyprus and to Israel by the end of September.

At 6:15 the following morning, we left Rhodes looking back at the walls of Old Town and its harbor where we had spent so long waiting, working, and learning. There was no wind so we motored smoothly with the new propeller. About noon I checked the bilge and was alarmed to see a substantial amount of water under the floor. It had been completely dry when we left Rhodes four hours earlier. A quick check revealed that the saltwater cooling pump, in which I had installed the new impeller, was leaking profusely. The screws holding the cover were in very poor shape, and I hadn't been able to find new ones of the right size in the Rhodes boatyard. I would need to work on this at the next opportunity. I noted that no amount of grease forced into the seal around the propeller shaft stopped the seawater from leaking in steadily as it previously had. We ran the bilge pump at least once an hour that day, worrying all the while.

We motored the entire eight-hour journey to the beautiful little bay of Yali Limna, about three miles west of Kalkan, Turkey. We were trying to get as close to the ancient harbor of Patara as we could. In Acts 21:1, Paul's ship left Rhodes and stayed the following night in Patara. We dropped the anchor in mid-afternoon among several Turkish *gullets*, then swam and relaxed for the remainder of the day.

The following morning, we concluded that the water in the bilge was roughly the same level as the evening before, which meant that it was only leaking when the engine was running. We decided it was safe to leave *SailingActs* at anchor, motor the three miles to the small town of Kalkan with the dinghy, and find a bus that would take us to Patara. While this had been a harbor during Paul's day, Patara is now accessible only by road due to silting of its harbor. The dinghy trip in choppy seas took 35 minutes. We found a place to tie up the dinghy in the tiny harbor, and a friendly man who ran a water taxi indicated that he would keep his eye on it for us. We hiked up the hill to the edge of Kalkan to find the bus to Patara.

When we boarded the crowded little bus, we noted that our guidebook seemed fairly accurate with its statement that Patara "attracts an interesting mix of Turkish and foreign eccentrics," for everyone on the little bus—except for Janet and me, of course—fit the description. All were headed for the long, white-sand beach that the tourist brochures claim is one of the best in the Mediterranean. The bus chugged over extremely rugged terrain among beautiful forests before dropping into a fertile river valley full of greenhouses. Before reaching the ruins or the beach, the bus stopped at a gate and everyone paid an entrance fee for a combination ticket to the beach and the ruins of Patara. We all paid, then as the bus wound its way through the ruins, we asked the driver to let us off. Janet and I were the only ones that got out of the sweltering bus in the stifling heat, and we and the beach-goers looked at each other with mutual pity.

The ruins of Patara are magnificently "undeveloped," as are many of the ancient sites in Turkey. We got the feeling, poking through the overgrown ruins with goats grazing in their shade, that we were discovering something for the first time. There were no signs explaining things. No tourists. No carpet-sellers at the entrance. Just the heat, the dust, the flies, and our own imagination among the overgrown, swampy ruins of baths, several temples, monuments, a theater, and a massive granary which once stored wheat for Roman soldiers on campaigns to the east.

When Paul's ship stopped here on its way from Rhodes to Jerusalem in 57 A.D., the river harbor was in the center of town. Visitors would find themselves surrounded by a grand showcase of human achievement and the gods' blessings. Patara would

35 | *The harbor at Lindos, Rhodes, Greece, where tradition has it that Paul's ship anchored during a storm.*

36 | *Repainting* SailingActs' *stripes in the boatyard on Rhodes, Greece.*

37 | *George, owner of Saint Paul's Supermarket in Lindos, Greece, and enthusiastic storyteller of local traditions on Paul.*

38 | *Repairing the seawater engine cooling pump. The temperature is over 100 degrees. I am covered with grease. The smile is fake.*

39 | *Admiring the granary built by the Emperor Hadrian (117-138 A.D.) at Myra's Andriace harbor in Finike, Turkey.*

40 *Janet on an early-morning sail toward Antalya, Turkey.*

41 *The impressive main street of Perga, Turkey, where Paul, Barnabas, and John Mark arrived on their first mission journey.*

42   *The main street of Tarsus, Turkey, boyhood home of Paul.*

43   *Traditional site where the first Christians met in Syrian Antioch (now Antakya, Turkey). A cave with ancient Christian symbols carved on the rocks gives credence to this tradition.*

44 *The ruins of Paphos on the island of Cyprus. SailingActs is anchored in the ancient town harbor and is just visible through the ruins of the arch.*

45 *Janet examines an early baptismal font in Salamis, Northern Cyprus.*

46 | *Navigating across the open water between Limassol, Cyprus, and Ashkelon, Israel.*

47 | *At home in the Ashkelon Marina, Ashkelon, Israel, where we lived on* SailingActs *from October 2004 to April 2005.*

later become famous as the birthplace of a certain Nicholas, who later became bishop in nearby Myra, and a saint. Born in the fourth century in the sun-baked southern coast of Turkey, Nicholas would be "converted" to a jolly icon of Christmas consumption. St. Nicholas, as Santa Claus, would become even more widely known than St. Paul.

After spending several hours among the ruins of Patara, we walked out to the beach to find a bus returning to Kalkan. It was early afternoon when we arrived back in Kalkan, retrieved our dinghy, and motored the three miles back to Yali Limna, where *SailingActs* was anchored. On one of the hottest days of the season, I decided to tackle the leaking water pump (see Photo 38). This turned out a much bigger job than I had expected because the water pump is located below the water line. Normally all one has to do is shut off the sea cock, the intake valve in the hull of the boat, and then disassemble the water pump. But when I attempted this, I discovered the sea cock was corroded and wouldn't budge. I couldn't shut off the water and needed to devise a creative engineering solution in order to keep seawater from gushing into the boat as I disassembled the water pump. Two hours later, covered with a black, slimy combination of sweat and grease, I was sad to see that it still leaked. I shut down the motor, tightened the worn screws on the cover as much as possible, tried again, and this time everything stayed reasonably dry. But was this good enough for the long passages off shore that we needed to make before arriving in Israel? What if I needed to quickly change an impeller but could not shut off the sea cock in order to do it easily? We reluctantly began to consider having *SailingActs* hauled out again when we were near the next boatyard.

We rose the next morning before daylight to sail east along the coast to the marina in Finike. From our base in the Finike marina, we planned to go overland to Myra and its harbor, Andriace. Myra is mentioned only once in the Bible, in Acts 27:5, as a stop and ship-change on Paul's ill-fated journey as a prisoner from Caesarea to

SailingActs

Rome in late fall of 59 A.D. Some scholars believe Paul also stopped in Myra after Patara on his voyage in 57 A.D. from Philippi to Jerusalem, but this is not certain. Although we intended to visit Myra on our own voyage to Rome in the following summer of 2005, we wanted to explore Myra while we had the opportunity.

The morning after arriving in Finike, we walked to the bus station and got a *dolmus* (minibus) to Demre, the town next to the archeological site of Myra. We started walking the one mile distance from Demre to the ruins of Myra. Another *dolmus* stopped and the driver persuaded us to take a ride. We arrived quickly at the entrance and were surprised to see the parking lot crowded with 10 tourist buses. We each paid a $7 entrance fee and entered the pleasant, shady, but tiny site. It was filled with throngs of tourists taking pictures of each other against the backdrop of spectacular Lycian tombs carved in the rock cliffs and the extremely well-preserved theater. The tombs reminded Janet and me of the Nabatian tombs in Petra, Jordan, and after considering that both the Lycians and the Nabatians had Phoenician connections, the similarities in burial practices and architecture between these two widely-distant places made sense.

Back in Demre, we stopped at the Church of St. Nicholas, where the good saint was once buried before his bones were carried off to Bari, Italy, in the 11th century. In the courtyard of the ancient rambling church stands a statue of Nicholas, a pack on his back, two adoring children at his side, looking like the Santa Claus of a 1950s Coca Cola commercial. The courtyard and church were jammed with Orthodox Christians from Russia, reverently taking pictures and crossing themselves. In a saint-popularity contest, St. Nicholas, not St. Paul, wins handily in Myra.

The more we discovered of St. Nicholas/Santa Claus in Myra, the more intriguing the historical saint became and the more absurd his transformation to Santa seemed. The legend about St. Nicholas in Myra, which forms the basis of Santa Claus, concerns a poor man who had three daughters, all eligible for marriage. But being poor, the father could not afford the required dowries.

When Nicholas, then the bishop of Myra, heard of this, he decided to help out anonymously, so he climbed on the roof of the poor man's hut and dropped three gold pieces down the chimney. Now you know the rest of the story.

St. Nicholas is not only the patron saint of Greece, Russia, and Sicily, but he is also the patron saint of children, prisoners, sailors, and travelers. I could well imagine that a Greek child running off to sea in order to explore the world, joining the Mafia while in Sicily, and being arrested and jailed while trying to smuggle drugs into Russia, would likely turn to St. Nicholas for help.

Having seen St. Nicholas's icon on several Greek boats while sailing the Aegean, I found sailors' admiration of St. Nicholas especially intriguing. Just why St. Nicholas became the patron saint of seafarers is not altogether clear, but the association likely has pagan origins. Myra, at the time of Paul's visit, was a center for worship of Poseidon, the god of the sea. Paul would have observed the sailors praying for protection and offering sacrifices of thanksgiving to Poseidon when his ship put in at the Myra harbor on his storm-buffeted voyage in the early winter of 59 A.D.

With the coming of Christianity, Poseidon was replaced by St. Nicholas, bishop of Myra, in popular seafaring superstitions. To this day St. Nicholas is accredited with many life-saving miracles at sea. St. Nicholas is referred to as the "mariner." Ships carry his icon, and islands, villages, capes, and lighthouses are named after St. Nicholas. Fishermen invite the local priest to pray to St. Nicholas to bless their fishing season. On St. Nicholas's Day, seamen toss boiled wheat into the sea for protection against storms and offer silver images of fish and ships at his church. This versatile saint, it occurred to us in Myra, had not only been co-opted by Christian seafarers to Christianize their pagan worship of Poseidon, but he had also been co-opted by entrepreneurs to paganize the Christian celebration of Jesus' birth.

Janet and I ate a *donar* (equivalent to the Greek gyros) wrapped in wonderful fresh bread, then took a *dolmus* out to

Andriace, the ancient harbor of Myra. Here, where the river empties into the sea, fantastic, unrestored ruins surround the silted harbor. As in Patara, we felt like explorers, wandering through the briars, sand, and swampy areas with no entrance fees or explanations. A large number of tourists were swimming off the beach at the edge of the ruins, while the Turkish *gullets* waited at anchor for them in the harbor. We seemed to be the only people interested in the ruins of this once thriving port. But Janet and I didn't mind. The most satisfying moment of the afternoon was finding, half hidden by overgrowth, the huge stone granary built by the Roman Emperor Hadrian (after Paul's visit, of course). It was simply the best preserved building of its kind that I had ever seen, and it demonstrated clearly the importance of this harbor for shipping grain (see Photo 39). The details in Acts of Paul's journey to Rome are substantiated by the archeological evidence in Myra's Andriace harbor.

In late afternoon, tired and limping from a massive thorn I had stepped on, we returned to Finike, satisfied with our findings. We showered, went out for an inexpensive meal, and paid the marina bill in order to leave at dawn the next morning.

We pulled out of the Finike marina at 6:20 and followed the unspoiled, rugged Turkish coast northeast toward Antalya, our final port in Turkey (see Photo 40). The air was absolutely still, so we motored, accompanied by 12 Turkish *gullets* in front of and behind us. We enjoyed breakfast in the cockpit, while the auto helm steered.

"Paul would have seen this very same scenery at one point or another," we commented. The unspoiled scenery of this part of the Turkish coast would have looked exactly the same as it did 2,000 years earlier. Paul had sailed from Paphos, Cyprus, to Perge, near Antalya, on his very first journey before going inland to Antioch, Iconium, Lystra, and Derbe. We would visit all of these places before leaving Antalya.

While the water leakage was not serious, it was still bothersome, and we began to notice a distinct vibration from the propeller shaft. We had worried that the cutlass bearing that held the end of the shaft under water might have been damaged when the workers used a heating torch to remove the old propeller in Rhodes. Now it seemed clear that had been the case. We would need to have *SailingActs* hauled out again in Antalya, a boatyard with a very good reputation for low-cost and quality work.

By 3:30 that afternoon, we had motored the 55 sea miles and entered the Antalya marina with its friendly and helpful staff that is typical of Turkey. I mentioned when checking in that we needed a haul-out for repairs, and two hours later, Ayhan, the boatyard foreman stopped by *SailingActs* to make the arrangements. "The haul-out fee is $280," he explained, "but if all of the repairs can be completed and we can re-launch your boat in the same day, the fee is $140. Which would you like us to do?"

"Go ahead and do the repairs as slowly as you can," I suggested to the fun-loving Ayhan. "That way we can delay our trip, spend twice as much money on the haul-out, and you can make a killing on the repairs." We all laughed and scheduled the one-day haul-out several days later, just before Janet and I would begin the long trip following Paul's overland routes.

We slept well that night, until a cat came aboard and began rummaging through our garbage bag at 3:40 in the morning. Janet's startled yell jarred me out of sleep, but it was pleasant lying there awake, knowing we would not be sailing the next morning, just resting and taking care of some minor maintenance tasks. I laid awake, thinking back on the day so long ago when we left Volos in a thunderstorm. We had sailed 1,150 incredibly intense and wonderful sea miles since then. *No matter how this ends,* I thought as I drifted off to sleep, *it will have been worth it all.*

CHAPTER 10

In the Footsteps of Paul in Turkey

"Paul sure picked pretty places to spread the gospel," Janet remarked as we explored Antalya the next afternoon. It was September 10. We had taken the *dolmus* from the marina for the 25-minute, 50-cent ride to the center of Antalya in order to visit the archeological museum and explore the old harbor. What a city!

The city of Antalya (called Attalia in Acts 14:25, 26) is mentioned in Acts only in connection with Paul's first mission voyage. Paul, with his two co-workers, Barnabas and John Mark, had left from Syrian Antioch in the northeastern corner of the Mediterranean in the spring of 47 A.D., sailed to Salamis on the eastern end of Cyprus, traveled overland until they reached Paphos on the western end of Cyprus, then sailed to Perge, located on the southern coast of what is now Turkey. From Perge, Paul and Barnabas had left John Mark behind to return to Jerusalem and traveled overland to Pisidian Antioch, Iconium, Lystra, and Derbe. Retracing their return route through the same cities, they arrived back on the coast about two years later, sailing for their home base of Syrian Antioch, this time from the main harbor of Attalia, about 10 miles west of Perge. From our base in Antalya, we would visit Perge and then follow Paul and Barnabas's route overland.

We found the excellent natural harbor that had made Antalya the commercial center of the southern Turkish coast from the second century B.C., and from which Paul and Barnabas had departed at the end of their intense mission activities inland. We had considered trying to bring *SailingActs* into this historic, cliff-flanked harbor close to the foot of Antalya's old center, but it was completely crowded with *gullets* and fishing boats. On the entire wharf around the harbor, tourists wandered among the hawkers in front of their empty party boats who pled with the tourists to take "the most enjoyable fantasy sail of your dreams."

Perge played a larger part in the story of Paul's early experiences in mission in Acts (Acts 13:13-14; 14:25). We set out for Perge the following morning, eager to visit the ruins of this once flourishing city. The local bus out of Antalya was filled with Turkish workers, at least 10 of whom, when they found out we were visiting Perge, became our team of self-appointed personal conductors, making sure we got off at the right stop.

We walked the mile to the site, paid the entrance fee, then joined a handful of other visitors on the vast site of a once magnificent city. Perge is located some distance from the sea on the Cestrus River, which in Paul's time was navigable and provided a safe harbor, protected from wind and waves of the sea, and easily defendable from pirates.

We walked down the 60-foot-wide colonnaded Roman street and imagined how it would have looked when Paul, Barnabas, and John Mark walked here in 47 A.D. (see Photo 41). The shops that lined this magnificent street behind the columns would have been doing a thriving business. The channel, fed by springs through an elaborate fountain at the top of the street, would have been flowing with sparkling water down the center of the street. The temple of Pergaean Artemis would have gleamed from the steep hill behind the fountain. If an athletic event would have been occurring, Paul, Barnabas, and John Mark would have heard the roar of 14,000 spectators in the magnificent stadium close by, and would have gazed at the wealthy citizens frequenting the magnificent bath complex located near the center of Perge (or "Perga" in Paul's time). If Janet and I were impressed wandering through the ruins of Perge, we were sure that Paul, Barnabas, and John Mark were impressed by the glory of this city in its prime.

We paused in the shade and carefully reread the short description of events connected with Perga in Acts. Paul, Barnabas, and John Mark had just arrived from Paphos in Cyprus where Paul had met with Sergius Paulus, the proconsul of Cyprus. Following this meeting and the conversion of this high-ranking Roman official to Christianity, Paul was never again referred to by his Hebrew name, Saul, in the book of Acts. Paul, Barnabas, and John Mark had just sailed what was probably the longest voyage of their lives up to that point, 155 miles over the open sea from Cyprus. John Mark decided in Perga to discontinue with Paul and Barnabas and returned to Jerusalem, something about which Paul was not happy.

Among the ruins of Perge, Janet and I tried to make sense of the events. Why had John Mark discontinued with Paul and Barnabas? Could it be that the rapid and eye-opening experiences of extended exposure to the pagan world were stretching John Mark, the younger man from Palestine, to the limit? For Paul, the explorer and experimenter, these experiences may have been positive, and for Barnabas, the native of Cyprus, they may have been familiar. Could Paul and Barnabas's openness to the pagan Greeks and Paul's rejection by the Jewish community on Cyprus have caused John Mark to feel misgivings toward his missionary partners? Finally, could the total immersion in pagan culture, which included arriving in the magnificent, thoroughly pagan city of Perga following a voyage of at least 30 hours on a pagan ship, have caused a kind of culture-shock in the young John Mark? By the time John Mark reached Perga, he must have had enough of Paul and paganism. He would return to Jerusalem for recovery. Paul and Barnabas, on the other hand, were eager to push on northward to Antioch and they set out immediately.

Janet and I needed to return to Antalya for the haul-out and repairs to *SailingActs* before we could do the same. We caught a *dolmus* back to Antalya, then another one to the marina. That night on *SailingActs* we were jarred awake at 1:00 in the morning by what seemed to be a group of semi-drunk Turkish and Eastern Europeans on a boat close by. One woman kept shrieking in both English and another language, which I assumed was Turkish, "I want my money! Give me my money!" Several men were arguing with her in Turkish. We lay awake listening to the fight for a number of minutes. At last the woman screamed, "I hate you!" and everything went quiet. I tried not to imagine what was going on in that boat, but I suspected it was the kind of thing Paul encountered over and over during his travels. I suspected it was not love.

At 9:00 the next morning, a Saturday, we motored over to the slip where the travel lift was waiting. These men were professionals. Two men handily eased *SailingActs* out of the water in a matter of minutes and parked in the work area about 75 yards away. "The workmen will come by shortly," the crane driver promised. I set to work on the frozen sea cock and, with the help of copious amounts of WD 40 and a little coercion with a hammer, it soon was working freely. I disassembled the leaky water pump, hoping the shop would have new screws to replace the worn ones holding the cover. Three workmen soon arrived and within several minutes removed the propeller shaft bearing. I gave them my spare bearing and they took everything back to the shop for assembly.

I continued to work on everything I could think of that could possibly need repair while the boat was out of water. Deciding to fix the leaky seal around the propeller shaft, I removed the pressure flange that holds the water seal and was amazed to discover that the seal had completely disintegrated. The shop foreman in the marina rummaged around and found a new piece of the woven fabric, Teflon-coated packing material that happened to be precisely eight millimeters thick, a perfect fit. Pleased at my stroke of luck, I cut it to fit and replaced the flange. I reassembled the water pump with the six new stainless-steel screws the workmen had found. The workmen reinstalled the shaft bearing. We tightened everything down by 5:00, and one hour later *SailingActs* was in the water again. I started the engine, adjusted the water seal on the shaft, and examined the water pump and all the new fittings for leaks. Everything stayed bone dry! With *SailingActs* ready for off-shore voyaging, we could leave in the morning for a week of travel to Yalvaç (Pisidian Antioch), driving all the way to Antakya (Syrian Antioch), and back to Antalya.

At 9:00 on Sunday morning, we were packed and waiting at the marina gate for someone to deliver our rental car. At last, at 9:30, he drove up. We loaded our luggage and drove across Antalya to drop off the driver near his office, then headed north out of the city toward Pisidian Antioch. The streets weren't busy that Sunday morning, and we quickly left Antalya behind, climbing rapidly from the coast into gorgeous mountain scenery. We wound up through pine trees and passed pristine lakes with remarkable blue-green water. The air was fresh and cool. We reached the summit, then descended through about 30 miles of apple orchards. The trees were loaded with bright red and yellow apples which the farmers were selling in stands that lined the road for miles. Then, down out of the apple county, the topography changed and rolling wheat fields replaced the orchards, with magnificent, rugged mountains in the background. The wheat harvest was almost over, and with no large combines visible, Janet and I concluded that the small, stationary threshing machines at the edge of some of the fields had been used to thresh the grain.

We followed the route toward the town of Yalvaç which, according to our guidebook, was in the vicinity of Antioch. Once in the dusty little town, however, we drove around without immediately seeing any signs to the site of Antioch. Finally we spotted a battered yellow sign with "Antioch" barely legible, and drove in the direction it pointed. At the first intersection we came to, we had to guess which street to take, then guessed at the next one, and soon lost our way completely. So we circled back, looking for a battered yellow sign pointing to Antioch, triumphant when we saw another one. But this one was pointing slightly heavenward, at the third floor of a nearby apartment building. We circled and criss-crossed Yalvaç looking for more random, misleading yellow signs to Antioch.

We passed the archeological museum. "Let's visit the museum first," Janet suggested, "then we can ask the museum people for directions to Antioch when we leave."

This sounded like a good plan. The two friendly men at the front desk could not speak a word of English, but took our money and wrote our names down on the tickets they gave us, something that continues to baffle me. We were the only visitors in the museum and the men bustled about, opening doors and turning on the lights. The small museum contained a collection of artifacts from Antioch related to the story of Paul's activities, including some ancient images of gods and goddesses, and several carved stones mentioning the cities of Lystra and Derbe.

"Which way to Antioch?" we asked as we were leaving. The two men pointed down the road beyond the museum. We drove off in the direction they indicated, but lost our way as the street divided and deteriorated.

"Do you suppose Paul and Barnabas got lost looking for Antioch?" I wondered to Janet.

"Not likely," Janet guessed. "Unlike you, Paul probably didn't have any problem with stopping and asking for directions when he got lost."

"I'm not so sure. Why do you think Paul always took someone like Barnabas along with him on his travels? And besides, we did ask directions, but we still haven't found Antioch." An hour of circuitous meandering was making us peevish.

We stopped at a gas station on the edge of town. Janet went in, as she seemed to enjoy the flurry of social excitement that her request for directions always ignited in Turkey. Through the gas-station window, I saw men gathering around her, their arms waving. Several arm-waving men led Janet out into the parking lot. We took the road we guessed they were waving at, but it soon disappeared into a farmer's recently harvested field. We returned to the museum where the two men were surprised to see us again. This time they solicited help from a friend whose apparent job was to keep them company in the empty museum. Everyone seemed to be pointing in the same general direction, so we decided to just keep driving, using the topography and our past experience of finding ruins to locate Antioch. Within five minutes we found a large, promising-looking mound surrounded by a fence. There was no sign, so I asked at a small kiosk near the entrance and, sure enough, we had found Antioch.

It's unclear to me how the antiquities and tourist people in Turkey decide to promote their fantastic wealth of archeological ruins. Some, like Ephesus, are well publicized and packed with tour groups. Other entire ancient cities are unmarked in vast and almost empty sites. Antioch, a truly exciting place to explore, is such a place.

While Pisidian Antioch is mentioned for the first time in scripture with the arrival of Paul and Barnabas (Acts 13:14), it was an important Roman military and administrative center of the region long before then. At the time of Paul's arrival, Antioch was a city of ethnic diversity, home to Jews, Greeks, local Phrygians, and Romans, speaking a variety of languages. Temples to the primary deities of the region, the goddess Cybele and the god Men, stood next to Jewish synagogues.

We gaped at the temple remains that once dominated the city. Dedicated to the Emperor Augustus, the huge arches surrounding the temple depicted the military victories of the Emperor. Across the street from this temple, the remains of a synagogue have been identified. Was this the site, under the shadow of the Roman temple, where Paul preached the long sermon recorded in Acts 13:16-47? we wondered. This sermon summarized the history of the Jewish people, declared that the ancient promises had been fulfilled in Jesus, and included the radical idea that "everyone who believes is justified." Farther down the hill, some distance away from the imposing temple, was another synagogue, over which a Christian basilica was later built—the traditional site of Paul's famous sermon. Was this the more conservative synagogue? Paul addressed his sermon to both "Jews and God-fearing Gentiles." Perhaps he was preaching to a more open and liberal group of Jews, who may have built their synagogue in a more prominent location next to the dominant temple. In any case, the listeners' positive reaction eventually provoked concern and resistance among the Jewish religious leaders, who may have been concerned that the crowd's enthusiasm listening to Paul would be interpreted as subversive by the Roman authorities. Perhaps the religious leaders feared this would jeopardize their good relations with their pagan neighbors, and their social standing in the community.

We explored the baths, the aqueduct, and finally the ruins of the massive early church. A group of about 100 Christian pilgrims from South Korea were gathered in the apse, singing and praying fervently. *How amazing, this gospel, that Paul preached here!* I thought observing the Korean Christians. *Two thousand years ago, Paul, the Jew from Tarsus, introduced the gospel to pagans in Antioch, who spread it throughout the Empire and shaped Western civilization. Western missionaries brought the story to Korea. These Koreans are now back in Antioch, worshipping where Paul preached.*

I was limping painfully through the ruins of Antioch. While exploring the area of Myra's harbor a few days earlier, I had stepped on a thorn bush and when I tried to pull out the thorn, it broke off under the skin and was beginning to fester painfully. Paul's own "thorn in the flesh," mentioned in his second letter to the church in Corinth (2 Cor. 12:7), alluded to some unnamed ailment that had caused him pain and humiliation. Biblical scholars have posited a variety of guesses as to what this malady might have been—epilepsy, poor eyesight, malaria, or depression. Sermons and articles have explored each one of these possibilities, but what if Paul's thorn in the flesh was just that—a thorn he had stepped on during his treks through the thorn-infested regions of Pamphylia? What if this thorn had broken off, become inflamed, and eventually caused serious damage to a nerve, causing Paul to limp for the rest of his life and inhibiting his journeys by foot? Luke, the doctor, who could have operated to remove a broken thorn in his foot, was not with him at the beginning of his travels.

"That's just another guess," Janet responded when I told her my thorn theory, "but you know, that sounds more reasonable to me than most of the other explanations I've heard." In any case, it convinced us that understanding and appreciating Paul's physical and emotional challenges—the achievements of his immense overland journeys and long sea voyages—were crucial to understanding Paul and his accomplishments.

We read again the story of Paul and Barnabas's hurried departure following the riot: "But the Jews incited the God-fearing women of high standing and the leading men of the city. They stirred up persecution against Paul and Barnabas, and expelled them from their region. So they shook the dust from their feet in protest against them and went to Iconium" (Acts 13:50-51). We shook the dust of the Antioch ruins off our own sandals as we returned to our rental car to drive the 100 miles to Iconium (modern Konya) before dark. Passing through some of the most beautiful farming country Janet and I had ever seen, the "bread basket of Turkey," according to our guidebook, we thought of Paul and Barnabas walking the same stretch together, reflecting on their eventful ministry in Antioch. Did Barnabas urge Paul to avoid deliberately provoking the authorities in Iconium, as he seemed to have done in Antioch? Did the compassionate

Barnabas try to persuade Paul that a kinder, gentler approach might be more effective in his ministry? Perhaps. But Paul's provocative approach was getting outstanding results—dangerous to be sure, but guaranteeing a keenly interested audience.

Modern Konya, biblical Iconium, is a large, sprawling city that lies in the dusty summer plains, surrounded by hills. Its origins are ancient. The city was over 2,000 years old when Paul and Barnabas arrived. On the main overland trade route between Asia and Europe, it was overrun and occupied by every major power that dominated the area throughout history. By the first century, Antioch was far more important as an administrative center than Iconium. Now it is known as a center of conservative Islam and the place where the founder of the Whirling Dervishes was born and established his movement.

We arrived at dusk and faced the daunting task of finding a hotel room with nothing more to help us than the tiny map in the tourist guidebook. We immediately lost our way and stopped for Janet to ask directions, which might have worked had she spoken fluent Turkish. As the day grew dark we found ourselves in front of a four-star hotel. We were not yet desperate enough to pay the rate of $90 for one night's lodging, triple what we had budgeted. The owners were completely unoffended when we declined to check in, and even offered to send their bellhop with us in our car to direct us to a budget hotel. The hotel to which he directed us charged only $29 for one night. We parked in a no-parking area on the busy street, unloaded our bags, and checked in.

"I'll park your car for you," the bellhop from the first hotel offered. We gave him the key and wondered, as he drove off into the night, how we would find the car the next morning. I need not have worried. The next morning a hotel employee walked with me several blocks to a parking garage, where our car had been parked overnight.

After checking out of the hotel, Janet and I visited the tourist information office to inquire whether there were any remains connected to Paul's visit.

"I don't know anything about Paul," the woman in the information center said, "but wait here. I'll find someone who does." She left and returned a few minutes later with a young man from a nearby carpet shop who spoke very good English and seemed to know a lot about Paul.

"Come over to my shop," he invited.

We walked several blocks as Muammer explained that there was virtually nothing in Konya (Iconium) related to Paul's visit. "We are Muslims," he explained.

Muammer had an impressive English library of books on carpets. "Please look through these," he offered. "I think I have something on Paul in my library."

"Paul was a tent-maker, not a carpet-weaver," I told Muammer.

"Ah, but a friend of mine gave me a book on Paul once. It is here somewhere."

At last I found a book with the title *Issues and Insights into Church Planting in the Muslim World,* and browsing through it I discovered that it was, indeed, based on the work of Paul. "Have you ever read this?" I asked.

"No, what is it about?"

"It's a book for Christians seeking to evangelize Muslims," I explained.

Muammer seemed pleased. "Ron, the author, is my friend," he explained.

"Why don't you go out to Sille," Muammer suggested. "There is a church there." He found a tattered guidebook printed in 1960 and pointed to a vague reference to a "rock monastery of St. Paul, located between Konya and Sille." I thanked Muammer. We would explore Sille.

We worked our way out of Konya and drove up into rugged countryside toward Sille, where we were pleased to find several extremely early, now unused, church buildings. We found the church which, according to our guidebook, was founded by Helena, the mother of the Emperor Constantine. According to tradition, with God's help, Helena had located and had churches built over such sites as Jesus' birthplace (the Church of the Nativity in Bethlehem) and the place of the crucifixion (the Church of the Holy Sepulcher in Jerusalem). Why did Helena identify this site for a chapel? we wondered.

We reread the story in Acts (14:1-6) and searched for clues in the isolated, remote little village of Sille. The description of Paul's activity in Iconium reveals that his preaching, predictably, had divided the population and that the concerned citizens of Antioch had followed Paul all the way to Iconium to warn the people there against him. "There was a plot afoot among the Gentiles and Jews, together with their leaders, to mistreat them and stone them. But they found out about it and fled to the Lycaonian cities of Lystra and Derbe and to the surrounding country" (Acts 14:6).

We speculated that early Christians had established a community here outside of Iconium in order to avoid the harassment and intimidation they may have continued to experience after Paul and Barnabas left. This community would have claimed direct connections to Paul. Helena's identification of the significance of Sille in the fourth century may well have been rooted in the community's credible claims to have originated with Paul's ministry in nearby Iconium.

Indeed, another feature in Sille points to its possible history as an outgrowth of Paul's preaching in Iconium: the rock caves in the cliffs surrounding Sille that were reputedly used by early Christian monks. I climbed up to one of the caves, entered through a small opening, and was surprised to find passageways leading to rooms created by enlarging the natural caves. Several, I discovered, had Christian symbols carved into the walls. These cave rooms, with their dimensions and features of basilicas, had obviously been used for early Christian worship. We were getting excited as we set off for our next quest—finding ancient Lystra.

We expected that finding Lystra would pose a challenge. Our guidebooks and scholarly references did not completely agree on the actual location of Lystra. One book identified Lystra with Gilistra, about 10 miles off the main road, up in a remote gorge.

Another identified an unoccupied tell just off the same road as the site of the city. We drove south of Konya on the main route, then turned west on a route marked by two signs that read: "Lystra 2 km" and "Gilistra 16 km."

We drove slowly, measuring the distance on the odometer carefully, comparing the landscape to a photograph of a tell identified in William M. Ramsay's *St. Paul: The Traveler and Roman Citizen.* Away from the traffic of the main road, and far from any towns, the countryside had a remote, peasant feel. We passed a field with an old man plowing with a horse and a mule, then a little later, as we drove by again looking for Lystra, the animals were resting in the middle of the half-plowed field, while the Turkish farmer knelt beside them on a small prayer rug facing Mecca, praying.

We encountered two more Turkish farmers beside the road. I tried to show them the picture of Lystra in Ramsay's book, but they assumed we were looking for something more picturesque than a barren hill in a field, and immediately pointed in the direction of Gilistra, talking excitedly in Turkish of the wonderful things, I presumed, that we would find there. Janet and I concluded that Gilistra was probably not the site of ancient Lystra, but we decided to drive the extra 10 miles to see the village. We were grateful for the misleading advice of the Turkish farmers, because Janet and I had never visited a place like Gilistra in our entire lives. Entering the village of Gilistra, perched atop a rugged mountain, was like taking a step at least one century backward into a time of stone houses and dirt streets. Protective geese, suspicious dogs, and oblivious chickens roamed the streets. Besides seeing several small children peeping out from behind doors, Janet and I seemed to be the only humans stirring. From the edge of the village we could see caves in the cliffs across the valley where monks had once lived. Could this be Lystra?

We drove back toward the road, convinced that Gilistra was not the site of ancient Lystra. Lystra, as described in Acts and according to the scholars, would have been on the main Roman route, the Via Sebaste, that ran southeastward through Antioch,

Iconium, and Lystra. The site of today's Gilistra is well off of that ancient route.

We came to a hill that looked somewhat like Ramsay's photo. I climbed an adjacent hill through wheat stubble and tried to match the photo with the view from various angles, but it didn't quite fit. I decided to make one more climb to a nearby hill that looked like a tell. The location, near water and a main route, seemed to make it a good location for a city. I climbed to the top. A fire had recently burned the dried grass growing on the tell, exposing the surface, and I recognized immediately that this was where Ramsay had located Lystra. The top was covered with pottery and remains of buildings with handsome carved stones. I sat on the ashes of Lystra and reread the story of Paul and Barnabas in this place (Acts 14:8-20).

Lystra, in the district of Lycaonia, seemed to have been a rather unsophisticated town. While a Jewish community resided in Lystra, they probably had no synagogue, for Paul and Barnabas preached to the crowds in the public areas of Lystra. Here Paul healed the crippled man, and the crowd, convinced that the gods Zeus and Hermes had come to them in human form, tried to worship Paul and Barnabas by offering sacrifices to them. It was here that Paul and Barnabas, when finally aware of what was going on, tore their clothes and rushed into the crowd, trying to convince them that they were not gods at all.

But that particular problem, which most likely Paul had never experienced before or ever would again, was offset by a more familiar one. "Then some Jews came from Antioch and Iconium and won the crowd over. They stoned Paul and dragged him outside the city, thinking he was dead. But after the disciples had gathered around him, he got up and went back into the city. The next day he and Barnabas left for Derbe" (Acts 14:20). *Paul seemed to stir up and divide people wherever he went,* I thought, gazing across the fields from the desolate site of Lystra. *But only in Lystra did he experience being both worshipped and stoned by the same crowds in the same place. What Jerusalem was for Jesus, Lystra was for Paul.*

We left lonely, silent Lystra and drove onward in the direction of Derbe. At Karaman, a pleasant city of 107,000 inhabitants, we found an excellent budget hotel, a wonderful restaurant with unbelievably low prices, and a telephone booth from which we called our son, Jon, in the United States for a long, low-cost conversation. We liked Karaman a lot, but the remains of Derbe were our real destination.

A mere 15 words in Acts describes the experience of Paul and Barnabas in Derbe. "They preached the good news in that city and won a large number of disciples" (Acts 14:21). Perhaps Paul's battered body and swollen, bruised face from the stoning in Lystra decreased his ability to provoke. Perhaps he tried a new approach in Derbe. In any case, there is no record of miracles, or of being worshipped. There were no riots, expulsions, or stonings, only preaching and large numbers of believers. This was the farthest point that the group had traveled from the port of Attalia, where they had arrived from the island of Cyprus, and even the tagalong, anti-Paul detractors had returned home. From Derbe, Paul and Barnabas would do the same, retracing their steps through Lystra, Iconium, and Antioch on their way to the coast.

We set out from Karaman the next morning, searching for Derbe. We drove through rolling, recently threshed wheat fields, the stationary threshing machines next to piles of straw at the edges of the fields. Suddenly we spied a small sign pointing to Derbe, but without any indication of distance to the site. We turned off the main road and drove toward a series of low hills in the fields, winding through little farming villages with dirt side streets skirting around piles of manure, scratching chickens, and antique farming implements.

In one village we discovered another sign pointing in the direction of Derbe, which we followed for several miles, expecting another sign indicating the way to Derbe. But there were none. Our guidebooks were exceptionally vague as well. On the road ahead we saw a man who obviously was looking for a ride.

"Why don't we pick him up? Maybe he can tell us where Derbe is," Janet suggested. Her confidence in her ability to ask and receive accurate directions to obscure sites across language barriers from random people walking along roads was limitless. The large man hoisted himself into the car and immediately launched into a loud monologue in Turkish. Occasionally we recognized words: "Manchester," "Leeds United."

"Derbe," Janet said.

Another loud Turkish monologue. "Maybe he is explaining that Derbe has no English football team," I speculated to Janet, confident that the man could not understand our running interpretive conversation. By this time we had traveled an alarming distance through the wheat fields, away from the promising-looking tells. Our "guide" was gesturing as he shouted, working up a sweat, the pungent odor filling the car. We began to listen carefully. He kept pointing and repeating a word that sounded like "houk," as well as "Roman" and "Byzanti."

"He's trying to tell us where the ruins of Derbe are," Janet was sure.

I was equally sure of something else. "He's trying to get us to go as far as possible in the direction of his house before we catch on that Derbe is in the opposite direction."

Miles later, Janet began to agree with me. We stopped, thanked the man, and left him, still talking and gesturing beside the road. We turned the car around and somewhat dejectedly drove the 10 miles back to the village where we had last seen a sign to Derbe. At the edge of the village, a vanload of *polis* had set up what appeared to be a checkpoint, which seemed remarkable as we hadn't seen any other vehicles that morning. The *polis* regarded us with silent suspicion as we drove up.

"Derbe," I said through the open windows.

They instantly sprang into action, yelling and gesturing to each other. *I hope "Derbe" is not some anti-polis curse in Turkish,* I thought. Several *polis* trotted over and pointed to a nearby hill, then a dirt track that ran through the village in its direction. At that very moment, a farmer drove his truck onto the dirt track and they ordered him to stop, then commanded us to follow the farmer.

With dust flying and chickens running for their lives, we zigzagged through the village, out through the wheat fields, and up to a tell. The farmer stopped and in limited but clear English explained that this is, indeed, the site of Derbe. He was friendly and well informed and invited us to his house for a meal, but we declined, suspecting that he had work to do. He waved goodbye, and we climbed the hill. We saw pottery and building stones everywhere. We had found Derbe!

We gazed around at the rolling wheat fields and the Taurus Mountains in the distance, and thought of Paul walking from Antioch, through Iconium, Lystra, and all the way here to Derbe, then walking the entire distance back again through the cities where he had been attacked and evicted. He would walk all the way back to Antalya, from where we had driven several hundred miles during the past few days. There is really nothing much else to see, but I savored the moment of admiration for the commitment and courage of Paul.

Driving back along the dirt track through the fields, we saw a number of curbing and paving stones along the edges, evidence of a Roman road. We realized that this tractor track through the wheat fields was once the Via Sebaste, a primary route of the vast Roman Empire. We drove back through the village, then drove on toward the Taurus Mountains in the distance and toward Tarsus, Paul's home town.

The plain is vast. The modern road follows the ancient route through the rugged mountains, through the famous Cilician Gates, the gorge through which armies and traders traveled across the historic barrier between the Cilician plains and Asia Minor. Paul also traveled this route eastward from his home city of Tarsus at least twice, once in 50 A.D., on his second journey, and again in 53 A.D., on his third.

The traffic climbed the western side of the Taurus Mountains, then suddenly we reached the summit through the gorges and began descending slowly at the speed of trucks in low gear, snapping pictures out of the car window at the awesome, rugged scenery. "I never imagined this kind of landscape in Turkey," Janet commented.

We continued our descent, the magnificent scenery gradually giving way to the Cilician plains. We approached Tarsus, the city of Paul's birth and early boyhood (Acts 21:39, 22:3), and stopped at the gigantic postmodern bus station on the outskirts of Tarsus, which Janet thought might contain a tourist information office. Janet disappeared inside while I waited for what seemed like an eternity in the car. I was beginning to wonder just what kind of information Janet was getting when she appeared with several gesturing men in tow. One was an official tourist guide of some kind, his status indicated by an elaborate badge.

"There is no tourist office here," Janet explained, "but this man will ride with us into town and take us to one."

What was he doing in the bus station then? I had never heard of such personalized service for tourists and wondered how he would get back to his office. Would we have to bring him back? Would he charge a fee?

"No, no, nothing," the man said, reading my thoughts.

We drove into Tarsus, winding through terrible, rutted, dusty streets through depressed and impoverished-looking neighborhoods. Paul had described Tarsus, correctly, as "no ordinary city," meaning it was above average in the first century. In the 21st century, Tarsus still appeared to be "no ordinary city," but this time because it was well below the average city in this part of Turkey.

We had reached the center of Tarsus. "There," the man said, pointing to a parking spot in a dusty lot. We got out and looked around. There was a small fenced-off area with a tiny kiosk in one corner and a group of college students milling around inside.

The tourist information man had accompanied us to the one site in Tarsus dedicated to Paul, St. Paul's well, which has dubious connections to Paul. We said goodbye and he disappeared on foot. Janet and I entered the area, but found little information explaining its significance. There were several guides, but they were busy arguing with the student group. It was 4:00, time to find a hotel.

"Let's find the tourist information office," Janet suggested. "There is one marked here in our guidebook."

We found the "tourist information" booth at the corner of the excavation site in the center of Tarsus, but it was vacant and locked. No one seemed to know if or when anyone would ever be there. From the looks of things, it may have been a month or two since it was last used.

"Wait," a helpful man insisted, and disappeared, then triumphantly reappeared several minutes later leading a reluctant man with a key which, it turned out, opened not the information booth but the archeological site behind it. *Good,* I thought, *at least we can go in there.*

"No," he said as he unlocked the site. "Forbidden." Then why did he open it? we wondered. We stood around looking at each other for a few minutes. "Okay, you can go in now," he offered. We thanked him and wandered around over the Roman pavement, a nice specimen of Roman road in the city, taking photos and thinking of the boy Paul running down the street (see Photo 42).

With no official information available, finding a hotel was the next hurdle. We asked, and helpful people pointed. It was obvious that independent tourists in Tarsus were as rare as Paul being speechless. One man sent his young son to show us a hotel, Hotel Mersin. We followed him on foot through dusty alleys and eventually emerged onto a large street. "This way," he pointed.

Janet and I walked for blocks before realizing the hotel was not in the near vicinity. We retraced our steps, found our parked car, and drove in the direction the boy pointed. Sure enough,

Hotel Mersin, huge and ugly, dominated the otherwise beautiful park where the Cydnus River breaks over the falls above Tarsus. I went into the vast, empty lobby and inquired about a room. "Yes, certainly," the elegantly dressed receptionist responded. "We can give you one for $95 dollars." *I'll take all 350 vacant rooms you have here at that price,* I thought sarcastically. "I'm sorry," I managed, "that is a little over our budget." We were back to square one with the hotels.

Back in the center of Tarsus, we continued to ask unsuspecting pedestrians for directions to cheap hotels. At last an off-duty policeman led us several blocks to Hotel Saray, a "budget hotel" which had a room for $73 *less* than the Mersin. We checked in with gratitude and spent the rest of the daylight hours on the streets of Tarsus, looking for anything related to the city's most famous citizen, Paul. In spite of wandering for miles, we found nothing except "Cleopatra's Gate," sometimes referred to as St. Paul's Gate, although it supposedly had nothing to do with either. Eventually, exhausted, we gave up and ate an excellent *donar* in a restaurant. The total bill came to $5.

We returned to the hotel, discussing the unusual feeling Tarsus had about it, an indescribable aura of sadness and depression. Was it just the dust and general dilapidation? Were we simply tired? While the people of Tarsus were friendly and helpful, we sensed a lack of vibrancy. I couldn't name it, but it seemed that Paul had been genuinely forgotten by Tarsus and that this collective amnesia made the lonely Paul site we had visited seem as artificial and empty as Treasure Island in Disneyland.

The next morning we enjoyed a fine breakfast of cheese, olives, bread, jam, and tea that was included with the room in Hotel Saray. The young boy who served us breakfast had tried, in expectation of a tip, to carry our bags to the room the night before. I had carried them myself, much to his disappointment, and felt guilty about it. So I tucked a million-lira tip (about 65 cents) under a dish on the table, and we left to collect our luggage and check out. Moments later there was a knock on the door. The boy had seen the bill on the table and was bringing it back, thinking we accidentally left it there. "No," we said, "it's for you." He was delighted, my guilt disappeared, and we left the hotel in high spirits.

We thought about Paul growing up in Tarsus as we explored the environs of the city the next morning before leaving to Antioch on the Orontes. Tarsus in Paul's day was on the main trade routes between East and West, North and South. Paul could have observed seagoing ships coming and going into the harbor of Tarsus on the Cydnus River from all over the Empire. He could have seen the famous Cilician Gates from the town, up in the mountains surrounding Tarsus, and would likely have observed the travelers, traders, and armies, and listened to tales of the great world beyond those gates. Without a doubt, Paul's curiosity for the world was fostered already as a child in Tarsus.

We left Tarsus and drove on the modern toll road toward Antakya to visit the ancient site of Syrian Antioch, or Antioch on the Orontes. This launching point of Paul's mission journeys, tucked down into the southeast corner of Turkey, close to Syria, would be the final site we would visit on this road trip. What distances Paul walked! Sailing the routes of Paul, we often marveled at his stamina. But driving the vast land stretches made us aware of the amazing tenacity and physical endurance of the apostle. *Some 50-year-old should hike the routes of Paul some day,* I thought. I was glad we were doing the sailing part.

We arrived in Syrian Antioch in the afternoon, with time to visit St. Peter's Church, the cave sanctuary which tradition claims as the meeting place of the early community of Jesus, followers of "The Way," who came to be known as Christians (see Photo 43). If this was, indeed, the site, Paul would have been part of that congregation that met there, and Peter would have preached in that very room when he visited Antioch. We paid the $3.50 entrance fee, and spent a long time contemplating the power of the movement that began in Nazareth and was carried by Paul and others from Antioch throughout the Roman Empire.

We found our way to the bustling center of Antakya, checked into a hotel, then explored on foot the old Jewish quarter of Antioch, where Paul would likely have stayed when he lived in Antioch. We visited the fine archeological museum, with its excellent mosaics that demonstrated the wealth and beauty of Antioch, and saw a number of images of local Greek gods and deities, including an impressive river god from about 100 B.C.

It was the harbor of Seleucia, on the coast about 18 miles west of Antakya, that I was especially eager to see. This was the harbor from which Paul, Barnabas, and John Mark began what could be called the very first overseas Christian mission trip in history. We drove west out of Antioch, getting lost only for short periods of time, out toward the Mediterranean coast, then turned north and drove several miles until we found the ancient harbor, with its old rock jetty still visible in the water. I climbed up the cliff to the ancient temple site that overlooked the harbor from which Paul left to sail to Cyprus with Barnabas. Looking out over the Mediterranean, I thought of the many harbors in the Empire, of which Paul and I had sailed into and out of. Several times on this trip, the significance and inspiration of Paul's life were overwhelming. This was one of them. I sat until the sun descended into the sea. Then Janet and I drove back to Antakya in silence.

At 8:00 the next morning, we began the 500-mile drive back to Antalya, following the rugged coastline up over the headlands and down to the beaches. This route existed in Roman times, and the modern road wound up and down with hairpin curves through the coastal towns, some of which have become sprawling resorts. It was a fantastic view, with pine trees and silence above, and the beautiful craggy coastline and excellent beaches below.

On that ancient and scenic coastal route between Tarsus and Antalya, I got my first speeding ticket ever. I had many excuses—

there are no posted speed limits along the roads, we were on a two-lane road, and I was being passed by cars with Turkish license plates. But the radar picture showed that my speed was 102 kilometers-per-hour (61 miles-per-hour) in a 90 kilometer-per-hour zone (about 55 miles-per-hour). Thirty minutes of protesting, pleading, and stalling did no good. They drew a sign with "90" and another one with "102," which is what I allegedly was going when the radar picked me up. Six miles-per-hour above the limit—surely that would be tolerated. But no. Technically they had me and they clearly were going to be technical.

"Okay," I finally asked. "How much?"

"Fifty dollars," one of the officers wrote on a piece of paper.

"No way," I said. "Way too much money."

They called the radar man and he drove up impatiently. I climbed into the radar car and looked at the digital image of Janet and me in our rental car with the speed of 102 in the digital read-out on the corner of the screen. It was us all right.

"Okay," I said. "I agree I was going slightly over the speed limit, but there is no sign posted as to what the speed limit is."

The radar man gave me a paper in English, explaining the speed limits in Turkey. "Ninety kilometers-per-hour on regular roads," it read. Another handwritten note read that 99 kilometers-per-hour would be the actual limit. I pointed to that note.

"You 102," the officer said.

"Very small," I said. Back and forth we went.

Then they saw we were in a rental car. They called the rental company and handed the cell phone to me when the owner of the rental agency answered. "You must pay," he told me with urgency.

I was still arguing when suddenly one of the policemen noticed that the car was registered as a *Kombi* (minivan), which the tiny Fiat Panda we were driving obviously was not. They pounced on this, as their literature said that the speeding ticket for a *Kombi* was about $100, double the amount for a car. Now we were really stuck. They called the owner of the car-rental agency again, then triumphantly handed the phone to us again after talking to him. This was getting ridiculous.

"Please, please pay the fine," he pleaded. "They will take my car if you don't. We'll pay you for the extra fine when you get back."

We had no choice. I went back to the car and rummaged through our luggage until I found enough cash to pay the fine. As soon as I paid, the policemen became jovial, having achieved, I assumed, their cash goal for the day.

"What do you do?" one policeman asked me.

"Professor," I said.

"Professor, ha, ha, professor," they laughed uproariously, slapping their knees, slumping on their patrol cars, gasping for air. They continued to banter in surprisingly good English, and by this time I was too disgusted to do anything but banter back. We left, laughing and waving at the highway robbery we had just facilitated. I couldn't help thinking, driving down the road toward Antalya as the laughter turned to sullen silence in the car, that the "perils of robbers" Paul mentioned in 2 Corinthians 11:26 still exists in Pamphylia.

We came back from a profitable trip a little subdued and very grateful for learning about Paul, his world, and ourselves. We reflected on the experiences of the journey since we began in June: We had a comfortable sailboat with a diesel motor for the times no wind blew. Paul sailed with freighters without passenger services at the mercy of the weather. We drove scooters and cars over mostly paved roads. Paul likely walked the thousands of miles through heat and over rugged mountains. We received a sabbatical salary and could withdraw cash from an ATM whenever it got low. Paul supported himself during his travels by working and relying on the generosity of others. We were doing research and, wherever we went, friendly people helped us in many ways. Paul preached the good news to everyone, including some who violently opposed him. We had been singled out unfairly to pay a speeding ticket, but Paul's false accusers almost killed him. We were broke and worn out, but everything we were doing was easy compared to what Paul did.

One thing had become clear to me. Paul was, among other things, one of history's great travelers.

CHAPTER 11

Cyprus and Israel

The prospect of sailing across open water in the dark of night was weighing on our minds the next morning after we arrived in Antalya. We had a day to prepare for what was terrifying for most people in the first century. We had talked to many sailors about night sailing.

"You either love it or hate it," one veteran told us. "Just make sure you have everything ready to go. You don't want any emergencies in the middle of the night."

We spent Saturday heeding his advice, deflating and stowing the dinghy, moving equipment, fuel, and water containers to balance the boat, checking the rigging, then finally driving the rental car to Migros—a huge, modern mall complex—for stocking up on groceries and other supplies.

"First-century pagan sailors would go to the temple to sacrifice to the gods for protection," I observed to Janet. "Going to the mall before the voyage is sort of the same thing."

"That's dumb," Janet responded. "We're just buying groceries."

But we weren't. We stayed a long time in the mall. Its sparkling marble floors would have rivaled Aphrodite's temples. Its toilets smelled like the pine forests of the Taurus Mountains, only better. The food court did not only have *donar kebab* stands but a Burger King, Arby's, and McDonalds, and their crisply-uniformed staffs of eager young Turks were smiling and eager to please. The throw-away plastic utensils and paper wrappings were whisked immediately by vigilant, uniformed men into garbage containers shaped like some variety of a gigantic Asian rodent. There was a cinema complex showing the latest

Hollywood movies, and teenagers with gelled hair and bare midriffs loitered around the entrance. This was the first mall we visited in three months and we tarried in its safe, cool, predictable, and friendly atmosphere, soaking up the familiar. We returned later that evening to eat our first Burger King hamburger in eight months, followed by a sundae at McDonalds. Now, like the pagan sailors sacrificing to their gods in the harbor temples, we were prepared inwardly for the dark and lonely sea.

We lingered in the glittering Migros Mall in Antalya, and I thought about the dingy, dirty streets of Tarsus, the veiled women in Konya, and the temple ruins in Antakya. The crowd in the mall was young, Western, and optimistic, surrounded by promises of abundance, health, beauty, and happiness. I thought of the temples, *agoras*, and theaters of the pagan world 2,000 years earlier and realized that the mall was a new version of the old. It doesn't matter if people in the Mediterranean hate American policy in the Middle East; the owners of malls don't care what political agenda their shoppers embrace, or even their religious identity, as long as they frequent the mall. The promises of globalization are irresistible. For an hour after eating our sundae at McDonalds, we watched laughing Muslim families enjoying Western globalization.

Upon awaking the next morning, I instantly thought, *Today we leave Turkey and sail for the first time all night!* I lay for a moment, listening for wind, looking at the sky through the hatch above the forward bunks. It was completely clear and calm. We motored to the fuel pumps across the harbor and filled the tank and two jerry cans with diesel. If necessary we could motor for 27 hours, the whole distance of 155 sea miles to Paphos, Cyprus. At 9:00 a.m., we left the marina, set the auto helm to the coordinates of the harbor entrance in Paphos, then sat back and watched the rugged coastline of Turkey slowly recede.

"When Paul left here for Antioch, he would have looked back and seen exactly what we are looking at," I commented to Janet. "Except none of the buildings we see were there," Janet reminded me.

"I wonder how he was feeling, returning to Antioch from his first voyage over land and sea, surrounded by the power and glory of Rome and pagan worship for over two years. Do you think he might have recognized that he had changed and maybe was feeling some trepidation about returning?"

We became silent as we looked at the open sea ahead and the gradually fading shoreline of Turkey. It is a different feeling altogether to leave a place in the morning, knowing that when the sun sets and darkness covers the face of the deep, you will be there, surrounded by a vast expanse of open water and darkness rather than a safe anchorage or protected harbor. I thought about the faith and hope involved in setting out across the unpredictable waves with no turning back, and how this moment is symbolic of such moments when we embark on something new. Facing the imminent darkness, I thought of how much the voyage had become a 15-month version of an entire lifetime.

Turkey disappeared and we saw no land from any direction. It was just Janet and me on *SailingActs*, a very small dot in a vast sea. The sun became a flat disc, a silver dollar slowly sinking into the Mediterranean piggy bank, and the day faded to twilight in various shades of blue and silver. With the wind light and the sea smooth, Janet was able to prepare a delicious meal of salad and potatoes. We dined in the cockpit as the blue day faded to purple.

I would take the first shift from 7:00 p.m. until 10:00 p.m., while Janet would try to sleep in the main cabin. She would then stand watch from 10:00 p.m. until 1:00 a.m., while I slept. I would take over again from 1:00 a.m. until 4:00 a.m., and finally Janet would take her turn again until 7:00 a.m. She would have the privilege of watching the sun rise. With this arrangement, we reasoned, each of us would have one complete shift in the dark, and one shift in partial darkness. But Janet couldn't sleep, so she stayed outside in the cockpit through my watch.

Night crept in from the east, eventually occupying the last resistance of light in the west. The moon, just a sliver, sank into the black waters at about 8:00 that evening, and it was dark. The stars in the black sky were gorgeous. We watched in wonder as the stars rotated around the North Star, and others rose and set. The glow of the instrument lights, the lights of the stars, and the flicker of phosphorescence in the water replaced the light of the sun and moon, and somehow we felt peaceful and secure as *SailingActs* rose and fell on the unseen waves.

I didn't feel sleepy when my shift ended, so I stayed on in the cockpit until 11:00 with Janet, then finally slipped into the bunk in the main cabin and fell asleep for 90 minutes. I awoke in the darkness and saw Janet through the open gangway, alert and watching. We greeted each other as if we had been separated for several days. We were making good time, and were precisely on course.

With the engine throbbing and the auto helm steering, the main responsibility on watch is to keep an eye out for the many freighters that ply the waters of the Mediterranean. These swift, steel, deadly monsters give the night sailor about 15 minutes from the time their lights first appear on the black horizon, to the time they bear down directly in front, behind, or on top of you. Janet had been tracking each light as it appeared through the binoculars, using the built-in lighted compass to take a bearing on the approaching ships. By charting the sightings over a period of several minutes, it was possible to determine whether the ship would pass in front of or behind *SailingActs*, or whether the paths of the two vessels would intersect. In this case, the person on watch must change course or speed accordingly, for it could never be assumed that there were alert crew on the bridge of the freighters.

Janet went to bed and fell sleep instantly. I continued to follow the progress of the lights on distant ships. At 2:00 a.m., a well-lit freighter appeared on our port side and I watched it come slowly in our direction for about 10 minutes. Soon another freighter appeared to be approaching directly at us from starboard, and I followed it for about five minutes, momentarily forgetting the freighter on the port side. This was a huge mistake. When I looked back to port at the ship I had been following earlier, I was stunned to see the freighter off the left of the boat, bearing right down on us, so close that no navigation lights were visible to indicate, at a glance, whether one is on a collision course or not.

Growing up in the Cascade Mountains of Oregon, I had sometimes seen the proverbial paralysis of a "deer in the headlights," which my alert father always managed to avoid hitting with our Ford. But this time I was the deer, and the man on watch in the freighter, now only 20 seconds away, might not be alert, or worse yet, there might not be anyone on the bridge at all. The tiny clunk *SailingActs* would make as the bow of the freighter sliced her in two or more chunks of mangled fiberglass would barely be noticed by the crew. For three seconds I froze. Should I slow down? Speed up?

In the fourth second, adrenaline finally overcame paralysis and I grabbed the searchlight we kept in the cockpit at night and pointed it directly at the bow of the ship. I can shut my eyes as I write this months later and still see two things vividly from that ship just 100 yards away: the gigantic white letters "MSC" on its bow, and the huge wake from the bow plowing through the water. I looked closely at the wake and was flooded with relief as I realized that the wake was slightly larger on one side of the bow than the other. The ship was not going to hit us! I kept the spotlight aimed toward the ship, and someone from the bridge flashed a light back. Then several others shined lights from the deck, and I realized their radar must have picked up *SailingActs'* radar reflector, and that the freighter had altered its course just enough to pass behind us. I waved the spotlight gratefully at the crew of the good ship MSC as she thundered past in the darkness. I would have appreciated a little more space between the two ships passing in the night, but a miss, even a near miss, was enough to make me alert and cheerful for the next two hours of my watch.

The time passed quickly. At 4:00 I did not feel like waking Janet, so I kept going until about 4:30. Then I was suddenly sleepy and woke Janet, who became wide-eyed with alarm as I told the story of the near collision with the MSC. I crawled into her warm bunk in the main cabin and immediately fell into a peaceful sleep.

An hour later, I was wide awake again. It was 5:30 and getting light. Janet had been enjoying the gradual dawning since shortly after 5:00. There was something so rewarding and blissful about dawn at sea after a star-filled night. Sailors on small boats know the vastness of the universe and their own tiny selves in a way that few others can. From the cruising sailors we have met on this voyage, it seems that this awareness pushes them to become either humble about their own limitations and quietly confident about their abilities, or crusty, independent, and fearless mavericks. I see a little of both traits in Paul and his writings. I think the experience of the sea, including the rare night passages, had something to do with Paul's personality.

We had met Reinhardt, a crusty, independent, fearless maverick and veteran cruiser from Austria in Antalya just before we left Turkey. He had arrived with his cat in an ancient, wooden, leaky, barge-like sailing vessel. Although signs of sailing genius were evident in his various contraptions—such as a rocking chair on deck and what looked like wheat growing on the cabin roof— Reinhardt's boat was mostly a barely-floating demonstration of human eccentricity. Reinhardt, I discovered within 30 seconds, had an instant opinion on everything. We chatted in German until he discovered I was American, then switched to English, which Reinhardt mangled commandingly.

"What you do? Where you go?"

"We're following the routes of Paul, visiting every place mentioned in Acts."

"Ha, stupid. Everyone does!"

"Really?" I leapt clumsily for Reinhardt's taunting bait. "In my 50 years of life I have never met or heard of anyone sailing all the destinations of Paul, doing research."

"Researscht?" Reinhardt spat. "What kind researscht?"

"Comparing the story in the New Testament to the physical evidence, the traditions, and the geography described in Acts."

"Ha, I read Bible, too," Reinhardt countered. "I do researscht, too!"

Having obviously concluded that he had won that round handily, Reinhardt demanded, "Where you go next?"

"Paphos."

"Paphos! Don't go Paphos! They will mess you up! They are the worst people in the world!" he said, peppering his indictment with expletives.

"If you read the Bible, you should know that Paul went to Paphos," I said testily.

The conversation with Reinhardt, especially the part about the officials at Paphos, weighed on our minds as we approached the Paphos harbor on the western end of Cyprus near noon. We knew the harbor would be crowded and the last thing we wanted at the end of this voyage across open waters was to face hostile officials. As we entered carefully between the modern jetty and the rocky ruins of the ancient harbor, we were dismayed to find not only a boat tied in every available berth, but the harbor crowded with boats at anchor at well. We circled slowly, calling out to boat owners, who all told us our only hope was to drop an anchor in the middle of the crowded harbor.

With fatigue overcoming caution, we worked our way in, uncomfortably close to a number of other yachts, and dropped anchor. I unpacked and inflated the dingy, then rowed ashore with our passports and ship's papers, found the harbor police, the harbor master, customs office, the police again, and finally the health official. All were helpful, even friendly. Only two hours to almost clear customs—a record! *Ha, Reinhardt! The officials in*

SailingActs

Paphos are friendly. You must not have done your "researscht" in Paphos!

Aside from being crowded, Paphos harbor was a delightful place. The ruins of old Paphos of Acts loomed just above the ancient harbor next to where we anchored. The modern town of Paphos, with all of the amenities, began within walking distance. All of the events of Acts 13:6-12 had occurred within several hundred yards from where *SailingActs* was anchored. We would visit the site in the morning. For the rest of the afternoon, we explored the modern town of Paphos, finding an ATM to get Cypriot currency and an Internet café to catch up on correspondence. We tumbled into our bunks early that night and woke the next morning, refreshed and ready to explore the ruins of Paphos.

When Paul, Barnabas, and John Mark arrived in the strategically important and wealthy city of Paphos in approximately 47 A.D., they had walked 90 miles through Cyprus from Salamis on the eastern end of one of the Mediterranean's most beautiful and important islands. The island of Cyprus is about 140 miles long and 60 miles wide, and was famous for its rich deposits of copper and thriving ship-building industry. Its strategic location had made it a target of conquest by each and every empire seeking domination of the eastern end of the Mediterranean, and by 22 B.C., Rome had made it a province. Barnabas, a native of Cyprus, had undoubtedly acted as the world's first Christian tour guide, recounting Cyprus history and pointing out the pagan wonders of the Hellenized island to Paul and John Mark as they moved between one Jewish community to another on their way to Paphos from Salamis.

It was in Paphos where Paul began to hit his stride. Up until Paphos, Luke, the writer of Acts, refers to the mission team as "Barnabas and Saul." Beginning in Paphos, it is "Paul and

Barnabas" for the rest of the journey. What had happened in Paphos?

Up until this point in Cyprus, the two had preached in Jewish synagogues exclusively. While Greeks attracted to Judaism may have been present in the synagogues where Paul had preached, it was in Paphos that Paul first preached to a non-Jewish audience. And what an audience—Sergius Paulus, the proconsul, or Roman governor of Cyprus, in his palace, accompanied by his attendants! One of the attendants was Bar-Jesus, a Jewish magician who seemed to be worried that the interest of his employer in the gospel Paul was preaching might cause him to lose influence with Sergius Paulus, or perhaps even his job. In any case, Paul introduced himself to the Roman proconsul by his Greek name and faced down Bar-Jesus, denouncing him as a fraud and condemning him to blindness. Bar-Jesus most likely lost both his influence and his job, Sergius Paulus believed in Jesus, and Paul's ministry among the non-Jews of the Roman Empire was launched.

Janet and I explored the ruins of Paphos under a blazing sun (see Photo 44). The roofs above the famous mosaics in the villas of the wealthy provided welcome shade. I noticed that almost all of the mosaics depicted Greek gods seducing, fighting, killing, loving, or celebrating. The most popular scenes included Aphrodite and Dionysius.

"Wouldn't you like to look at the celebration of drunken lust on your living-room floor every day when you come home from work?" I mused to Janet. "Do you suppose Sergius Paulus had his floor redone after that meeting with Paul?"

As in the first century, Paphos is a tourist destination. Today Cyprus attracts sun-starved Britons to its beaches and discos, with just enough vestiges of British culture to make the Mediterranean feel somewhat like home. In Paul's day, Aphrodite attracted crowds of pilgrims to Paphos, looking for love. Cyprus was Aphrodite's island. Not far from the harbor is the place that Aphrodite supposedly stepped ashore after emerging out of the sea foam. Close to this spot was the site of the great temple to Aphrodite, which, along with the "priestesses" that worked the place, attracted a great many, especially male, pilgrims from all over the Mediterranean. The place where Aphrodite bathed, according to ancient legend, is a short distance north of Paphos.

Under the shade of a tent covering a mosaic, Janet and I reflected on Paul's experience in Paphos. Paul would have heard about Paphos and Aphrodite long before arriving in Paphos. Indeed, eager males seeking a little "spiritual renewal" in one of Aphrodite's temples may have trotted eagerly past the trudging missionaries on the road to Paphos. Paul's very first pagan convert was the highest-ranking Roman official of Cyprus. Could this positive experience among pagan worshippers of Aphrodite in Paphos have caused a change in Paul more significant than which name he used to introduce himself? Could Paul's observation of the irresistible power of love have changed his understanding of God, pagans, and the good news of Jesus? After living in Corinth, another center of Aphrodite worship, Paul would write a lengthy, revolutionary treatise on love to those former worshippers of Aphrodite. Out of faith, hope, and love, Paul wrote, the greatest is love! This is a truly remarkable thing for a former Pharisee to write to former pagan admirers of Aphrodite.

After several hours in the ruins of Paphos, we walked north on Apostolos Pavlos Avenue, the main road from the harbor to the new town of Paphos, to the Chrysopolitissa Church to see St. Paul's Pillar, a marble column in the church courtyard where Paul was reputedly lashed 39 times. This lashing is not recorded in the story in Acts, but knowing Paul, it's completely possible that he may have been lashed for some reason, and this could have been close to where it happened. The pillar, however, made from marble imported to Cyprus in the fourth century A.D., could not have been used for Paul. This fact made very little difference to the laughing British men lined up, arms cruelly "lashed" to the column, faces contorted in "pain," to get their pictures taken.

By 6:45 the next morning, we were motoring out of the Paphos harbor in time to watch the sun rise, heading east toward Limassol. Motoring along the southern coast of Cyprus in windless conditions, we were able to identify the site of Aphrodite's temple by tourist busses parked nearby. Soon we could see the long beaches of Limassol with a thin line of hotels and resorts separating the beach from the hills. Following directions from our cruising guide, I called the upscale marina a number of times on the VHF, but got no response. We found an arrivals dock, tied up, and I set off to find the marina office. The whole place had a lethargic feel to it; when I finally found the office and pushed open the door, I was greeted by a look of surprise, as if I had accidentally walked into someone's bedroom.

"Hello," I ventured, glancing quickly around to make sure I really hadn't wandered into a bedroom. "We just arrived. You probably got my reservation I e-mailed several days ago."

"No, we did not get your e-mail," the woman behind the counter yawned.

"That's funny," I replied. "I got a message back from the marina stating that I had correctly reserved a berth." This was true.

She shrugged. It didn't make any difference. There was plenty of space. We finished the paperwork, cleared customs, and I went back to the boat pondering the mystery of why the most expensive marina thus far on the trip offered the least assistance and amenities for their guests. Before securing *SailingActs* in her berth, I pulled alongside the fuel dock and filled the tank and spare jerry cans with diesel. Then, with everything secure, we took a bus to the center of Limassol to get transportation information for our trip to Salamis the next day.

At 6:15 the next morning, we were out of our bunks. We hurriedly ate breakfast and then hiked up the hill to the main road to catch the early bus to Nicosia, where we would need to get a 24-hour visa, walk across the "Green Line" into the Turkish Republic of Northern Cyprus, and find transportation to Salamis.

SailingActs

We would visit the archeological ruins there, and then reverse the whole process in time to get back to Limassol that evening.

Our cruising guide had effectively discouraged us from attempting to sail from Greek Cyprus to Turkish Cyprus. The ports in Northern Cyprus have been closed to all international shipping since October 1974, when Turkey began to occupy this area. The Cyprus High Commission warns that the master, crew, or owner of any ship calling at the ports of Northern Cyprus may be liable to prosecution under Cyprus laws. Janet and I, as master, crew, and owners, were not about to take this risk. We decided to obtain a one-day visa to Turkish Cyprus, a possibility for visitors to the island since 2003.

We flagged down the bus with "Nicosia" on the front and hung on as we charged around tight corners of secondary roads, through small villages, over terraced hills full of olive trees, arriving in Nicosia 90 minutes later. Using our little map in the back of the pocket guide, we found the Cyprus exit point, walked through the U.N.-controlled zone between the two bellicose neighbors, and arrived at the entrance point to Turkish Cyprus. Nicosia is the only capital city in a world still divided like Berlin had been until 1991.

In 1974, Turkish military forces invaded the northeastern side of Cyprus, occupying about 40 percent of the island. The "republic" they established is recognized only by Turkey. They have remained as unwelcome, bitterly-resented neighbors of the Greek south. Greece is a member of the European Union; Turkey is not, but would like to be. Turkey's acceptance is contingent upon a settlement of the Cyprus stalemate.

The formalities went quickly. The signs on the Greek side leading up to the border protested the international crime of Turkey's occupation. The signs on the Turkish side called the Turkish Republic of Northern Cyprus "a touch of heaven" and declared it would be Turkish "forever."

Once on the Turkish side, we decided, in the interest of saving time, to bargain with a taxi driver and for a mere 120 million lira ($75), we had our "limo," an ancient, extra-long black Mercedes, with an affable, personal chauffer, Enver, for the day. Enver drove out of Nicosia through the flat, dusty, monotonous countryside. Enver was driving a left-hand-drive car as they do in Turkey, but in Northern Cyprus the roads are laid out for driving with right-hand-drive cars, as in Britain. This means that everyone drives on the left side of the road in cars with the controls positioned for driving on the right side. But just to keep things really interesting, some of the cars have controls on the British side, keeping drivers guessing which person in the front seat of approaching cars is actually the driver.

Enver suggested several tourist sites. "Just take us to where St. Barnabas is buried, then on to Salamis," we instructed.

"What do you know about the Apostle Paul?" I asked as we drove toward the church and tomb of St. Barnabas.

"I think he used to run the monastery with his two brothers," Enver said with all the importance of a licensed travel guide.

We wandered through the somewhat neglected and rather forlorn little church and museum of St. Barnabas, with its extensive collection of icons of Barnabas, then across the dusty parking lot to the shrine built over the grave of the Salamis native. We descended a set of stone stairs that ended in pitch darkness. After our eyes adjusted, we noticed a stand with some matches, a bottle of oil, and a container with a wick next to the entrance of a cave leading off the room at the bottom of the stairway. We lit the oil lamp and walked into the darkness and gloom of the grave, feeling like Indiana Jones, half expecting a snake to slither across our sandals. We saw nothing at all in the blackness.

"I'll just take a photo into the black void," I suggested to Janet. "Maybe we'll see something there." As the camera flashed, we saw a stone sarcophagus decorated with burnt candles and icons. We were, indeed, standing in the burial place of the saint, and for a split second, we had actually seen it.

Enver drove us on to Salamis. Now in spectacular ruins by the sea, Salamis was the first port where Paul, Barnabas, and John

Mark landed after leaving Antioch on their first mission voyage. During the 130-mile voyage from Seleucia, the port of Antioch, Paul and John Mark were sailing out of sight of land for probably the first time in their lives. Both, no doubt, eagerly anticipated entering the harbor at Salamis and the prospect of familiar, solid land to walk on.

"Let's find the harbor and see if we can determine what Paul might have seen as he entered," I suggested to Janet. We carefully studied the topographical and archeological evidence, and made a list of the buildings flanking the harbor: a theater, stadium, gymnasium, and several villas. A short walk from the harbor and Paul would have been in a magnificent *agora* dominated on one end by a temple to Zeus. Salamis was the first of many showcases for the wealth, power, wisdom, and pleasure throughout the Mediterranean Roman Empire that Paul would explore. Paul would observe in almost every port in the Mediterranean in the next 10 years variations of what he saw entering the harbor in Salamis.

We admired the buildings, some of the best preserved we had seen in two months of visiting archeological sites around the Mediterranean. (See Photo 45 showing an early baptismal font.) The gymnasium was especially impressive, an incredible building with an open courtyard surrounded by columns and an image of Caesar Augustus in the very center. Around the edges of the courtyard was a whole pantheon of the important Greek gods. These images are now on display in the Cyprus Museum in Nicosia. Later that day I listed the gods that once graced the gymnasium in Salamis: three beautiful Aphrodites, the River God, Zeus, Hera, two images of Asklepios, Dionysus, Hygeia, Nemesis, Hercules, Isis, and Meleager.

While Salamis was the first of the many ports Paul would visit on his mission voyages, it was the last of the ports of Acts that Janet and I would visit that season during our three months of sailing. We had visited all of the cities and all of the ports north of Cyprus that Paul had visited according to the book of Acts.

I thought about Aphrodite and Paul for a long time after the visit to Salamis. Her statues abound everywhere in the Roman Empire, but in great abundance in Cyprus. Lovingly sculpted by many different artists but always stunningly beautiful, Aphrodite is recognizable and attractive wherever she appears. We had not seen one single statue of Paul in Greece, Turkey, or Cyprus. Whenever he appears, which is rare, it's in the form of an icon—somber, sober, scowling, and squat. Aphrodite would win any beauty contest with Paul. The gospel he preached, however, with radically different promises than that of Aphrodite, was attractive to people in Salamis, throughout Cyprus, and to Sergius Paulus, the first pagan convert in Paphos. It was in Cyprus, I believe, that Paul discovered the attractive power of the gospel for pagans. Paul would encounter the power and glory of the Roman Empire and discover that it was no match for the power and glory of the kingdom of God.

Enver drove us back to Nicosia, we re-crossed the Green Line, visited the museum and several churches in Nicosia, then caught the bus back to Limassol. We would spend the next day preparing for the longest voyage of our first season, the 36-hour, 195-mile passage to Ashkelon, Israel.

During the following day, as Janet and I finished the purchases and preparations for leaving Cyprus, we recalled our conversation with Wendy and Chris, an American couple we met in Antalya, Turkey. The night before we left Turkey, we had met this seasoned sailing couple in the marina restaurant for dinner in order to get their advice about sailing into Israeli waters, which they had done several years earlier.

"It was very intimidating," Wendy had said. "We were sailing at night about 50 miles away from the Israeli coastline when I got a funny feeling that we were being watched. I sensed something out there, but there were no lights. Then out of nowhere, in one instant, the night lit up like daylight. We couldn't even see the navy boat, because the lights were so bright in our eyes. Then they followed us for the next couple of hours, asking us the same questions over and over."

We decided that night in Turkey that we would try to time the passage so that we would enter into Israeli waters during the daylight. Walking back to *SailingActs* in the Limassol marina on the day before we left, Janet and I passed two couples speaking Hebrew. It turned out that they, too, were leaving that evening for the passage to Israel. "We're a little anxious about sailing into Israel," we admitted.

"Oh, don't worry about it," they encouraged us. "Sure, the navy will show up, but just answer their questions. You won't have any problem at all. Think about it this way. If you need any help, the Israeli navy will be right there." Somehow this conversation made us feel better.

So on Saturday, September 25, at 1:15 a.m., we eased *SailingActs* out of the marina in Limassol, Cyprus, trying not to give the impression to the noisy partiers on the boat across the dock that we were leaving because of them. We calculated that this departure time would give us the best chance of meeting the Israeli navy in the daylight and allow us to arrive in Ashkelon, Israel, by mid-afternoon Sunday in order to clear customs. Once out of the marina entrance, I adjusted the auto helm with gratitude for the inventor of the tiny gadget that would steer *SailingActs*, hour after hour, all the way to Israel.

We settled down for our three-hour watches under an awesome canopy of stars. The night flew by. I passed the time reflecting on how my understanding of Paul had changed while sailing the routes he had so long ago. I understood why his experiences of sea travel were useful metaphors in his writings. It was on the sea, on calm nights like this, when he must have seen and understood the world, his call, and God most clearly.

The sun rose, reached its zenith, sank, and disappeared as we relaxed, slept, snacked, and sailed on Saturday. Someone had told us earlier in the summer that time seems to pass more quickly the longer you are away from land. I am not certain this is true, but that Saturday felt like one of the shortest days of my life.

The second night at sea was even better. Contrary to our expectations, there were very few freighters. Janet was supposed to take over at 4:00, but I was enjoying the night so much I let her sleep, and watched light grow slowly over the eastern horizon. The old term for the lands of the eastern Mediterranean is "Levant," meaning the area of the rising sun. I watched the sun rise over the Levant from the Mediterranean for the first time in my life.

I thought of Paul, tired, inspired, beaten, triumphant, eagerly searching the water line for the first sight of land, impatient to be "home" after his first mission voyage. He thinks of tiny Palestine, once the kingdom of Israel, now a Roman colony. He sees Palestine with new eyes now, because he has seen other colonies throughout the Roman Empire. He has seen the grandeur of pagan temples with their images of beauty and power, and the cities with their magnificent theaters, fountains, and villas.

I imagined his excitement as he thought of sharing the news of the journey with the church in Antioch and Jerusalem. "Even the Roman Proconsul, Sergius Paulus, believed!

"Greeks and pagans all through Pamphylia and Cilicia are believing in Jesus!

"I was beaten and stoned in Antioch, Iconium, and Lystra, but I went right back through these cities again!

"I sailed all through the night!"

Yes, Paul was eager to tell the story, but he also saw the people of Jerusalem, the elders of the church, with new eyes. These were Paul's people, people of the land. These people, especially those from the mountains of Jerusalem, were resistant to the seductive invasion of Hellenism and Roman power that enticed so many into cooperation and compromise with the Roman system. Paul would have understood his fellow Jewish Christians in Jerusalem, for he was once one of them. Now he was returning with experiences that made him see with new eyes the ethnic animosity his brothers in Jerusalem had toward the pagan Greeks and Hellenistic Jews. And so he arrived in Israel with eagerness and apprehension.

Sailing toward Israel from the west, I saw Israel, Jerusalem, and her people in new ways as well. Like Paul, I had lived in Jerusalem and had been in Israel long enough to have a sense of the deep attachment that Jews have for the land of Israel. And like Paul, I had just sailed the Mediterranean of the Roman Empire, visiting its harbors and cities, talking with the variety of intense, paranoid, opinionated, aggressive, and wonderful people that have fought for space for thousands of years around the Mediterranean rim.

Sailing toward Israel, I recognized that the Jews and the Palestinians are like the other peoples of the Mediterranean. Like all other invaders before them, they belong to the area. Like the others who drifted in by land and by sea in order to establish themselves in the area, they bring their respective cultures with them. Like the others, they are unique. Hebrew and Philistine. Jew and Greek. Israeli and Palestinian. Paul had seen and appreciated the ability of the Roman Empire to incorporate and unify these disparate cultures. Each time Paul sailed back to Antioch and Caesarea following his mission voyages on the Mediterranean, I believe he saw, just a little more clearly, the potential for the good news of the kingdom of God to reconcile the natural enemies of the Mediterranean.

Janet woke up, amazed at the daylight and how close we were to Israel. "We have 32 miles until Ashkelon," I told her when I checked the GPS (see Photo 46). The wind was gently blowing as we enjoyed a fantastic breakfast of scrambled eggs and hash browns in the cockpit that Sunday morning, with the sweet strains of Vivaldi's *Four Seasons* wafting out across the empty sea.

"I don't think it has ever sounded better," Janet said fervently.

The Israeli navy still hadn't approached us, and we were getting a little concerned with their laxness. I had radioed the

Israeli navy with our coordinates at about 50 miles off the coast of Israel and received no response. I tried again at 40 miles with no reply.

At 30 miles I called again, and this time a woman's voice answered, asking us our destination and instructing us to keep the radio on. Three hours later, we spotted a speck on the horizon coming straight at us. "I think we're getting our navy visit," I commented to Janet as I watched through the binoculars. The patrol boat kept coming, spray flying, a huge wake following. It didn't slow down. I turned off the auto helm that had steered the course since Cyprus, ready to throw the wheel one way or another, but then realized that the navy boat would be the one swerving. I would just keep going straight. The boat kept coming and it occurred to me that, in a game of chicken with the Israeli navy, *SailingActs* would come out on the losing end.

A second or two before crashing, the patrol boat—with six grinning, tan, youth on the bridge, looking more like fashion models than military in their designer sunglasses and beachwear—swerved slightly, just missing us, but sending a wall of water from the wake that violently jarred and rocked us. For some reason, all six navy models found this amusing. The patrol boat looped around and headed at us from behind. We got ready for the second wave of water from the stern, but this time they slowed down, matched our speed, and followed us in silence about 30 feet behind. We looked at each other for a couple of minutes. Finally they addressed us on the loudspeaker, instructing us to reply on our VHF. For the next 30 minutes, we entertained a series of questions.

"What is the name of your boat?

"What flag are you flying?" (Were they all wearing sunglasses because they were blind?)

"Do you have weapons on board?

"Why are you coming to Israel?"

Finally they left, still grinning. "Sorry about the waves. Welcome to Israel."

"That wasn't so bad," Janet and I said to each other. But we still needed to clear customs in one of the tightest security areas in the world; Ashkelon is about 10 miles north of Gaza. Based on previous experiences entering Israel, we expected hours of interrogation and inspection on the wharf in Ashkelon. So, with some apprehension, we approached the harbor entrance at exactly 1:30 in the afternoon. I called the marina and was told to pull up to the arrival dock and wait. We spotted a casually dressed young man on the dock as soon as we entered the harbor.

"Hello, welcome to Israel," he called out. He helped us with the lines. "My name is Rami. Could I come aboard?"

Rami briefly glanced around the cabin and, apparently convinced that we had not rigged a bomb to blow *SailingActs* to smithereens as soon as we were in Israel, said "okay" to the customs officer who had just arrived. He, too, was dressed casually and appeared to be barely out of high school. On board he swabbed the door handles for drugs and poked into the nooks and crannies of *SailingActs* while asking questions nonstop.

"Why do you want to winter in Israel?"

"We are following the Apostle Paul. I want to do some additional research and a lot of writing this winter."

"Can you prove you are doing this project?"

This was a novel question. "Look at the name of the boat. Look, here are my notes." I gave him a bookmark with the description of the sabbatical project. "And we have a Web site, too."

"What is it?"

The customs official made a telephone call and repeated the Web address. Somewhere an assistant checked it out immediately.

"Okay, we believe you," he said. *Don't mess with Israeli customs,* I reminded myself, *even if they do look like they barely finished high school.*

"Who was Paul?" he asked looking at the icon of Paul on the cabin wall that Captain Steve and Jenny had given us in Volos.

"A Jewish believer in Jesus. The world's first missionary to pagans."

"What did he do that was special?"

I was beginning to suspect that the questions no longer had anything to do with security. "Well, his biggest contribution was to get the Jewish believers in Jesus to accept pagan believers into their churches," I explained. "This is what made him controversial."

"Why would that be controversial?" the customs boy asked. "That sounds like a good idea to me."

"Yes, I agree with you completely," I replied, relieved that we were not going to be barred from Israel because of our theology or opinion of Paul.

*Our ease thus far must all be part of the preliminary formali*ties, I thought to myself as we headed to the marina office for passport control. *The real problems will come from passport control.*

I was mistaken. We had feared the worst, but the Israeli officials were by far the most friendly, helpful, efficient customs officers of anyone on the trip. The passport official stamped our passports within five minutes and offered to help us with anything we needed. Michal, the marina office matron said, "No problem," when we asked about payments. Hillel, the marina manager, explained that the mission of the marina was to make our stay as pleasant as possible. We were given a berth between two boats whose owners, Hillel assured us, could speak English. "We want you to feel at home here."

Janet and I secured the lines of *SailingActs*, then sat in the cockpit, looking around and at each other. Three-and-a-half months, 1,500 miles of sailing, 36 different ports, and we were "home" at last (see Photo 47).

We were also tired and hungry. We needed to find an ATM, get some Israeli shekels, then find a place to eat before we collapsed from exhaustion. We found an ATM at a shopping area in Ashkelon about a mile from the marina, and were standing on a street corner looking for a restaurant when a black car pulled up alongside. It was dark by this time. The window slid down silently and the man behind the wheel spoke to us. *Is he asking directions?* I thought. *Or is he one of the Russian mafia who reputedly work in Ashkelon and is hustling us to have a "free drink" in his bar in order to fleece or rob us?*

"We just arrived," I explained. "I'm sorry I can't help you."

"No, no," the shadowy figure protested. "I see you are new. I want to help *you.*"

"We're looking for a restaurant."

"Get in the car. I'll show you restaurants and Ashkelon," he ordered.

Janet and I exchanged should-we-go-with-a-stranger glances. Something from my background screamed urgently, *Never get in a car with a stranger!* But that was a long time ago and we were in Israel and dead-tired, so we got into the plush, air-conditioned car and sped away.

What happened in the hours following was a completely enjoyable and unique introduction to Ashkelon. Uri took us everywhere, pointing out restaurants, shopping areas, prisons, and banks, all the while giving us a short course on the history of Ashkelon. Then he took us to his beautiful home, introduced us to his wife, who did not seem either shocked or resentful, and offered us food and drinks on the patio. We stayed for over an hour, visiting, using their Internet connection, and other land-based amenities such as running hot water and flushing toilets. We discovered that our host was a semi-retired computer representative and traveled regularly all over the world. Later, after Uri had driven us back to the marina, we ate a celebratory dessert in the marina's outdoor café, and finally by about 10:30, we made our way back to *SailingActs*, completely exhausted, grateful, and amazed. We were in Ashkelon. It wasn't just a good beginning, it was fantastic.

In the days that followed, we became acquainted with our sailing neighbors. We discovered we were the only non-Israeli boat in the entire marina. On one side was Reuben, a former diver for the Israeli navy, a sailing instructor, and a walking audio-encyclopedia (with no "off" button) of sailing trivia. On the other side was

Henry, a South African-Israeli. He lived on a nearby *moshav* and ran a dairy. On the next boat over was Moshe and Panni, Moshe's Thai wife. All were sailors, people of the sea, and secular.

We explored Ashkelon during the first week, which is built on the site of an Arab village. We discovered that its population has a high percentage of Russian immigrants and a non-kosher supermarket where one could buy pork chops and bacon every day of the week, including on the Sabbath. There were also several synagogues. Ashkelon is a seaport with an artificial harbor. Most of Ashkelon's inhabitants are tan, secular, tolerant people who wear shorts. It's a long way from Jerusalem, the holy city built on the holy Mt. Zion, populated by many pale, holy people in large hats and long black coats.

Biblical Ashkelon was one of the five major Philistine cities mentioned in the Bible, usually in connection with the ongoing battles with the Israelites. The city was never part of the kingdom of Israel. The Philistines were people of the sea, perhaps from the Minoan culture of Crete, who controlled the southern coast of Israel during most of its biblical history. They were bitter enemies of the Jews. The word "Palestine" is derived from the Philistines.

We would have liked to winter in Caesarea, where Paul had spent two years in prison awaiting his trial and voyage to Rome, but Caesarea's ancient harbor no longer provides adequate protection from the wind and waves that pound the coastline in winter (see Photo 48). Ashkelon, we discovered, was a good alternative, for although its modern, artificial harbor is the farthest port from Caesarea on the Israeli coast, it resembles Caesarea during the time of Acts. Herod the Great had built Caesarea and its artificial harbor. Pontius Pilate had made his home there. The two years that Paul spent in Caesarea's prison was more time than he spent in Jerusalem following his conversion. Like Caesarea in the time of Paul, Ashkelon is a modern city built on someone else's village. Its orientation is also toward the west rather than toward Jerusalem. And its inhabitants are also immigrants and people of the sea.

We could not winter in Caesarea, but we would winter in Ashkelon, surrounded by people of the sea, sailors, travelers, tradespeople, soldiers, and secular Jews. Among these people, Paul felt at home. So would we. In Ashkelon, like Paul in Caesarea, I would write and we would dream of the voyage to Rome.

CHAPTER 12

Wintering Like Paul and Dreaming of Rome

Our routine in the early winter months on *SailingActs* in Ashkelon developed quickly and varied little. From Sunday to Friday at about 6:00 a.m., as the light of dawn crept stealthily into the forward cabin through the Plexiglas hatch above the bunks, I would awaken. The bunk where Janet and I slept, shaped like a V, is appropriately called a "V-berth." Maybe V stands for "very"—as in very small, very worn, and our very matted foam-rubber cushion. Certainly very satisfying, anyway. The wide point of the V is six feet tapering down to an alarming 10 inches where our feet end.

"How do you manage to sleep in that?" everyone who visited us would ask.

"We really don't know," we'd reply. But somehow we slept in that tiny space just as well as on our queen-sized bed in Harrisonburg, Virginia.

A narrow shelf runs along the cabin wall above each side of the berth. All of our clothes that were not hanging in the locker were neatly folded and stacked on these shelves, along with books and sundry other items. The bunk in the forward cabin takes almost the entire space. With the little V-shaped filler cushion removed from the bunk, we had just enough room to stand and get dressed with the cabin door closed, which was only necessary when guests were on board.

On most mornings, I'd slip out from under the warm fleeces, step into the main cabin, and carefully close the door, trying not to waken Janet. If the mornings were chilly, I'd flip on the switch of our little electric heater, pull on jeans, a T-shirt, and a fleece that I would have lain out in the main cabin the night before. I'd check the barometer on the wall, then open the hatch and survey the weather.

We were living in an area that measures 5 x 6 feet of floor space, with a large table in the middle that folds down so that one can walk around it. My entire morning routine up to this point involved walking maybe 15 feet.

The chart table area on the port side of the main cabin served as my writing space. I'd carefully take the laptop computer out of its place above the port settee and remove it from the carrying case where it always stayed, unless in use, for protection against moisture and minor contusions. I'd place the computer on the chart table, plug it in, turn it on, and let the memories and discoveries of the summer wash over me for several moments, then I'd begin to write.

When Janet got up later, I'd take the little V-shaped filler cushion off the bunk and fit it into a groove on the back of the chart-table seat and continue to write in padded luxury. The entire chart table area is exactly 40 x 40 inches.

Directly on the opposite side of the cabin, in precisely the same position, and with identical measurements as the chart-table area, is the galley with a two-burner gimbaled gas stove and oven. The sink measures nine inches wide and 14 inches front to back, and has running hot and cold water that works either with an electric pump from the batteries or manually with a foot pump. There are 12 inches of counter space and an icebox used for storage. The electric refrigerator is under the starboard settee in the main cabin. The floor space in the galley is 18 x 24 inches.

Soon thereafter Janet would waken, dress, and come into the main cabin. She'd remove the cover above the stove, and insert it into a bracket above the starboard settee where it provided extra counter space while she cooked. She'd turn on the gas, light a burner, and begin heating water for coffee. We'd have fresh bread, soft-cooked eggs, cheese, and coffee made in a French press. The quality and variety of delectable meals she created while standing in that tiny space always astounded me.

During this whole time, Janet would not say a word to me. We forged a carefully crafted agreement: While I was writing, she'd speak to me only if there was an emergency. We would chat over breakfast, but silence reigned as soon as I got back to work. In the confines of a boat, we discovered, we needed to create private space by patterns of routine and silence. These patterns worked incredibly well most of the time, although Janet and I discovered that we had somewhat different perspectives on what, exactly, constituted an emergency.

One such difference of opinion occurred during the first winter storm of the season in Ashkelon. Torrents of rain had slashed against the deck, and I had gotten up on three different occasions that night to check for leaks. Back in May, when we had first purchased *SailingActs*, almost every porthole leaked copious amounts of water during even gentle rains. During the summer and into the fall, I had repaired 16 portholes on *SailingActs*, and so I was quite pleased, as I inspected them during the night, to find no water coming in from any of these once-leaky portholes.

But life, especially on an old boat, is never quite perfect. For the first time since we had been living on *SailingActs*, water had somehow leaked around the anchor windlass that is mounted on deck directly above the narrow point of the V-berth, just where our feet come together. The water had run down the wall, under our mattress, then harmlessly into the bilge. I had not noticed this problem during the night and was blissfully writing the next morning when Janet appeared at her usual rising time.

"Our bedding is wet," she announced.

Now this might be an emergency depending on *why* the bedding of two adults in their 50s is wet in the morning. "Why is the bedding wet?" I asked suspiciously, seeking to determine if we had a genuine emergency or if Janet was flaunting the Rule of

Law necessary for the order and stability of our mini-civilization on *SailingActs*.

"I don't know," Janet explained. "Water just leaked in from somewhere."

"Couldn't you just have told me at breakfast?" I countered with growing impatience as I sensed any creative inspiration I might have had, dissipating.

"I thought you would want to know about it right away," Janet countered reasonably.

"If the boat were in danger of sinking, I might," I retorted unreasonably. This might be theoretically true, but in reality, there are no good times for me to hear bad news about the boat that I thought I had, finally, brought into near-perfect repair.

If you are thinking that mature adults should be able to quickly and calmly reach a consensus on what constitutes an emergency, you probably have never lived for a winter on a sailboat with only 30 square feet of floor space on which to develop and defend a definition of "emergency." You might think that it would be far quicker to just fix the problem than to debate the issue for an hour. And you would be right. But that is not what happened. I fixed the problem in 10 minutes by covering the windlass with a piece of plastic, but only after an hour of debate, tears, sullen silence, and apologies. After all, a bunk that measures 10 inches for two pairs of feet is not big enough for unresolved conflicts.

Thankfully, our "Pax Stutzmana" worked well almost all the time. We'd eat our leisurely breakfast between 9:00 and 10:00, and on good days I'd return immediately to the chart table and write until 1:00 or 2:00 in the afternoon, and on excellent days until 4:00. Most days—eyes tired, shoulders aching—I'd check our e-mail at the computer in the marina office, then we'd go for a walk on the beach, or I'd do a small project on the boat until dark.

Almost every day Janet would walk 10 minutes to a small grocery shop for fresh bread and vegetables. Once every week or two, she'd walk 25 minutes with our little folding cart for major provisions, and to buy the *Jerusalem Post* and *Herald Tribune*. She'd wash the clothes in the marina laundry every week, and hang them out to dry on the deck of *SailingActs* by stringing rope from the stays. We'd get lots of sunshine in Ashkelon, and by evening they were always dry. For the first time in years, Janet had time to read for hours, just for sheer enjoyment.

Darkness would settle in early. By 4:30 or 5:00, we'd be back on board. In the warm glow of 12-volt brass lamps in the cabin, Janet would prepare dinner. I'd help or read until dinner was ready, then we'd savor the food and talk about the day, and listen to and discuss the world news on the BBC. We'd clean up the dinner table and read until we couldn't stay awake, which on some nights was as early as 8:30. With no TV, social schedule, car, or appointments, *SailingActs* was either like a prison or a retreat, depending on one's perspective.

On Friday evenings, even in secular Ashkelon, even among agnostic Jewish sailors, *Shabbat* begins. Janet would prepare a special meal of chicken soup with the tiny *Shabbat* crackers, *Shabbat* bread and wine, and meat and potatoes. She'd light the candles and recite the blessing. I'd bless the wine and the bread. We'd bless each other and our families and thank God for the amazing gift of this sabbatical—sharing 30 square feet of floor space on *SailingActs* that had taken us this far on the journey with Paul. We'd linger over the meal.

On *Shabbat* morning, I'd wake up as usual, but with no sense of urgency to get out of bed. We'd sit at breakfast for hours, reading aloud from the Bible, books, and the newspaper. Then, if the weather was nice, we'd go for long walks along the beach, exploring and reflecting. Down the beach from the marina are the 4,000-year-old ruins of Philistine Ashkelon, with the remnants of the oldest arched gate in the world and its city ramparts (see Ashkelon's ruins in Photo 49). Near the harbor is a place for sailors to offer their sacrifices of gratitude to Baal for protecting them on their voyages. In the evening, when *Shabbat* ended at dark, the markets opened back up, and we'd sometimes buy a frozen pizza, bake it in the oven, and eat while watching a DVD movie on the tiny computer screen. *Shabbat* on *SailingActs* was a touch of heaven on earth.

Each month I'd pay the mooring fees for the marina. For the equivalent of $125 we had a secure berth with water and electricity, clean toilets, and showers 50 yards from the boat, garbage collection, and 24-hour security. We could use the Internet in the marina office for free. The only extra expenses were for electricity, but sailboats are energy misers and we averaged $5 per month.

Occasionally, sometimes in the middle of the night, we could hear helicopters clattering southward overhead. Gaza is only 10 miles to the south of Ashkelon, and sometimes we heard the *whump* of an explosion from far away. The first time this occurred, we were standing on the dock talking to our neighbors. "What was that?" Janet asked in alarm, thinking this would certainly be an "emergency."

"What?" the Israelis answered, as if they hadn't noticed a thing. "Oh, that noise? That happens all the time. Those are just sonic booms. Nothing to worry about."

But we found it odd that helicopters were breaking the sound barrier, and noticed that the booms occurred shortly after they had passed overhead. We'd often buy a newspaper the day after we'd hear repeated "sonic booms," and inevitably we'd read of yet another Israeli military strike within Gaza in response to a Palestinian terrorist attack on Israelis—a seemingly endless tit-for-tat cycle of violence.

We saw the infamous Wall on many occasions that winter whenever we traveled to Jerusalem and the West Bank. The ugly, concrete Wall of separation between Palestinians and Jews is, among other things, a visible reality of the mutual fear and rage toward the ethnic, religious, and cultural "other" here in the Middle East. In some ways, the contemporary Wall that divides the land and its peoples today resembles the wall of division between "Jews" and "Greeks" (Jews and non-Jews), for which Paul risked his reputation and even his life to breach.

Once, just before Christmas, I traveled from Ashkelon to Jerusalem, and then the short distance from Jerusalem to Bethlehem to visit some friends who live in Beit Sahour, a family of Palestinian Christians. The distance between Jerusalem and Bethlehem is about five miles but sometimes can take hours, for one must go through the checkpoint in the Wall that divides Israel from Palestine. I had brought several small presents along for the children. When I had delivered the gifts, Saba, a charming, generous boy of 13, immediately searched the house to find a Christmas present to give to me, and within a few minutes had found an olive-wood cross with the word "Jesus" carved to form the cross piece. After a delightful visit, I stuck the cross in my backpack and walked back across the muddy checkpoint, showed my passport to the bored soldier, then looked for transportation for the ride into Jerusalem.

A few hundred yards from the checkpoint, a group of ultra-orthodox, Hassidic Jews were waiting at a bus stop, returning from their visit to Rachel's Tomb on the edge of Bethlehem. I joined the waiting group, the only male passenger who was not dressed entirely in black. Soon the bus arrived and filled, the men sitting in the front and the women occupying the seats in the rear, a pattern I had not noticed until a woman asked me to move to a vacant seat in the front next to a man so she could sit down in the vacant seat next to mine. One row ahead of me, in the men's section of the bus, an American Orthodox Jew with a New York accent was seated with his four excited children. The oldest I guessed to be about 13 years old, the same age as Saba, the Palestinian boy who had just given me the cross. The two youngest children were pestering their father with questions. "Do Arabs live on the other side of the Wall?" one asked.

"Yes," the father replied, "I'm afraid they do."

"Not for long," the elder son piped up from across the aisle.
"God willing, not for long."

On the bus back to Ashkelon that afternoon, I thought of the
two delightful, intelligent, religious, 13-year-old boys I had met
that day, growing up without knowing each other. I took the cross
out of my backpack and thought of Paul's vision of reconciliation
between divided people.

Imprisoned in Caesarea following a riot in the Jerusalem temple, Paul dreamed of intervention far more radical than *Pax
Romana*, military occupation, terror, or compromise when he
wrote from prison to the church in Ephesus: "For he himself
[Jesus] is our peace, who has made the two one and has *destroyed
the barrier, the dividing wall of hostility. . .* His purpose was to create in himself one new man out of the two, thus making peace,
and in this one body to reconcile both of them to God through
the cross, by which he put to death their hostility. He came and
preached peace to you who were far away and peace to those
who were near" (Ephesians 2:14-17, my emphasis).

What had Paul done to incite the riot which got himself imprisoned when he wrote this anti-wall treatise? He had just completed his final mission voyage in the Aegean and, after landing in
Caesarea and spending some time there, had gone up to
Jerusalem in spite of the warning that he'd find serious trouble
waiting. Paul entered the city walls through Joppa Gate the day
before Pentecost began, sometime toward the end of May, in 57
A.D. (Acts 21). He had arrived in Jerusalem facing, as usual, a
mixture of acclaim and controversy from his fellow Christians
there. In order to appease the Jerusalem Jews who were convinced that Paul had completely abandoned his Jewish religious
identity, Paul had agreed to do what the leaders of the Jerusalem
Christian community suggested in order to demonstrate his
Jewish identity. They suggested that Paul sponsor and join four
men who had taken a special religious vow that ended with a ritual in the temple area. While concluding this ceremony in the

temple, Paul was spotted by some religiously zealous Jews from out of town who loudly accused him on the spot of bringing a Gentile into the temple area reserved exclusively for Jewish males. "Men of Israel, help us!" Paul's accusers had shouted. "This is the man who teaches all men everywhere against our people and our law and this place. And besides, he has brought Greeks into the temple area and defiled this holy place" (Acts 21:28). The penalty for any non-Jew found in this part of the temple, according to Jewish law, was death.

Did Paul actually do such a provocative act? Luke, breathlessly recording in detail every move and word of the event, is non-committal. The accusers, he writes, "had previously seen Trophimus the Ephesian [a Greek] in the city with Paul, and assumed that Paul had brought him into the temple area" (Acts 21:29).

Would Paul have done such a thing? I think so. Such an action fits Paul's many previous bold, dramatic, provocative challenges to the xenophobic attitudes of his fellow Jews toward Gentiles. It corresponds to his theology. Luke does not directly deny the accusation, and Paul, speaking in his own defense to the crowd, makes his case, not by denying the charge of bringing a Gentile into the temple, but by reviewing his Jewish credentials and his clear commission from Jesus *to take the good news to the Gentiles*. He appeals to the Roman legal system, not to the Jewish religious law, for protection and judgment. By taking a Gentile into the forbidden area of the temple, he would have violated Jewish temple law, but he would not have violated Roman law.

Perhaps Paul played it safe in Jerusalem, but the Paul we had been following throughout the Aegean for the summer never played it safe. One might naturally assume that the success of starting flourishing Christian fellowships around the Mediterranean would have mellowed him. Or that the aging Paul, returning to Jerusalem after 10 years of constant hardships and dangers of travel on the pagan roads and seas of the Empire, and after facing hazards of hostility in the cities, would have been ready for rest and relaxation. Or that he might have been considering retirement options in Jerusalem, ready to enjoy some well-earned respect and prestige along with the rest of the apostles in Jerusalem. One might assume—but one would be mistaken.

Why? Because I'm convinced Paul would never have stopped taking personal risks until his Gentile brothers and sisters were fully accepted by his Jewish brothers and sisters. Never. I think the evidence supports the possibility that Paul actually did take a Gentile into the temple. From the moment Paul arrived in Jerusalem and during the time he was cooperating with the Jerusalem leaders to prove he was still faithful to the law, he was acutely aware that the situation had not really changed. Gentiles were still second-class believers.

How little the situation has changed in Israel/Palestine today. Since the beginning of the *intifada*, which began in September 2000, it has become increasingly difficult for Palestinians to travel outside of the West Bank. Permits are required to travel into Israel, confining many Palestinians to ghetto-like enclaves. Palestinians found to be in Israel without a permit are subject to prosecution, as are those who assist them. The resulting economic, social, and personal suffering of the majority of Palestinians who neither support nor believe in terrorism is incalculable.

I had just reread the story of the temple riot incited by Paul's alleged act of taking a Gentile into the temple, and renewed a debate with Janet that we'd been having for some time. We were on our way back to Ashkelon after visiting some of our Christian Palestinian friends in the West Bank town of Beit Sahour, next to Bethlehem.

"Why don't we sneak some of our Palestinian friends down to visit us in Ashkelon?" I asked in what I thought was a convincing Paul voice. "Our Palestinian friends have showed us such gracious hospitality and have taken so many risks for us and our student groups over the years. We can bring them on board *SailingActs*, take them for a sail, and have a meal together afterwards. They never get a chance to do something like that. What a gift that would be! This is a chance for us to return some of

48 *The beauty of winter storms off the coast of Ashkelon, Israel.*

49 *Ashkelon's ruins date back to the time of Abraham. Modern Ashkelon is in the background.*

50 *At Cnidus on the Turkish coast, sailing toward Rome in the spring of 2005.*

51 *The massive temple of Apollo at Didyma, Turkey.*

52 *Reminders of Paul on the bluff overlooking the traditional site of his famous shipwreck on the island of Malta.*

53 | *Lowering the Greek flag for the last time on the voyage as we approach the island of Malta.*

54 | *Janet demonstrates the first-century Roman crosswalk in Pompey.*

55 | *Contemplating the story of Odysseus and the Sirens as we approach the Galli Islands and thinking of Paul, sailing the same route toward Rome.*

56 *Examining the marvelous Roman brickwork of the amphitheater in Pozzuoli, Italy.*

57 *Walking to Rome on the Appian Way.*

58 *In the prison cell of the Mamertine Prison, where tradition has it that Paul was once incarcerated.*

59 *The massive interior of St. Paul's Church, built above the traditional site where Paul's remains were buried.*

Sailing off the coast of Israel.

their hospitality, to take some risks for them for a change." I was getting warmed up. "It would be something like Paul would do. It will also help us appreciate his personal efforts of breaking down the walls between Greek and Jew, just like they need to be broken down between Palestinians and Israelis."

"You promised me that you wouldn't try to 'understand' Paul by being shipwrecked, thrown in prison, or beaten," Janet reminded me with accurate memory of some long-ago conversation. Her memories could be genuinely inconvenient for conducting solid academic research with a humanitarian-heroic spin.

"Let's just talk about it with our friends the next time we go to Beit Sahour," I suggested. "If they think this is a good idea and that it can be arranged, would you be open?"

"I'll have to think about it. It's not that I am afraid, but if we're caught doing something illegal, maybe the Israelis wouldn't let us back into the country in the future. Would you want to jeopardize being able to lead future groups of students on the Middle East cross-cultural program just because you think Paul might have done something like this? Don't forget, you aren't Paul." Janet had a point.

"I'll have to think about it," I said. But I was pretty sure Paul would have already decided.

Whether or not Paul violated laws, he managed to get thrown in prison quite often, it seems, by offending religious sensibilities and violating social and ethnic codes of separation. In the Roman Empire of the first century, prison was generally not used as a penalty for a crime, but as a holding place where the accused awaited trial or execution. Imprisonment, especially for a Roman citizen, was an extremely humiliating and shameful thing to suffer. Paul, with his usual creative challenge to conventions, used his imprisonments as a way to demonstrate his authenticity, establish his authority, and write letters. At least four of his major letters were written from prison. There is reason to believe that Paul's letters to the churches in Philippi and Ephesus were written from a prison in Caesarea.

SailingActs

In October, Janet and I visited Caesarea, trying to imagine the conditions of Paul's imprisonment there for two years from 57-59 A.D., as he awaited transfer and trial in Rome. We surveyed the ruins of the governor's compound and the surrounding area, where Paul had likely been imprisoned. To the west was the sea; Paul could likely hear the roar of the waves from his cell. To the south, just a short distance away, was the theater; Paul could likely hear the laughter and applause from the crowds. To the northeast was the hippodrome; Paul would have certainly heard the roar of the spectators as they cheered the chariot racers. In Caesarea, Paul, a Jewish believer in Jesus, was surrounded by pagans.

In his mind's eye, Paul could still see the view of Caesarea from the sea where he had arrived at the end of his second and third mission voyages. When he arrived in Caesarea, he saw not the temple of Jerusalem but a pagan temple dominating the harbor just as he had seen everywhere else in the Mediterranean. But this temple was in the land of the one God.

Paul spent two winters in prison in Caesarea. He never wrote about being a prisoner of Rome or about being imprisoned unjustly. Rather, he wrote as a "prisoner of Christ Jesus." It almost sounds as if his imprisonment was voluntary, that he lived and acted in such a way as to end up in jail.

I could imagine Paul's experience in prison in Caesarea. The living and working space aboard *SailingActs* was roughly equivalent to the size of a prison cell in Herod's palace. We could hear the wind and the waves. I sat and reflected on the voyages and dreamed of sailing to Rome in the spring. But in the meantime, there was nothing to do but write. I, too, was in prison, voluntarily. I thought of others besides Paul who wrote from prison, incarcerated because they had lived out their convictions and sense of calling—Martin Luther King, Dietrich Bonhoeffer, and a host of others. Their writings, too, helped change the world, just like Paul's. I was in good company, but I did not talk about this very much to Janet. "Not only are you not Paul, you are also not Martin or Dietrich," she would have said.

In Ashkelon, the sea was also near, and the sailors were international. We were the only non-Jewish, non-Israeli boat spending the entire winter in Ashkelon. And I was very pleased. Jerusalem was always my favorite city in Israel, but having voyaged with Paul, Ashkelon felt like home. Unlike Paul, we would wait until spring to sail for Rome.

By November we learned why the sailing season in the Mediterranean traditionally ends before the middle of that month, and why Paul was shipwrecked when he was sent on a voyage that started in November. The first winter storm, mentioned earlier, struck with fury on the evening of November 21. Winter storms affected first-century shipping far more than they do today. The great sailing ships transporting wheat from Egypt to Rome during the first century would normally make one round-trip voyage each season, but daring ship-owners could make a small fortune if they could squeeze in two round-trip voyages in a season. This could only be done by sailing into late fall when winter storms suddenly threatened. Often they were successful. Sometimes they were not.

The marina in Ashkelon, located at the eastern end of the Mediterranean on a coast with no natural harbors, has a huge jetty that protects the harbor. This jetty is an artificial breakwater made with gigantic concrete objects that resemble children's playing jacks. While the jetty, which is about 20 feet high, protects the harbor from the waves, it does little to slow down the wind. For 24 hours during that first storm, the waves rolled in from the sea, thundered against the jetty, and exploded into white foam that washed completely over the top. The wind howled through the marina, shrieking through the masts of the sailboats leaping like furious Rottweilers against their tethers. Loose ropes in the rigging slapped crazily. A furled headsail on a nearby boat somehow worked loose and began to disintegrate in the fury of the wind. All the boats heeled for hours, as if under sail, as the wind pushed against the bare masts.

The stormy and sublime boat-bound days of early winter flew by, punctuated by trips inland. In November, Janet and I finally were able to celebrate our 32nd wedding anniversary. We have a tradition to never celebrate this important event twice in the same place; in fact, we have celebrated in a different state, country, or island every one of those 32 years. Our first anniversary had been in Israel in 1973, memorable because the Yom Kippur War was fought during that month as well. We celebrated that time by running to the bomb shelters on the kibbutz, where we had gone for the duration of the war.

Being in Ashkelon, we decided to go to Jordan. A friend of ours had recommended a resort on the Dead Sea, and we decided to live in two days of luxury. As always, travel in the Middle East is as unpredictable as any sea voyage. The "weather" is fickle, the "climate" unstable. We caught a bus to Jerusalem, took a taxi to Damascus gate, found a *sherut* to the Allenby Bridge, then transferred to a taxi to take us to the Israeli crossing. "Do you have a Jordanian visa?" the guard asked at the preliminary checkpoint.

"No, we'll get one at the Jordanian border," we answered with the confidence of seasoned travelers.

"You can't get one there," the guard explained in a tone that indicated he was not impressed by people who were simultaneously confident yet clueless. "You must go to the Sheikh Hussein Bridge crossing."

We didn't want to do that. This northern crossing would take at least another 90 minutes and would be expensive because we'd need to take a taxi. "We'll just try crossing here," we told the guard.

He allowed us to go through, but the moment we left we knew we had made a mistake. If we were allowed through the Israeli border and were to take the bus through no-man's land across the Allenby Bridge, only to be sent back, it would cost even more time and money, not to mention confusion. So, just before entering the Israeli border crossing, we decided to cancel the whole trip. The hassle of getting through the borders was not worth it. I called Rami, a travel agent and a good friend from the West Bank, who had made the reservations at the Mövenpick Resort for us.

"Oh," Rami said when I told him our predicament, "you should just go anyway."

"But we can't afford the extra expenses," I explained.

There was a moment of silence. "I wasn't going to tell you this," Rami said, "but we made the reservations and paid for them already. This is a gift to you and Janet for your anniversary celebration. I knew you wouldn't accept this if I told you what we were doing ahead of time."

I was stunned. Rami was right. We wouldn't have accepted such a generous gift from people who have suffered economically and in so many other ways since the beginning of the *intifada*. There was only one thing to do. "Thank you, thank you," I told Rami. "Don't bother canceling the reservations."

"We decided to go to Sheikh Hussein after all," we explained to the bewildered *sherut* driver. "Can we get out? We want to find a taxi to take us there."

What ensued is hard to grasp by those who have never traveled between Israel and the neighboring Arab countries. We were in a *sherut* full of both West Bank Palestinians and Israeli Arabs. They feared that if we left the vehicle in the border zone between Israel and Jordan that the guards would notice the absence of two passengers, and this would cause trouble for all.

"Please go to the border people and have them change the number of passengers in the vehicle on the permission slip," an old Palestinian gentleman begged.

So, with hands raised, Janet and I walked back and forth between the *sherut* and the border crossing as the other passengers watched anxiously. Finally we succeeded. But, in the meantime, we created another situation when we secured another *sherut* to take us to the Sheikh Hussein Bridge border crossing rather than wait until the one we rode in from Jerusalem was free. A grand, verbal *sherut*-driver fight broke out. We hurriedly threw our luggage into the trunk, the ancient Mercedes roared to life, and we lurched away from the near violence behind us toward the Sheikh Hussein Bridge crossing.

Ninety minutes later and $50 poorer, we were waiting to go through the border crossing for the second time that day. The young female Israeli officer looked with bewilderment at our passports. "Where did you enter Israel?"

"Ashkelon."

"No, I am not asking where you are living now," she replied impatiently, "I am asking where you entered Israel."

"We *entered* in Ashkelon," we tried to convince her. "We arrived on a sailboat and went through customs. Don't you know that Ashkelon is an international harbor?" It was obvious she had never seen an entry stamp from Ashkelon in any passport before in her life. She refused to take our word for it, and we spent 10 minutes standing restlessly in the ugly surroundings at the depressing window while she made telephone calls to verify that, yes, it is possible to arrive in Israel through Ashkelon.

Once through, we got our Jordanian visas without a problem, found a taxi that would take us all the way south, past the Allenby Bridge where we had been hours earlier. By early afternoon we entered the lush oasis of the Mövenpick Hotel at the Dead Sea. We instantly noted the contrast between the watered lawns, palm trees, and smartly-dressed staff eagerly working for tips around the grand entrance of the resort, and the dusty poverty of the surrounding area with its goat herders and stray donkeys. It reminded me of Herod the Great's opulent palaces that had once given testimony of Rome's power and glory. Herod the

Great's palaces demonstrated the good life in this very region on the Dead Sea shores not far from where John the Baptist in his camel skins was baptizing in the Jordan. We spent two wonderful nights soaking up the luxury among the wealthy, the privileged, and the pampered, recognizing that, in terms of wealth and privilege, we were far closer to Herod than John the Baptist. We returned to *SailingActs* personally refreshed, but with lingering sadness about the way the world is divided.

CHAPTER 13

Foreign Interludes

And so our winter progressed. As we neared the middle of December, our one-month interlude in Virginia began to loom large, inserting its demands into our simple schedule. For some reason, the prospect of spending Christmas at home with friends and family was at once exciting and daunting. Life, we remembered, was busy and complex on land, especially in the United States. But we had our tickets and began to prepare *SailingActs* for our absence

The evening before we left, our Israeli boating neighbors invited us, along with the Dutch couple who were also leaving for the winter, over to their boat for Thai food. We sat in the cockpit and shared sailing adventures, joked about our mishaps, and laughed about life's absurdities that become so clear on boats. Moshe had ordered a taxi to take us to Ben Gurion Airport at 2:00 a.m., and insisted that he would waken to make sure the taxi driver came. "No, no," we said, "we'll be fine." But we knew our Israeli friend well enough to know that protesting was futile.

At 1:30 the alarm rang and Janet and I, as in a dream, shut off the gas, disconnected the electricity, locked the hatches, secured all the portholes, and walked to the marina gate with Moshe, glancing back at *SailingActs* rocking in the dark waters. The taxi arrived. We threw our bags into the trunk. *Maybe I can nap until we arrive at the airport,* I thought to myself, but my spirits sank when the very orthodox Jewish taxi driver commanded, "You sit front." He had heard our English and limited Hebrew conversation and was determined to utilize the hour-long journey by reviewing Hebrew conjugation rules of grammar.

"You say, *'ani rotsay, at rotsah, anachnu . . . ,'*" he ordered. On and on, relentlessly, he covered the vast combinations of tense and gender-specific Hebrew verbal endings until I got it right. By 2:30 that morning, I had conjugated far more Hebrew verbs than I thought possible in the middle of the night.

"Please," I pleaded in Hebrew that I thought I had long since forgotten. "I am very tired. I do not want to speak anymore."

"Fine," the taxi driver said. "I stop." Thirty seconds of wonderful silence transpired before he loudly resumed his conjugational torture. *Has he taken some kind of kosher stimulant?* I thought darkly. *Is there a law in the Torah that goyim are supposed to learn Hebrew in the middle of the night before flying from Israel? Perhaps he is really an Israeli secret-service agent trying to extract a "confession."* Nothing I said or did seemed to lessen his enthusiasm, so I ended up submissively conjugating until, mercifully, we arrived in front of the airport with the delightful prospect of grammatical freedom. I did not tip the driver and did not quite understand his muttered Hebrew response, although I was pretty sure that, grammatically, it was in the second-person male singular, present tense.

We boarded the plane to Athens as the sun rose in the east. Then, after a 24-hour layover, continued on across the Atlantic to Dulles airport near Washington, D.C. Janet's sister, Dorothy, met us at the airport and took us to her small townhouse in Alexandria for the night. It seemed so large, so stable, so strange to be sleeping on land again. The next day we arrived at our own house in Harrisonburg. Five EMU students had been living in it the whole semester and were away for the Christmas holidays. The key they had hidden for us did not fit any of the outside locks. I wandered around, trying to figure out how to break into our own house without doing too much damage, eventually entering by shinnying up to the second story front porch and entering an unlocked door, thanking the negligence of students. Once inside Janet and I padded around flushing toilets, opening taps, flipping light switches, adjusting thermostats in wonder and awe at the ease of life on land. We had never gone through that kind of adjustment before. This was more than cultural shock; it was a social, spatial, existential shock, and the adjustment took days.

The cultural, linguistic, and lifestyle differences between the Ashkelon Marina and small-town Virginia at Christmas is vast. During the seven-hour flight from Athens to Dulles, I had thought of Paul traveling back and forth between the pagan and the Jewish worlds and wondered if he struggled each time he crossed these boundaries. His immersion in the pagan world didn't end when he boarded a ship sailing from the Aegean toward Palestine, for it was a pagan ship. Nor did it end when he arrived in Caesarea, for that was a pagan port. The transition would have been the most acute on the two-day journey between Caesarea and Jerusalem.

What made these transitions especially dramatic was that the Paul who returned to Jerusalem after spending years in the pagan world was not the same Paul who had departed from Jerusalem. He always brought with him a perspective on the land and its people that was influenced by his time with the sea-going pagans of the Empire. The Jerusalem audience thought they knew the pagan enemy, and Paul's sympathetic descriptions were shocking and infuriating to them. The polarization among the Jews as Paul explained his views on the "enemy" pagans belonging to the chosen people through their faith—without going through the Jewish rites of initiation first—was too much for even liberal Jews to accept.

Janet and I felt a little like Paul must have felt on occasion as we tried to explain to Americans over the following weeks what it was like to be Americans and Christians in a part of the world where U.S. foreign policy has produced outrage, especially among Muslims. Some American Christians, thinking they know the evil of the enemy, believe they are being realistic in their justification of violence in return for evil.

On January 19, 2005, Janet and I flew to Frankfurt, Germany, to spend several days with our oldest son, David, who was working in Heidelberg. Four days later I flew on to Israel, a week ahead of Janet, to get as much writing done as possible without alarming announcements about wet bunks or any other kind of "emergency." I flew into Tel Aviv, then took a bus to Ashkelon, arriving several hours later in the dark. *SailingActs* was exactly as we had left her five weeks earlier.

Without a wife on his travels, Paul must have known loneliness, I realized during that week alone on *SailingActs*. Late one lonely afternoon, too tired to think clearly enough to write, I decided to try to relate to the fishermen who, the local yachting neighbors complained, were taking over all the free space in the marina. "They are smugglers, criminals, and rude, uncouth people," the neighbors had told us. "Be sure to lock your boat when you leave it if the fishermen are in the marina."

I wandered onto the wharf where the fishermen were preparing their nets for later that evening. They eyed me and my camera with suspicion but gave me permission to observe and take pictures, telling jokes in Hebrew at my expense when they discovered I couldn't follow the conversation. As I was leaving, another fisherman strode purposefully from an adjacent wharf, "Why you take picture?" he demanded. "You from tax?"

"No, no," I replied. "Just a neighbor, friend." He walked away muttering.

I thought about these crude and unruly fishermen and their animosity toward outsiders, especially tax officials. I thought about Jesus, getting these fishermen and tax collectors together in his little band of followers through whom he was going to share the good news. *What was Jesus thinking when he selected them? What was he thinking when he called Paul?*

Janet returned "home" from Germany. Life, again, was good. Sometimes the fishermen even grunted a *"shalom"* when I walked past during the following days.

SailingActs

Spring comes early in Ashkelon, and by mid-March the weather had become mostly sunny and warm, luring sailors out of their boats, chatting, puttering, and planning. My writing plummeted to three hours before breakfast, and then I was out in the sunlight and breeze, getting *SailingActs* ready for the voyage to Rome. I removed the tarpaulin that had covered the cockpit all winter, cleaned the bilges and the engine, and changed the oil. I made minor repairs and major plans.

I somehow managed, one day while adjusting the cables on the steering system of *SailingActs*, to gash my ankle on a sharp piece of metal in the cramped, dark, curved, and unstable working conditions. One look at the half-inch-deep wound and I knew it required a trip to the hospital. Eight stitches later and about to be released, I looked around for Janet and discovered her lying in a hospital bed. She had fainted! She had left the surgery room feeling dizzy, fallen on the floor, struck her head, and needed medical attention herself. We looked at each other, shook our heads, laughed, and hobbled back to the boat.

"You know," Janet reminded me several times in March, "it's time we put *SailingActs* up for sale. We need to find a buyer by August when we are finished with the sabbatical."

"Yes," I always agreed, "I'll do it real soon." But somehow neither Janet nor I felt any real motivation.

"Keep the boat," all our sailing neighbors encouraged us. "She's a real ocean cruiser. You can sail her back to the U.S., and then you have a boat to sail anywhere in the world if you want."

And so we stalled and delayed, considering the options. November is the best month to sail west across the Atlantic from the Mediterranean, but that would be impossible for me to do. I'd be teaching full-time during the fall semester after we returned.

"I'll sail her back myself," Janet suggested one day. "I could get a couple crew members to help me and we could be in the Caribbean before Christmas. Then you could fly down over Christmas vacation and we could sail up to the Chesapeake."

Something about selling a boat that has been your life, your world, your refuge, and salvation makes it different than selling a home on the land. No wonder that ships have been used as a symbol of salvation and the church in history. It's like selling your faith or one of your best memories to a stranger. So we dawdled and stalled on the future of *SailingActs*, focusing instead on the usual last-minute repairs, stocking up on supplies, and making preparations for the voyage to Rome.

But we still had not been to Damascus. We had longed to visit the famous city of Paul's conversion since we'd begun sailing Acts, and two weeks before leaving Israel, I finally had the chance. Because of international and regional politics, violence, and military conflicts, this short journey of 250 miles took 12 hours—a bus to Tel Aviv; a short flight from Tel Aviv to Amman, Jordan; a taxi to central Amman; and finally a service (shared taxi) from Amman to Damascus. But it was worth every minute of travel, security checks, and border crossings.

My hosts in Damascus, Mennonite Central Committee workers Eldon and Jane Wagler, were incredible as were the many Syrians I met. I discussed Paul with Patriarch Zakka of the Syrian Orthodox Church, and with Patriarch Ignatius of the Greek Orthodox Church. I walked Straight Street, visited the sites of Annanias's house and the famous basket-over-the-wall escape. The traditional site of Paul's conversion, Kawkab, was the highlight. The old Roman road rises slightly at the site, and one can catch the first glimpse of Damascus ahead, and the snowy profile of Mt. Hermon behind. It's a peaceful and marvelous spot and I lingered with my hosts, thinking of the impact of Paul's conversion on history as we sat in the shade drinking tea served by Father Matthew, the resident monk, and discussing Paul and his conversion.

I left Damascus on Easter morning. The sun was still low in the east as our service pulled out and headed down the Damascus road toward Amman. The driver was Syrian. A Druze man, who had fled his village on the Golan in 1967, was riding in the front seat. Next to me in the back seat was a couple from

Fallujah, Iraq, refugees living in Syria, whose home, they told me, was possibly destroyed.

I do not know if you can imagine what it is like to be an American passenger under such circumstances. Here we were— Muslim, Druze, and Christian speaking Arabic, English, and even Hebrew, riding together in a small car for four hours on the Damascus Road. I was overwhelmed by the kindness, especially of the Iraqis, as they described their shattered lives and explained why the Americans are so resented in the Middle East.

I thought of Paul, Roman citizen, on the Damascus Road. I introduced Paul and his nearby conversion briefly when they asked why I was in Syria.

"Isn't today some kind of Christian holiday?" the Iraqi man asked.

"Yes, it's Easter," I replied.

"What happened on Easter?" he inquired seriously.

"Jesus' resurrection," I explained. We continued to talk about suffering and hope, evil and Easter, life and death, until we reached Amman. That car ride and the conversation, the road, the refugees, and the resurrection have been on my mind ever since.

The next day an e-mail was waiting from "your Iraqi friend." I opened it. "Happy Easter!" it said. I wish we all, especially American Christians, could travel the Damascus Road with Paul and refugees from Iraq.

I rejoined Janet at the Jerusalem University College in Jerusalem, where she'd been volunteering in the library during my time in Syria. The next day we caught a bus at Jaffa Gate and made the short journey from Jerusalem to Bethlehem in order to say goodbye to our friends in Beit Sahour. For the last time of the trip, we experienced the familiar shock of crossing cultures and walls between Israel and the West Bank, and for some reason were more deeply saddened this time than ever as we observed the workers putting the final touches on the Wall, the guard tower, and the massive gates.

Back in Ashkelon, visitors who had been waiting until spring for a promised sail dropped by. Two former EMU students, Dave Landis and Eric Kennel, moved aboard with us to help us sail to Turkey as part of their year-long, round-the-world trek. The luxury of spare time vanished. We would begin the 40-hour sail toward Cyprus on Sunday, April 3, we decided.

On the evening before our scheduled departure, the weather began to deteriorate. According to the weather maps on the Internet, a massive storm system was building, giving us favorable wind in terms of direction but with heavy seas and near gale conditions. On top of that, my ankle wound was becoming very painful, turning red and swelling. Everyone who looked at it agreed that I should see a doctor and get more antibiotics. I also lost a nose piece from my glasses. The case for delaying at least 24 hours strengthened rapidly.

During the night, I laid awake listening to the wind scream through the rigging and the waves crashing into the jetty. At 6:30 I got up to look at the harbor entrance. Janet woke up as I eased out of the bunk. "I'm not feeling right about leaving today," I admitted.

"Neither am I," Janet replied immediately.

We called the marina and rescheduled our departure for 24 hours later. "You wouldn't be able to leave the marina today if you wanted to," Michal, the woman in the office, confirmed. "The weather is just too bad to clear the marina entrance."

That forenoon, instead of leaving, I visited a doctor, got more antibiotics, and had my glasses repaired. Janet and I bought bags of groceries. We consulted weather charts and discussed options. The wind was still howling when we went to bed. I woke on the morning of April 4, knowing that we would wait another day.

The following morning was the same. The Mediterranean, as always, was still in control of our voyage to Rome, just as it had been for Paul's.

CHAPTER 14

The Voyage to Rome

For Janet and me, and our two crew members, Dave and Eric, the hours leading up to our departure from Caesarea for the voyage to Rome were joyful and expectant. Within hours after arriving in Ashkelon in September, Janet and I had forgotten about the fear, loneliness, and discomfort of long voyages. Dave and Eric, having never sailed, could not imagine them. *This must be how Paul felt after two years of waiting in prison for his voyage to Rome,* I thought as I went to the marina office to pay the final bill, check the weather, and read our e-mail for what I thought would be the last time in Israel.

We carefully studied several different weather forecasts on the Internet and were heartened that they all seemed to agree. Hillel, the marina manager, gave us his predictions. Seth, the old man of the sea with a boat on the next pontoon, came by with a sheath of weather updates and predictions, and Henry, who kept his boat next to *SailingActs*, called from his *moshav* to explain the weather report that he had faxed to us in the marina office. There was a veritable squall of weather reports—all favorable. At 11:00 that forenoon, the four of us were waiting for the customs official, and 15 minutes after he arrived we finished and were walking in the bright warm sunshine to *SailingActs*. We said goodbye to our wonderful neighbors, Panni and Moshe, and Orestes and Zoa. As we backed out and headed out the channel, others came out from below deck and stood in the cockpits of their boats, waving to wish us a pleasant voyage to Cyprus while we slowly motored toward the marina entrance.

Janet and I waved back with tears in our eyes as we cleared the marina entrance. Holding our breath as we scraped the bottom on the sand that had washed in during the winter storms, we pushed through with a burst of power and we were on the sea. The wind was brisk, the water blue, the waves three to four feet high. We were on our way to Rome!

The euphoria didn't last long. Did I think the first day of the voyage to Rome would be different than the first day of the voyage last year? Did I forget that the voyage to Rome was, to put it mildly, somewhat challenging for Paul? Did we think that we could learn of his sufferings at sea by cruising effortlessly on a predictable and gentle Mediterranean Sea? Had I forgotten that, in spite of all the repairs I had made in the six months we had wintered, *SailingActs* was still an old boat with her own middle-aged mind, body, and soul?

Yes. I had forgotten all this and more. Optimism had infiltrated my spirit like seawater through portholes, corroding my mental capacities, and there we were, blissfully sailing toward one of our worst days at sea.

Subtly, imperceptibly, the waves began to build as the wind increased. The four weather reports we had studied and compared so carefully the previous day were soon as irrelevant and inaccurate as an average political campaign speech. Eric was the first to get sick and the rest of us resolutely tried to look the other way and ignore his retching as he leaped to the rail, time after agonizing time. Soon I, too, began to feel a little nauseous as I worked on the heaving deck, now starting to wash a little. We changed tacks and headed away from shore. The seas were confused and the wind strong so that within an hour after leaving, sheets of spray drenched everything in the cockpit. I was soaking wet before I came to my senses and pulled on foul-weather gear. I, too, began the dreaded downward spiral toward full-blown seasickness, eating pretzels and chunks of strong ginger candy that Janet had purchased on a random piece of anti-seasickness advice she had come across. I was dabbing evil-smelling, oily liquid behind my ears, which a man at a long-ago boat show had convinced me worked for "80 percent of the people." I was one of the 20 percent for whom it did not.

By now Eric was huddled in a pathetic, stoic ball in a corner of the cockpit, immobile except when charging to the lifelines to heave every 10 minutes. The wind rose and I, the sickening captain of this rolling, cold, wet, nauseous prison, needed to put a reef in the mainsail and furl the headsail. I began with the headsail, which should have been the easiest, but somehow the furling rope had swollen during the winter and kept jamming. I struggled into a harness, clipped onto a jack-line, and went forward on the sea-washed deck that erratically rose and fell 10 feet every few seconds like a first-century carnival ride. Hanging on with one hand, working with the jammed roller with the other, struggling to tame the flapping ropes and sails, battling wind, waves, chill and exhaustion, I did something for the first time in my life: I heaved the contents of my stomach over the rail, not once but repeatedly.

Only 43 more hours of sabbatical hell to go until we reach Cyprus, I thought grimly. *It has got to get better soon. One thing is certain— it can't get much worse.* Precisely at that moment, Janet announced that a copious amount of water was leaking around every one of the portholes in the main cabin.

"They can't be leaking," I out-shrieked the wind. "They didn't leak a drop all winter. Try tightening them."

"I have already," she yelled up to the cockpit. "Why don't you come down and try?"

In nauseous misery I descended into the dripping, rolling cabin covered with towels and trays that Janet had strewn around in an attempt to catch the water, but it was no use. The gaskets must have all dried and hardened during the winter in Israel. Water was pouring in. It was getting dark. *Only 42 hours and 50 minutes left until we reach Cyprus.*

Then, there in the gathering doom, shivering in a water-logged cabin in which we could not stand, we did something for the first time of the voyage. We changed our destination. "We're heading in," I informed the crew. By this time we were only four miles off the Israeli coastline and the lights of Tel Aviv beckoned. Checking the GPS and our chart, we changed course, setting the auto helm on course for the Tel Aviv marina, shivering and rolling our way through the darkness of the sea toward the string of lights on the land.

Dave and Janet, in the closest thing to a mutiny we ever had on *SailingActs*, consulted with each other in the wet cabin and decided, correctly, that Tel Aviv harbor was too dangerous to try to enter in the dark, especially during a storm. The guidebook stated that the Tel Aviv Marina was treacherous and that incoming boats should call for a pilot boat and enter only in the daylight. "Okay, we'll go to Herzlia," I announced when they made their case, and we changed course once again. It would be eight additional miles of miserable pitching in total darkness.

We could see the lights of Tel Aviv and Herzlia stretching out along the shore above the billowing waves; foam; screaming wind; sick, huddled bodies; and dripping cabin. The VHF radio crackled as the familiar voice of an Israeli navy official called repeatedly for a vessel whose position was much farther out at sea than ours. Due to the extremely high security along Israel's coast, we were a little unsure of the consequences of checking out of Israel, reporting our route to the navy, then changing our minds and returning to Israel without permission. We hoped that our circumstances would justify our decision.

Anxiously we sailed on. Suddenly I remembered that Rick and Tsippy, as well as Bruce and Pam who spent some time on their boats in Ashkelon, were now in Herzlia. "Why don't you try to call Bruce or Rick," I yelled down to Janet. And somehow in that wet, dark, rolling cabin, Janet found Rick's telephone number, dialed it on the cell phone, and began a series of conversations over the next hour. Rick assured us we could enter the marina safely, gave us instructions for how to do so, called Bruce who volunteered to meet us and help tie up, and promised to have hot soup waiting for us when we got in. Such words of comfort and hope I had never heard, such sweet consolation. We began using the VHF to talk to Rick and realized, when the navy interrupted, that we had been off their radar screen and it was us they had been trying to call earlier. "I'll call the navy," Rick offered, "and explain your change of plans."

Following the guidance of the GPS, we cautiously approached the marina entrance on rolling waves, then we were in and gliding in suddenly calm waters into the channel. We spotted Bruce and Pam's flashing light signals and pulled into the slip next to their boat. Dave, Eric, and Janet threw them the dock lines and we were at once secure and safe. Oh, blessed land! The sickness disappeared.

Rick and Tsippy arrived with some of the most delicious soup we had ever eaten, and we wolfed it down as they sat in our dripping, disheveled cabin and chatted. "You did the right thing," they assured us as they left an hour later then returned with their key to the marina shower block. Soon we were warm, dry, and very tired. We collapsed into bed, thankful for life, safety, and friends. We would assess the damage, check into the marina, worry about the navy, and finish recovering in the light of day.

Lying in the warm, safe bunk the next morning before getting up, I thought about how Paul's own course changed due to weather and sailing outside of the normal sailing season. We had started the voyage to Rome, experiencing—in spite of the significant technological advances since first-century sailing—the dominance of the sea and the powerlessness that Luke described so well in Acts 27. I thought of Bruce and Pam, Rick and Tsippy, people of the sea who came from Florida, Iowa, and Israel, whom we barely knew and who had shown us such generosity and kindness. I realized new possibilities for why Paul had defended the people of the sea to his landlubber Christian brothers and sisters.

After checking into the marina that morning and paying the fees to process our visas back into Israel, we went to work drying out the boat and making the necessary repairs to the leaking portholes. By evening we were ready to sail again but decided to wait until the weather reports were favorable before attempting the long sail to Cyprus. On April 9, three days after we arrived in Herzlia, the weather forecast seemed ideal and we left at noon with very strong winds from the east, which made for excellent sailing. We followed the coast north of Herzlia. The unexpected change of plans several days earlier had created an opportunity to sail to the ancient harbor of Caesarea from which Paul had left for his voyage to Rome. For years I had dreamed of sailing toward Rome from the harbor of Caesarea, which, next to Selucia, had played the greatest role of introducing the gospel to the Mediterranean.

The gratification of the slow sail-by from the great artificial harbor built by Herod the Great in Caesarea, just before Jesus was born, made the discomfort of the previous days seem insignificant. Janet and I had visited Caesarea on numerous occa-sions, but to see Caesarea only from the land is like looking at a theater set from backstage. The real display is from the water. Anyone arriving in Palestine by sea in the port of Caesarea would have been impressed at the triumph of paganism over Judaism. Caesarea was the port that figured so importantly in the book of Acts, and it was to and from this port that Paul went with his message. *When he left for the last time, did he look back? Did Paul admire Caesarea's splendor and wonder how magnificent Rome was going to look? Did he imagine himself walking the streets in the heart of the Empire?*

We turned *SailingActs* toward the open sea, into the wind and the waves, away from the marinas, our friends, and the land at about 5:00 p.m. Pope John Paul, we learned as we listened to the BBC broadcast that afternoon, died about the time we had left Ashkelon. We would be going to Rome, but we'd see neither the Caesar nor the beloved Pope John Paul there, for leaders of empires, in spite of their power and glory, die like everyone else.

Paul, setting off for Rome from Caesarea, was no longer a young man. He knew that he could not expect to live many more years. He was aware that his appeal to Caesar might end in punishment, perhaps even execution. Paul knew that both his own life and Caesar's would end in death. Paul, however, had seen the risen Lord, and I am quite sure he left Caesarea for Rome with confidence and anticipation.

The winds died off at nightfall and we motored for 12 hours. At about 7:00 in the morning, the wind came up and we sailed all day on the open sea, completely alone. In fact, for 24 hours we did not see a single ship, something that surprised us sailing on the Mediterranean with its crowded shores.

Early Sunday morning we were approaching Larnaca, Cyprus. I had seen the glow of light in the night sky from about 4:00 a.m., and an hour later the lights themselves twinkling from the land. As the sun came up, the puny, human lights disappeared, the only visible evidence of land. At precisely 7:30 that morning, just as we had planned a day before, we arrived at the Larnaca harbor, 43 hours after leaving Herzlia. The formalities went smoothly and we soon were enjoying rest, hot showers, and solid land. Because of the delay in Israel, we decided not to sail from Cyprus back to Lebanon as originally planned, but instead I would fly to Beirut that evening in order to visit Tyre and Sidon, two places mentioned in Acts that we had not been able to visit during our time in Israel. In late afternoon, I caught a taxi at the marina gate to the airport and bought a ticket to Beirut.

I had noticed, checking through customs that morning in Larnaca, that the agent who cleared us had not stamped our passports. Because we arrived on Sunday, outside of regular office hours, I needed to pay 30 Cypriot pounds (about $68) in extra fees to have the customs official come to the marina. Fuming inwardly about the extra expense, I failed to ask why he handed our passports back without stamping them. Now, in the passport control booth at the airport, the man slid the passport through the computer scanner, looked puzzled and asked, "Are you crew?"

Crew of what—the airplane to Lebanon? I thought. "What do you mean?"

"You arrived by boat today?"

"Yes." *What kind of information do they get when they run your passport through that little slot?* I wondered.

"If you are leaving Cyprus, you need to have a Cyprus entrance stamp in your passport. Wait."

Another man appeared and told me to follow him into an inner office. "Why didn't you check through customs when you arrived in Cyprus?" he asked.

"We did," I said, "I paid 30 Cypriot pounds for a guy to come, and he never said anything about stamps."

"Okay, I'll stamp your entrance and exit both right now." In a few minutes, I had the stamps and was on my way.

The flight to Beirut lasted 45 minutes, roughly one minute in the air for every hour it had taken us by sea to make the crossing. It was 10:45 at night when the plane landed in Beirut at what seemed to me like the strangest airport in the world. It was a gleaming new edifice, with clear signs guiding the traveler to airport facilities—all fine, except that none of the facilities were actually there. Theologically, these would be called "prophetic signs," but for tired passengers, the prospect of a future hope does not satisfy immediate hunger or the desperate need for coffee. There were hardly any passengers, just uniformed workers waiting, it seemed, for the time that they actually would have services to offer. There was no information about transportation or hotel options, so I decided to spend the night in the airport and get an early start at dawn.

I slept well despite the glaring lights and seats designed to keep people from trying to sleep on them. I was awake at 5:30, hungry and craving coffee. A sign with a cup of steaming coffee gave clear directions to a gleaming but deserted, non-functioning café. Then my heart leaped for joy when I spied a brand-new coffee machine and I eagerly fed the only Lebanese coins I had with me into the slot, pressed the "double espresso" button, and watched in horror as the cup dropped under the little spigot *upside-down*, the coffee gushing onto the bottom and running down the sides into the drain. My caffeine-starved reaction was lightning-fast, but I ended up with only one-quarter inch of coffee in the bottom of the cup by the time I righted it.

Having woken up and paid one dollar to smell the coffee, it was time to get going. From the moment I awoke, a taxi driver had been doggedly pestering me to let him take me anywhere in Lebanon. Due to lack of sleep and caffeine, my resistance was weakening. "How much to go to Tyre and Sidon for the day?" I asked.

"One hundred dollars."

"I can rent a car cheaper."

"No you can't."

"Okay, I'll check." Four rental-car offices had just opened and I moved toward them, the concerned taxi driver following one step behind. Four uniformed agents looked at me hopefully. I was the only potential customer in the airport.

"Seventy-five dollars," the taxi driver said at 30 feet away from the rental car counters.

I kept walking. At 15 feet from the car-rental counters, his price was $60 and, standing right at the counter of Hertz, the price was $50.

"Okay, I'll do it for $50." We shook hands in front of the disappointed agents and walked to the driver's battered yellow taxi.

What followed was a wonderful day of exploring the beautiful southern coast of Lebanon with its storied biblical sites of Tyre and Sidon. Paul had stopped in Sidon, the first port after leaving Caesarea on the voyage to Rome. I sat looking out across the harbor for a long time. Paul quite likely never came back to the eastern Mediterranean after leaving for Rome. This was his last seaport this close to his home of Tarsus that he ever sailed from.

I pondered the parallels between Paul leaving from Caesarea and stopping in Sidon, and us leaving from Ashkelon and stopping in Herzlia. Sailors still must use the winds and the safe harbors to their advantage. Paul had friends in Sidon (Acts 26) and reading this made me wonder if Paul had not stopped here often on his way to and from Antioch and Tarsus to Jerusalem. For the traveler, friends are priceless.

Leaving Sidon, the driver stopped at a roadside kiosk that sold coffee and the flat *manaeesh*, a pizza-like pastry that, in my ravenous state, tasted like the best thing I had ever eaten. "Where are you from?" the proprietor asked.

"U.S.A.," I replied between huge mouthfuls of *manaeesh*.

"Everyone here hates Bush and the U.S.A.," the proprietor stated. He had obviously not taken a course in public relations, but his comment came as no surprise. That morning in a bookstore at the airport, I had noted that nearly 50 percent of the nonfiction books in English were anti-American treatises denouncing the alleged self-serving and unjust policies of the U.S. in the Middle East. I paid for the *manaeesh* without saying much. What can you say to a poor man when you feel like a first-century Roman citizen in Palestine?

As we drove farther south toward Tyre, the violence of the past and the ongoing tensions of the present became more visible. Checkpoints, bombed-out buildings, and general disrepair indicated the massive conflicts and associated problems of recovery.

Tyre has some impressive ruins and I spent the better part of my allotted two-and-a-half hours—which I negotiated with the taxi driver—exploring them, trying to imagine the city at the height of its power and glory. Tyre figures significantly in biblical and non-biblical history. Ezekiel 26-27 describes the wealth and importance of Tyre as a major trading port on the eastern end of the Mediterranean: "Tyre, situated at the gateway to the sea, merchant of peoples on many coasts" (Eze. 27:1).

So influential was the city of Tyre that the Mediterranean was once referred to as the "Tyrian Sea." Alexander the Great had besieged Tyre, building an earthen causeway from the mainland to the island to get his great siege equipment, the largest in the world, within battering distance of the city walls. The city of Tyre today is built on this causeway, and I noticed the lower elevation between the original island Tyre and the mainland of Lebanon.

Tyre became a Roman province in 64 B.C. It was the first city in the region to accept Christianity. The Arabs launched their Mediterranean conquest from Tyre. Their first target was Cyprus. I thought of Paul leaving Selucia for Cyprus and his desire to go to the farthest reaches of the Mediterranean. Tyre was where Paul landed at the end of his third journey and received the prophecy not to go to Jerusalem. He chose to ignore the prophecy and went anyway. In Jerusalem, he was taken into Roman custody then transferred to Caesarea, where he appealed to be tried before Caesar in Rome. On the transfer to Rome, the ship stopped in Tyre. He was finally on his way to Rome.

Tyre was the highlight of the day. I walked until my feet ached and was glad when the taxi driver, spotting me limping from the other side of the harbor, drove around to pick me up. We made it back to the airport in time to catch the flight back to Cyprus.

By 9:00 that evening, I was back in Larnaca, Cyprus. I caught a taxi from the airport to the marina, surprised to see Janet waiting at the marina entrance as the taxi pulled up. She had bad news. "I had to have a tooth pulled while you were gone!" she lamented. This tooth had been giving her problems for some time. I had, in fact, filled Janet's tooth using our emergency dental kit on the boat just a week earlier when the old filling fell out. It had become painful and she had visited a dentist who declared that the tooth was cracked and could not be saved. He extracted it on the spot. "It looks terrible," Janet informed me, close to tears.

"Now we can't tell everyone that we made it in one piece," I commented. Janet laughed and I hardly noticed her missing tooth. In fact, I noticed Janet's smile was getting more beautiful the more she triumphed over the daily adversities of our voyaging. But I felt sorry for Janet, coming back to Cyprus that day, as well as a twinge of pity for Paul for not having ever experienced the joy of returning home to a wife.

The Cypriot passport drama was not over. The next day I need-ed to go to the port police with my passport and exchange it for the card we were to have received when we entered. While there, Janet and I asked about checking out of Larnaca the next day and were assured that we could come to get our passports just before we left in the wee hours of the morning.

The following afternoon we dropped by the marina office to pay our bill and finalize the checkout procedure. "You will have to pay the overtime fees to get the customs man to come this afternoon and check you out," the woman said.

"What? We are only sailing to Paphos tomorrow, not leaving the country!"

"Yes, but you still must do this, or else you must wait to leave until 7:30 in the morning, or delay your departure by a day," the women explained.

We had planned on an early 4:00 departure in order to make it into the crowded Paphos harbor during daylight hours. Before we knew it, Janet and I were negotiating in a way we had seen work so effectively in this part of the world—yelling. "This is ridiculous," I shouted. "Why didn't the port police explain this last night when we asked them about checking out?"

The director of the marina, hearing the commotion, joined in. "This is the law," he said defensively. Janet burst into tears.

"What if we just leave in the morning without checking out?" I asked.

"You could do so, but I would not advise it."

But as we talked further, it became clear that the marina direc-tor agreed completely that the law was senseless and absurd. "Just go ahead and leave without the customs stamp," the mari-na director offered. "I'll write a note of explanation to the port police in Paphos and sign it. When you get to Paphos, if the offi-cials give you any trouble, tell them to call me."

At 3:30 the next morning, I was awake. I dressed hurriedly in the darkness, then walked to the port police with the boat documents and temporary visa cards in order to get the passports back. I wondered if we'd have any problems, but the two officers were engrossed in what appeared to be a black-and-white American sitcom from the '50s as they stamped and copied documents, their eyes glued to the TV the entire time. In 15 minutes, instead of the usual 30 to 60, I was back on board *SailingActs* with our passports.

Eric and Dave were up and we quietly slipped out of the marina and were soon cruising in the darkness toward Paphos. Fourteen hours later, we arrived in Paphos on the eastern end of Cyprus, just before sunset as we had hoped. We dropped the anchor in the crowded little harbor, inflated the dinghy, and I rowed ashore with the paperwork, which went without a hitch in spite of the unconventional checkout in Larnaca.

Right after breakfast the following morning, I rowed in with the dinghy to arrange to have some diesel delivered. Within an hour a tiny, three-wheeled "truck" that sounded like a garden tractor delivered three huge, plastic jerry jugs to the wharf. I loaded them into the dinghy, rowed out to *SailingActs*, and siphoned the contents into the fuel tank, amazed that it took all 100 liters to fill it. We hadn't used the motor that much, had we? We had started from Larnaca with a full tank. Even if we had motored all day, the total consumption should have been less than 40 liters. Something was wrong.

In making the final checks just before our departure from Paphos, Cyprus, for the long voyage to the Turkish coast, I was startled to discover that the bilge was far too full. What was going on? I dipped my finger into the liquid and sniffed. Diesel! The large amount of diesel that I thought I used motoring to Paphos was actually in the bilge. A quick check revealed that the fuel return line had been leaking. We had checked out of customs and were ready to go, but I could not start with diesel leaking into the bilge at that rate. I would have to change it now, maybe even delay our departure.

"Why don't you change it as fast as you can and we can still go today?" Janet suggested. Earlier I calculated that changing the line would require up to a half day's work, and I wasn't sure I had all the parts I needed. But I decided to go for it. Stripping down to my work shorts and grubby T-shirt, gathering all the tools around me and unloading the locker, I discovered the job was not as difficult as I thought and that I had all of the supplies and spares I needed on the boat. In 45 minutes the job was completed, and by shortly after noon, almost right on time, we were underway toward Finike, Turkey, 144 miles distant, the motor purring, the engine room completely dry.

The wind was perfect so we shut the motor off and sailed. An hour out of Paphos I noticed that the floor of the cockpit locker containing the fuel tank was covered with liquid. Oh no! What now? Should we turn back or keep going? I plunged down into the locker and discovered quickly that the liquid was motor oil, not diesel, which seemed to be even worse until I discovered, to everyone's great relief, that one of the oil containers stored in the locker had fallen upside down and the lid had worked lose. As I mopped up the oil in the slippery bilge in the rolling seas, with 29 hours of voyaging ahead of us, I once again got seasick. This was starting to be a pattern. But glorious sailing and Dramamine soon had everyone, except Eric, feeling well again. We made the voyage to Turkey with little problem until the next day at dawn when the wind and waves built to a roar, making the final hours approaching Turkey seem endless. But at last we were in the protection of the marina at Finike. We slept for 10 hours straight that night, happy that the open sea voyages were behind us for a while and confident that we could now relax with plenty of time to sail up the Turkish coast to Kuşadasi. There we would leave *SailingActs* in the excellent marina while we took the ferry to Athens in order to meet the EMU student group to begin their three-week cross-cultural study program in the Aegean that Janet and I were leading.

This three-week program would take us off the route Paul took from Caesarea to Rome. We would rejoin it later. It had taken Paul six months to make the journey from Caesarea to Rome due to the shipwreck on Malta. We had decided that by skipping the shipwreck, we could easily make the same passage in three months, with plenty of time to lead the cross-cultural study program in May.

SailingActs

We spent several days in the stunningly beautiful marina of Finike. With the backdrop of snow-capped peaks, Finike had an alpine feel to it and we soaked up the friendly atmosphere of the international sailing community. We met a couple from Canada who 18 years earlier had set sail for a year-long sabbatical that lasted two years. They had kept their boat and, ever since, returned each summer to the Mediterranean to sail. "Don't sell your boat," they advised. "They don't make well-built boats like yours anymore."

Having spent several hours that day trying to fix the persistent leaks around the portholes, I wondered if the term "well-built" applied to *SailingActs*, but I knew deep down they were right. Janet and I had received a lot of advice in the past year, but there in Finike, the advice to keep *SailingActs* seemed to make perfect sense.

After several days of cleaning, e-mailing, filling tanks, buying supplies, and enjoying the social life of the marina, we left the comfort and safety of Finike and spent the second half of April working our way west along the Turkish coast. Before we left Ashkelon, several of our Israeli boating neighbors had recommended their favorite anchorages and harbors, which we carefully marked down on our charts. The first such recommended anchorage was at a little village of Uçagiz in Kapi Creek, allegedly the "best protected harbor" on the southern Turkish coast.

A strong westerly wind was blowing when we entered the harbor in mid-afternoon and dropped the anchor in front of the village. Eric and Dave were eager to take the dinghy ashore and hike up to an old fortress that guarded the harbor entrance. With the wind whipping up the waves, we decided that Dave would take Eric to shore first then return to pick me up, as I wanted to explore the village. The winds had increased in the few minutes it took them to row ashore. I stood helplessly watching as Dave wore himself out trying to row back to *SailingActs* to pick me up. Every time he'd almost fight his way within range of where I could throw him a rope, a powerful gust of wind drove him backwards. Just as Dave was about to give up and let the wind blow him across the bay, a young Turkish boy who had been watching from the shore jumped into a power skiff and offered to tow Dave to *SailingActs*. When I offered to pay for the rescue, he refused but invited us to dine at his father's restaurant on the waterfront. "Just call us on the VHF when you are ready, and I will come pick you up," he said.

The wind continued to build. Captains of the large Turkish *gullets* anchored in the bay stayed on their boats all afternoon, ready to motor out if the anchors gave way. The stainless-steel fastener on the snubber rope that I had used from the beginning of the voyage to secure the anchor chain broke in the gale.

Later that evening, the winds subsided enough for the young Mahmet to ferry us to shore with his power skiff. Everyone in the restaurant was discussing the wind. "It was blowing at Beaufort-9," Ibrahim, the restaurant owner stated. "That never happens here."

Now we knew why Dave could not make it back in the dingy. Beaufort-9 is a severe gale of up to 50 miles per hour. On the open sea, waves can build to over 22 feet. When we tried to pull up our 45-pound CRQ anchor the next morning, we were amazed to see that it had buried itself so deep that it took 10 minutes to work it loose. "We are tracing Paul's shipwreck route," Janet and I assured each other several times in April, "not the shipwreck itself." Fifty-mile-per-hour wind at anchor was all the insight I needed to appreciate Acts 27.

The rugged, pristine Turkish coast slipped by on our starboard side over the next few days (Acts 27:5a). We anchored in Kalcan close to Myra (Acts 27:5b). We spent nights at anchor at Kapi Creek with its remote mountain-goat-herding village, and at Bozuk Buku, where the owners of the tiny restaurants on shore frantically hailed us from their dinghies, hoping we would tie up to their makeshift wharf. We selected the one where the enterprising tout, using binoculars, had spotted our American flag from a great distance and ran a tattered Stars and Stripes up a pole on the end of his wharf. It was more out of appreciation for his creativity than a sudden patriotic impulse that attracted us in.

Then it was on up the coast, with a stop in Cnidus (Acts 27:7) to explore the fascinating ruins above the harbor (see Photo 50). We lingered as long as we could in Cnidus before sailing on to the marina at Bodrum where we spent several days stocking up on supplies, making repairs, and visiting the outlying area. We were now within two day's sailing of Kuşadasi, ahead of schedule and confident of arriving in Athens well before the student group. We continued from Bodrum and by early afternoon were anchoring off the beach in Altinkum, an ugly, dusty town with discos and bars advertising "full English breakfasts" strewn along the other-wise beautiful Turkish coast. Altinkum is near the sacred town of Didyma, the home of the world's biggest Ionian temple (see Photo 51). This temple to Apollo, built by Alexander the Great, was famous for its oracles. Didyma was connected to Miletus by a Sacred Way that began in the Miletus harbor. Pilgrims would walk to Didyma from Miletus on this special road. While Paul never visited Didyma, he would have heard all about the wonders of this magnificent temple and would have observed the throngs of pilgrims on the Sacred Way during the time he was in Miletus more than two years earlier.

We anchored some distance off shore because of the shallow waters, and I decided to dig our battered outboard motor from the locker where it had been stored since September. I filled the dry tank with fuel and tried to start it. After about 50 pulls of the cord, after taking out the spark plug to check the spark (good), with the hopeful crew offering positive reinforcement ("I think I heard it sputter a little"), it dawned on me that I hadn't opened the fuel valve. So I turned it on and didn't exactly tell anyone about my oversight, but I let them applaud and think I had fixed something when the outboard snarled to life.

Dave, who elected to stay with the boat, shuttled Eric, Janet, and me ashore, where we negotiated with a taxi driver to take us to Didyma. He drove us about five miles out of Altinkum, across some open landscape, then stopped in front of a bunch of carpet shops with owners desperately inviting us to step inside for a cup of tea. But we had not come to buy carpets, so we battled our way directly into one of the most awesome temple areas we had ever seen outside of Egypt, with towering columns, massive walls, and intricate stone carvings. We spent the full hour wandering the site and taking pictures.

At 5:30 the next morning, I pulled anchor while the crew slept and eased out of the anchorage in the darkness for our final day of sailing with Dave and Eric. In Kuşadasi they would leave us to begin the bicycling phase of their year-long, round-the-world travel adventure. I put the sails up and made good speed in light winds using the motor. The sun arose and we turned north, heading through the Samos straights. We waved to the Turkish soldiers on the lookout, then, emerging from the straights, we encountered our first really favorable sustained wind for the whole trip and we sailed in high spirits, with Eric and Dave steering, for a magnificent run into the Kuşadasi marina.

During the next several days, we made arrangements to take a ferry to the nearby island of Samos, Greece, then another ferry to Athens. Eric and Dave offered to spend a day working on *SailingActs* as a thank-you present to us, an offer I could not refuse. When they were finished scrubbing the deck, oiling the teak, polishing all the metal, and waxing the fiberglass, *SailingActs* looked better than we had ever seen her look, and we all stood there, admiring not only our own work, but the little vessel that brought us the 700 miles from Israel to Kuşadasi. That evening the marina put on their annual spring barbecue and the four of us, freshly showered and very relaxed, joined for an excellent free meal.

SailingActs

Dave and Eric said goodbye the next morning. Janet and I used the next few days to prepare ourselves and *SailingActs* for the cross-cultural program.

The trip from Turkey to Athens was a two-day maritime travel adventure. First we needed to take a small ferry from Kuşadasi, Turkey, to Samos, Greece, a very short distance, but requiring a tedious customs process. Then, because the ferry schedules did not mesh, we needed to stay overnight in Samos, taking the overnight ferry to Athens on the following day. Our journey happened to be on the weekend following the Orthodox Easter, and it seemed all of Athens must have spent their Easter holiday on Samos. We had planned on getting a cabin for the crossing, but when we got on the ferry, we heard an announcement that every cabin was full. This was easy to believe because hundreds of people were staking out every seat and every remotely suitable place to stretch out on the floor. The ferry looked like a floating emergency shelter following a natural disaster. Janet and I quickly found a decent-looking area near the front of the ship, spread our belongings around to secure two places, then defended our territory against encroachers for several hours before it was time to sleep. *This,* I thought to myself, trying to get comfortable on the narrow bench at 3:00 in the morning, *must be close to the conditions of travel that Paul endured for weeks on end aboard cargo ships crammed with passengers.*

We arrived early in the morning, took the metro to the Omonia Square in Athens, and checked into the Golden City Hotel in which the students would be staying when they arrived. Over the next three days, Janet and I finalized the program while I prepared my lectures. Then on May 9, both of us were at the airport to meet the excited and exhausted students. The three weeks that followed were packed with travel, learning, minor glitches, and celebrations. Beginning in the Areopagus in Athens, where Paul had preached his famous sermon about the unknown god (Acts 17), we explored the ruins of once-gleaming temples, bustling *agoras,* and noisy theaters in well-known places such as

Corinth, Ephesus, and in lesser known ones like Miletus, Priene, and Didyma. The students explored the islands of Samos and Kos on smoky, noisy scooters, and the serene island of Patmos on foot. We enjoyed the cuisines of Greece and Turkey, and the conversations and endless cups of tea with descendants of pagans, Crusaders, and invaders. And we were fascinated by the visible, public faith of the Greek Orthodox Christians in Greece and the Muslims in Turkey.

During the three weeks, we traveled together over 500 miles by ferry. For 11 nights, Janet and I hosted two students at a time overnight on *SailingActs*. All of the students made at least one voyage, ranging from 20 to 50 miles, under sail. No one got seasick. Everyone participated in handling the boat and, at the end of the day, helped bring the sailboat into harbor like seasoned sailors.

We had the usual challenges. One student lost his wallet to a pickpocket while riding the metro following a soccer celebration at the Olympic football stadium. One scooter-driver suffered a minor scrape with a car on the island of Kos. One student broke out with a severe case of hives and was taken off a large ferry in the middle of the night in a wheelchair. The ferries do not have doctors on board and the captain did not want to take any risks with his passengers.

"I'll take responsibility," I pleaded to the assistant captain as they began to transfer the student into an ambulance waiting in the darkness on the wharf.

"I'm an adult; I'll take responsibility," the student added when she realized that she was about to be left behind. She rose dramatically out of the wheelchair like someone instantly healed by a faith healer. And so it was that the group remained together.

In the end, the risks and struggles were worth it. In the final session before leaving for the airport, I told the students: "You have been on the Mediterranean, the most fascinating sea in the world. You have sailed the 'wine-dark sea' of Odysseus and Paul, both heroes determined to reach their goals. Life is like a voyage. Don't be driven aimlessly by the wind and the waves, but sail

SailingActs

with purpose. But don't try, like Odysseus, to sail back home from where you started. Sail instead toward the future, the 'rosy-fingered dawn' of the kingdom of God, like Paul."

We said goodbye to the students, grateful for the opportunity to learn more about the Greeks, the Jews, and the world today by being with 12 great students for three weeks in the Mediterranean. But even before we were out of the airport, I thought of *SailingActs* rocking gently in the Kos marina, the open seas, and the call of Rome. Suddenly I felt like the students leaving on the airplane, eager to go "home" once again, to be aboard *SailingActs* on the Mediterranean, headed toward Rome.

CHAPTER 15
And So We Came to Rome

A light rain was falling in the pre-dawn darkness when the ferry from Athens arrived in Kos. Dorothy, Janet's sister, had joined us in Athens and would sail with us for the next 10 days. We picked our way through the dark streets of Kos, around puddles of water, toward the marina. As usual, when we returned to *SailingActs* after being away on land for a day or two, we scanned the forest of masts as we approached the marina for the distinctive bronze-colored masts of *SailingActs*. As usual, we were relieved to see them.

To see *SailingActs* floating always felt good, but this particular leg of the voyage following Paul's shipwreck route, including the long, three-day stretch of open-water sailing between Greece and Malta, made us a little more sensitive to the state of *SailingActs'* safety equipment.

"How about your life raft? Has it been inspected lately?" Maria, the woman at the chandlery in the Kos marina asked when I stopped to pick up the Maltese flag I had ordered several days before. The old life raft lashed to the deck was not something I liked to think about. According to the little sticker on the ancient, ugly thing, it had been due for an inspection two years earlier.

"No," I said, "we want to leave in the morning. We'll need to do it some other time."

"I am a certified life-raft inspector," Maria said. "Let me take a look at it. I can do it cheaper for you here than you can find anywhere else. If you don't know the condition of the raft, I can tell you right away whether it is in good shape or whether it's worth fixing."

"Okay," I decided spontaneously. It would be another hour before Janet had dinner ready. I took a trolley from the chandler, returned to _SailingActs_, untied the old life raft from its place on the deck, and took it back to the chandlery. Maria loosened the cover, making those little clucking noises I hate hearing from experts. Then suddenly she gasped.

"There are no gas canisters at all on this raft," she explained, pointing to the rusty connectors dangling in space. "If your boat had begun sinking, you would have thrown this raft overboard and it would have sunk more quickly than your sailboat. This is not a life raft," Maria declared. "Life rafts are supposed to float." I was pretty sure the last statement was true.

Maria also just happened to be a dealer for new life rafts. "It will cost you as much to get this old one fixed as to get a brand new one," Maria said. "I'll sell you a brand new, six-person life raft, the best there is, for the price of a four-person one."

"How much are we talking about?"

"The cost is 1,140 euros. But think about it—how much is your life worth?" Maria was a gifted salesperson.

I gulped. _There go the earnings from leading the cross-cultural group,_ I thought. Back on the boat, Janet and I discussed our options and decided to go ahead with the purchase. The new life raft fit perfectly in the deck brackets where the old one had been fastened, and we felt a sense of peace knowing it was there. _Here we are, getting a life raft just before sailing the same stretch of open water that ended in shipwreck for Paul,_ I thought. _I hope we never have to use it, but if we do, I think the_ SailingActs _project wouldn't necessarily be a failure. It wasn't for Paul._

I thought more about shipwrecks and life rafts in the bunk that night. Those first-century sailors of the Mediterranean who, on their square-rigged grain ships, managed to sail one and sometimes two round trips each season between Egypt and Rome, must have been incredible sailors. The grain ship bound for Rome, carrying the usual number of passengers including Paul, was sailing far too late in the season. Whether this was a private grain ship or part of the Roman fleet, the voyage presented a chance to make a small fortune that tempted the daring seamen to risk losing everything, which is what happened on Paul's journey to Rome.

Janet and I began to struggle a little during the days after leaving Kos. Somehow, knowing that we were sailing toward the final destination was unsettling and sad. We knew that our lives would change when we reached Rome, but we weren't sure how. I began to imagine that Paul felt similar feelings of anticipation and anxiety as his ship progressed toward Rome. He was going to Rome, just as he had hoped, but he did not plan for his travels to end there. Perhaps his plans to go to Spain were his way of coping with the possibility that Rome might be his final destination.

Janet and I had our own coping to do and slowly made the decision that we, too, were not willing to stop our exploration of the Mediterranean when we reached Rome. We had half-heartedly put *SailingActs* up for sale but had done very little to follow up on the inquiries that came in by e-mail. We simply had no motivation. Discussing our options with Dorothy, we decided to keep *SailingActs* in the Mediterranean for at least one or two more years before selling her, returning each summer to sail for as long as we could. With that decision reached, the voyage toward Rome became enjoyable once again.

We arrived on the northern coast of Crete five days after leaving Kos, after having hopped from island to island—Astipalaia, where we anchored in the tiny fishing village of Maltezana; and Santorini of the Atlantis legend, the island shaped by the world's largest volcanic explosion in about 1400 B.C., destroying the Minoan civilization on the island of Crete 60 miles to the south. One day we were delighted by the largest pod of dolphins we had ever encountered in the Mediterranean. Usually the dolphins show up in groups of two to six, but this time I estimated somewhere between 50 and 100 of the acrobatic, leaping, diving, circling mammals. They were so close we could hear their quick gasps for breath when they surfaced. The main group stayed with us for about five minutes. Gradually, small groups left until a group of five played at the bow for another 20 minutes.

The island of Crete is beautiful from the water, with rugged, 7,000-foot mountain peaks covered in places with lush greenery that we could see from a distance of 60 miles off shore. Crete is home to the famous Minoan civilization and probably to the Philistines that invaded Palestine. Crete is Greek's largest island, the most southerly, and in some ways the most beautiful.

We had decided to deviate when prudent from the exact route Paul's ship took and avoid reliving other details of the shipwreck voyage. Because the prevailing winds in the summer are "on the nose" along the southern coast of Crete—that is, blowing directly from the direction we needed to sail *toward*—we would sail along the northern coast, where the winds, we hoped, would be slightly more favorable. Approaching from the east, we entered the picturesque harbor of Khania on the island of Crete in the afternoon of June 11.

The harbor seemed quite full when we pulled in and searched for a place to tie up along the wharf. Crowds of people on the wharf seemed to be waiting expectantly for our approach. *Too expectantly*, I thought uneasily. There were mooring floats in the water, which apparently could be used by visiting boats. We found an empty slot next to a huge motor yacht and decided to go in bow first instead of the usual stern-to. Janet and Dorothy got ready with the boat hook to snag the mooring line and I eased in.

A crowd of at least 25 eager spectators was waiting to watch us come in. Everything went well until we reached the floating mooring marker. When Dorothy tried to snag the line with the boat hook, it was pulled right out of her hands. Now we had no way of snagging the mooring line to keep the stern from swinging in the cross-wind that threatened to push us into the motor yacht. The owner and uniformed crew, naturally, were observing everything with concern. We had to act quickly while the delighted crowd looked on. Janet scrambled on the upwind boat that was moored next to us to secure a temporary line to keep us from swinging into the motor yacht on the downwind side. With the help of the crew next to us, *SailingActs* was eventually secured. The satisfied crowd began to disappear. "They could have at least applauded," Janet said.

Several days later, Janet and I told Dorothy goodbye. She would fly back to Washington, D.C., a few days later. We'd explore the island by rental car, searching for the places mentioned in Acts. Our first destination was the little village of Kali Limenes, the accepted site of Fair Havens, where Paul had warned the ship's officers not to try to continue toward Phoenix, a safer harbor. This was an incredibly remote place. We drove over 14 miles of dusty, rocky track, descending steeply down to the village, which consisted of a couple of dusty waterfront *tavernas* and a fishing-boat harbor. We read the story in Acts, snapped photos, and tried to get a feel for the dynamics of the story in the setting and agreed that the description in Acts 27 matched the place very well indeed.

Our next stop was the village of Loutro, the site of Phoenix, which the officers on Paul's ship had attempted to reach in order to winter there. According to the map, the road did not actually go all the way to this village. Loutro appeared to be accessible only by ferry from Chora Sfakion, just east on the coast. We drove for hours in the late afternoon, reached Chora Sfakion, lost our way a couple of times as the signs were often missing or hand lettered, then took an incredible, narrow, precarious winding road up and over the rocky mountain jutting right out of the sea, a road unlike any we had ever driven on. We finally arrived at a small town of Anapolis, right at the top of a steep cliff, then tried to find a road down to Loutro. Our map indicated that it was a walking trail. The trail led through a gate, across steep fields with grazing goats, and down the cliff to Loutro. A short walk on this trail brought us to our goal of looking over the harbor of Phoenix.

SailingActs

According to Luke (Acts 27:12), this was a harbor with two openings facing in different directions. It appeared, indeed, to be a well-protected harbor, with sort of two sides to it. One could use the eastern side and approach going northwest, for it faced northeast. Around a finger, one could enter going southeast, for it faced southwest. There are other theories about where the Phoenix harbor might be located, but Loutro seems to fit the brief description in Acts most closely.

We retraced our precarious route back to Chora Sfakion, then began the long, arduous route up over the craggy mountains, down the northern slopes to Rethimnon, and finally back to Khania. I returned the rental car after dark, worried that they would notice that it was completely covered with dust from our off-road explorations, but no one at the rental agency seemed concerned.

When Janet and I left Khania, Crete, for the two-day journey north to the southern tip of the Greek mainland, we realized that we were sailing alone for the first time since last fall. We had thoroughly enjoyed all our guests, but it was good to be back to just the two of us sailing again. With our auto helm, "Timothy," relieving us of the long hours of steering, two is plenty of crew.

Timothy, however, was aging. Only hours after leaving Crete, with some of the longest voyages ahead of us, he quit. No amount of coaxing, fiddling, or threatening helped, although I spent hours and exhausted every idea to revive the aged instrument. Finally I called Captain Steve for help, and within hours he had tracked down an auto-helm dealer in Athens. "Give them a call," he advised.

The following day, while sailing, I called the dealership in Athens on our cell phone. "Yes, we have a new unit in stock," the pleasant woman assured me.

"How much is it?" I asked.

"Let's see, with tax, a new control unit will cost 4,068 euros."

"What!?" That came to around $5,000—way too much for our budget. "Isn't that a little too much?" I asked, as if a dumb question would result in some kind of spontaneous discount. The woman agreed that it was, indeed, a lot of money but insisted this was the correct amount.

I called Captain Steve once more. "Call me back in 30 minutes," he instructed. When I called again, he said the price was about one-tenth of the amount the woman had quoted earlier. I correctly suspected that the woman had simply used the wrong English words when quoting the price—"thousand" instead of "hundred" in this case. We decided that when we reached Kalamata, I would take the four-hour bus ride to Athens the next day and pick up a new auto helm.

The day I went to Athens was Friday. I purchased the new auto helm and was back in Kalamata by evening. How lucky, we told ourselves, that we were able to get the new auto helm before the long Pentecost weekend. The next day I installed the new unit, filled up with diesel, water, and supplies for the 75-hour voyage to Malta. The weather forecast was ideal. We were ready!

The following morning was wind-still, ideal conditions for testing the new auto helm and for making adjustments as the manual described. According to the instructions, we needed to steer the boat in large circles until the digital readout indicated the compass had adjusted itself to the boat. For the next three hours we circled, made adjustments, and circled some more, but nothing happened and we finally conceded that the unit was defective. With heavy hearts we returned to Kalamata. Now what would we do?

We had made arrangements to meet guests in Malta—my cousin Byron Gingrich and his wife, Virginia, with their daughter, Roanna, from Oregon. Although we could not contact them about our delay, we agreed that we could not leave until getting the autohelm unit replaced or repaired in Athens. The dealership would only be open on Tuesday, for Monday was a holiday. I would have to catch the bus again on Tuesday, get the new unit repaired, then return by bus to Kalamata. If everything went well and if the weather cooperated, we would be able to leave for Malta on Wednesday morning.

*Sailing*Acts

On Tuesday morning, for the second time in four days, I got up at 5:00 to take the bus to Athens, bringing the defective unit with me to get replaced or repaired. Five hours later, I walked into the shop. The proprietor looked at me as if I was crazy when I suggested they just exchange the defective auto helm for a new unit. No, I would have to wait for Mr. Andonopolis, the technician. At 1:00 p.m., Mr. Andonopolis finally arrived at work. Within minutes he had replaced the faulty compass in the unit and I was off.

The water was smooth the next morning when we conducted the prescribed auto helm sea trials with bated breath. What if "Luke," as we named the new auto helm, would not work? But within minutes, it was doing exactly what the manual described. We made the adjustments and within 15 minutes were on our way, rejoicing, to Malta.

We slipped into the routine of voyaging easily. I thought of Paul on the voyage to Rome at the end of his years of sailing the Mediterranean. The sea—familiar now—the ships, and the waiting had changed him. By the time he was on his way to Malta, he was considered a veteran, for even the captain and crew listened to his advice. We, too, were becoming seasoned voyagers.

Because of the constant headwind, we motored continuously. Checking the fuel level and doing some careful calculations at the end of the second day of motoring, I realized that we would have to sail whether the winds were favorable or not. So at 3:30 on the morning of the third day, I shut off the motor and we began the slow process of beating, tacking back and forth across the headwind, making two knots of headway for every hour of sailing. This would add one whole day extra to our passage. We would arrive on Sunday instead of Saturday, but there was absolutely nothing that could be done otherwise. The sea always wins. We could not inform our waiting guests about the delay, but we had couched the promises of our arrival time in Malta with enough "ifs" that we were pretty sure they would not be too concerned.

And so the long days and short nights progressed. In spite of the slow progress, we were having a wonderful time. We recalled how, during the previous season, sailing at night had been full of anxiety—how the sight of land elated us.

This summer, by comparison, was relaxed and pleasant, especially the nights. We'd eat dinner at about 8:00 in the evening, just before the sun set. Janet would take first watch at about 9:00 or 10:00 while I tried to catch some sleep in the bunk. Between 2:00 and 3:00 in the morning, she would waken me and we would trade places. I would stand watch until late the next morning. With the stars in the heavens, the sparkling phosphorescence in the black waters, and the snacks, the night would pass quickly and the slow dawn was invariably a religious experience. After the sun rose, I would make myself a cup of coffee. Janet would awaken about 9:00 or 10:00, make a great breakfast, and then we'd settle back for satisfying hours of watching, reading, and dozing as we sailed along.

But it was not all easy. Once, in the middle of the night, Janet woke me.

"The headsail is torn!"

I couldn't believe it. This was the brand new, expensive one we had installed in Rhodes the previous summer. But when I inspected the sail with the spotlight, sure enough, there was an ugly gash. We rolled the headsail to about two-thirds of its normal size so the tear was not exposed. I went back to bunk, worried about how we would make it to Malta without the use of that vital sail. The next morning, in the light, I discovered that the little clamp I had put on the stay at the spreader had turned, and a sharp corner had cut the sail when it flapped against it. Now we had to repair that or it would endanger the sail. With some difficulty, we took the headsail down under fairly rough conditions and made emergency repairs that allowed us to use the full headsail. The next morning when Janet woke me at 3:00, the lights of Valleta were beckoning. I shut off the motor and sailed slowly, delaying the arrival until daylight (see Photo 53).

In spite of the satisfaction of voyaging Paul's shipwreck route without shipwreck, we were especially eager to get to Malta and finally connect with our guests. Within hours of our arrival, they had rendezvoused with us in the marina and moved aboard *SailingActs*. They were happy to see us, for they had arrived in Malta five days earlier and had waited for us ever since. During the next several days, we would explore Paul's legacy on Malta together, then sail together to anchor overnight in St. Paul's Bay, the traditional site of the shipwreck on Malta, before beginning the long day sail to Siracuse, Sicily. They planned to leave us then, and our son, David, and his fiancée, Rebekka, would join us from Germany where they both live.

The next day we went searching for Paul in Malta. "Paul (or "Pawl" in Maltese) shipwrecked here," the priest in St. Paul's Shipwreck Church in Valleta, Malta, explained with great pride when we visited the church. "This is Paul's island. Look, here we have a bone from St. Paul's wrist, and over there is the pillar from Rome on which Paul was beheaded."

Indeed, in an ornate case, with the official papal seal of authenticity, was a bone, and in another case atop a small stone pillar, a very dead silver head rested. Some may dispute whether the island on which Paul shipwrecked was actually Malta, but for the Maltese, there is no question. *Pawl was here!*

Leaving Valleta we drove out to the town of Rabat where, the Maltese claim, Paul spent the three months between the shipwreck in November and when he continued the voyage on toward Rome in February.

"We are very proud of St. Paul," the sextant at St. Paul's Grotto in Rabat declared as he showed us the cave where Paul allegedly lived. "He is the father of our faith." The sextant invited us to stay in Rabat, for on that very evening the annual, week-long festival of St. Paul was beginning. We had noticed an atmosphere of celebration in the decorated streets of Rabat. In addition to the statues, street names, and even small businesses that bore names in honor of Paul, we observed additional gaudy statues of saints and apostles. We decided to stay and the evening was amazing. Fireworks exploded as eight strong men carried an ornate statue of Paul on their shoulders to the main doorway of the cathedral. Confetti supplied by *Radju Pawlin* (Radio Paul, a local Rabat FM radio station) showered down from the roof. The bells clanged from the cathedral tower. The brass band in the plaza in front of the cathedral struck up a tune and the clapping crowd joined in singing lustily. As for Paul, he stood silently amid the raucous, spontaneous, adoring crowds, stone hand raised triumphantly above the sculpted fire into which he had shaken a small stone snake.

A year earlier I would not have been moved by this display of devotion. I would likely have dismissed it as misplaced religious enthusiasm. But after having followed Paul this far around the Mediterranean, I was startled to discover that I shared the enthusiasm of these descendants of the friendly "barbarians" who cared for Paul on the night of his shipwreck 1,945 years ago.

"I love Paul," one of the T-shirted youth volunteers explained when I asked him why he was helping with the festival. Having followed Paul to Malta, we understood and bought Paul T-shirts, too.

We sailed out of Valleta on Apostles' Day, a national holiday honoring Peter and Paul. The anchorage in St. Paul's Bay was crowded with Maltese boaters frolicking in the water under the gaze of a gigantic statue of St. Paul (see Photo 52). Byron and I inflated the dinghy, motored to the island, and inspected St. Paul close up. Paul had spent three months on Malta, waiting for spring and sailing weather. While the story in Acts does not indicate exactly how he kept himself occupied, according to the traditions of the Maltese, Paul accomplished incredible feats while there, including the miraculous preaching to *everyone* on Malta and the nearby island of Gozo from a single location in Rabat.

Sailing Acts

At 3:00 the next morning, we were weighing anchor for the 83-mile sail to Siracuse, Sicily. Now we were on the exact itinerary of Acts 28:12-13. Syracuse-Rhegium-Puteoli (Siracuse-Reggio-Pozzuoli today) were ports on the Egypt-to-Rome grain-shipping route. These three cities were powerful, strategic, and wealthy seaports, and we were eager to experience the cuisine, energy, charm, rugged beauty, and romance of southern Italy that are unparalleled in the Mediterranean. We entered Siracuse harbor 14 hours later, happy for the ideal weather and that none of the guests got seasick. We tied up on the public wharf next to a sailboat flying a rare American flag. "Where do I go for customs?" I asked our neighbor.

"You're in Italy now," our neighbor, Pete, explained. "Someone will come by after a while and check your documents. Don't worry about it." I knew I was going to like Italy.

The Egyptian grain ship that Paul was on from Malta, sailing under the protection of the twin gods Castor and Pollux on the prow, stayed three days in Syracuse. Luke writes nothing of Paul's activities during that time. Perhaps he was kept on board the ship, but we spent our three days in Siracuse exploring the impressive Greek and Roman ruins in the city.

A few days later, our guest now departed, Janet and I sailed for Rhegium (modern Reggio di Calabria) on the toe of Italy's boot. However, unlike the quick trip in the Acts story, after fighting our way to within 16 miles of Reggio, we had to return to the coast of Sicily to anchor for the night. The headwinds, current, and huge waves were simply too fierce to fight.

The next day we tried again and practically flew across to Reggio in favorable winds. We pulled into the harbor, looking for the free berth we had heard about. We thought we had found it when a man came running out of the fuel station shouting that we could not tie up there. "If you want free, down there." He motioned to the commercial harbor. We motored to the end but it seemed neither secure nor safe, so we decided to tie up in the nearby marina.

After resting a while,we walked several miles uptown to the train station to find the tourist information office and Internet café, then hiked up the hill above the harbor to San Paulo's church with its somewhat crude and fearsome statue of Paul outside, and a number of paintings inside the church depicting the important events of Paul's life. The little San Paulo Museo was closed, so we headed back, stopping at a supermarket to buy supplies for the following day. Tomorrow we would leave Reggio and sail through the Straits of Messina.

It was the Straits of Messina, the narrow channel between Italy's toe and Sicily, that had us worried. Made famous by Homer's *Odyssey*, it was here that Odysseus had encountered the fearsome twin perils of Scilla, with her six long necks and horrible heads with which she could pluck dolphins, swordfish, and sailors from the sea on one side, and on the other, Charybdis, a gigantic whirlpool that could suck down complete ships and its crew. The passage through the Straits is described in the *Odyssey*: "And all this time, in travail, sobbing, gaining on the current, we rowed into the strait—Scilla to port and on our starboard beam Charybdis, dire gorge of the salt sea tide. By heaven! When she vomited, all the sea was like a cauldron seething over intense fire, when the mixture suddenly heaves and rises." Clearly, Luke did not write this.

As we approached this legendary place, I wondered if the sailors on the Alexandrian grain ship, sailing toward Rome in February of 60 A.D., had regaled Paul and the other passengers with Homer's legend and tales of their own terrors of the Straits. But we hit the current and wind just right, flying through at speeds exceeding seven knots, even with a headwind and the motor idling. We were relaxing once we had cleared the heavy cross-traffic between Italy and Sicily, and were emerging from the Straits when we suddenly found ourselves spun around about 90 degrees. We had experienced Charybdis! But it had become tame, a mere momentary thrill, much closer to Luke's description than to Homer's.

SailingActs

To our left we could see the Aeolian islands of Stromboli, Lipari, and Vulcano. Because of the constant ship traffic coming through the Straits, we had to keep a good lookout, but everything went smoothly and by 1:00 p.m., we were nearing the little town of Tropea that a sailor in Siracuse had recommended to us as a good place to leave *SailingActs* for the winter. We could see already from the water that it was extremely picturesque, and as we entered the harbor we were impressed by the design, cleanliness, and scenery of the marina. It was just perfect. Janet immediately fell in love with it and we decided, more or less on the spot, to leave the boat there that winter if we could.

The day after arriving in Tropea was spent doing routine *SailingActs* maintenance. I changed the oil and, when I could not find a place to dispose of it, took the jug of used oil out and set it next to the garbage bin. With the jobs completed, I cleaned up, showered, and took a leisurely walk down the beach feeling very satisfied about my accomplishments that day. Back on *SailingActs* in the late afternoon, Janet and I were enjoying some cold drinks when four young men walked up. *"Prago,"* one said, and motioned for me to come out on the dock.

I was not used to people telling me to get off my boat. "What do you want?" I asked, not moving.

The tall one motioned to another one with *"Guardia Costiera"* embroidered on his shirt. "Come. Bring documents."

Were these guys for real? I wondered as I got the boat documents and followed them. Another man from a neighboring boat suddenly appeared to interpret. "What's going on?" I asked him.

"Someone saw you put oil in the garbage," he explained.

"I didn't put oil in the garbage," I protested. "I placed the container of oil on the outside of the dumpster."

The officials solemnly escorted me to their office and made photocopies of our passports and boat documents. "Let's go to garbage," the boss-type ordered, and I walked between two officers with some confidence, leading them straight around the end of the dumpster where I had conspicuously placed the jug of used oil. The jug was not there. Then one of the Coast Guard officials opened the dumpster lid with a knowing look. Sure enough, there was the jug of oil.

"I did not put it in there," I insisted. I was getting worried. The penalties for improperly disposing of used oil were significant.

The officers looked like they possibly believed me. "Bring," they said.

I dove into the dumpster and fished out the jug of oil and carried it meekly to the unmarked dumping station. They stood back and watched as I carefully poured the offending oil into the container. "Okay," they said, "that's all." Then they walked away.

I was more than a little relieved, but something did not seem right about the whole thing. Why did someone say they saw me put oil in the garbage when I had set it next to the dumpster? Was someone trying to get me in trouble by putting it in, then reporting to the Coast Guard that I had done the deed? Had someone seen our American flag and decided to engage in a little resistance to the Empire? I don't know, but I did think of Paul, accused of taking a Gentile into the temple in Jerusalem on his way to trial in Rome. Were the accusations that got him arrested a set-up, too?

In Tropea we planned the final weeks of our journey with Paul. We would work our way northward along the Italian coast toward Salerno, where we had heard the harbor had several fine, free berths for transient boats. From there we'd visit Naples and Vesuvius, sail on to Pozzuoli, the last harbor mentioned in Acts, then sail back to the Tropea marina. There Janet would stay on *SailingActs* while I took a train north in order to walk the last 30 miles or so into Rome on the Appian Way, the route Paul followed coming into Rome from Pozzuoli. I would then return to Tropea and spend the final days of the sabbatical finishing up writing projects and getting *SailingActs* ready for winter.

The voyage north along the sometimes spectacular Italian coast went smoothly. We spent one night in Cetraro on the municipal wharf where Janet tripped over a rope someone had strung across the wharf, bringing about eight French yachters rushing out of their boats to rescue her when they heard her startled yell. We spent another night at an anchorage near Cape Palinuro where we snorkeled and swam in the clear, warm water. When we arrived in Salerno, we were pleased with the excellent free visitors' berth near the center of town. It even had electricity and water available.

The following morning we took the train to Pompey. What a city! We had visited ruins of Roman cities all over the Mediterranean, but Pompey, destroyed in 79 A.D. by the eruption of Vesuvius, is more than just the ruins of public buildings. In Pompey you can wander around on intact streets lined with villas, fast-food kiosks, and small businesses. Paul never made it to Pompey, but he spent years of his life in cities all over the Empire just like it. We left, amazed and impressed by the brilliance and success of the Romans, the power and the glory of their cities, and the lifestyle of the citizens (see Photo 54).

The voyage up the beautiful Amalfi coast toward Pozzuoli (Acts 28:13) was bittersweet for us, as I am sure it was for Paul. Did Paul struggle with discouragement as a prisoner heading toward Rome? Our route toward Rome, like Paul's, took us within sight of the Galli Islands, famous as the place where the Sirens enticed unsuspecting sailors to their deaths with their beautiful singing. The last temptation of Paul was not the Sirens, but more likely the power and glory of Rome that was visible in every harbor, on each island of the Empire. And now he was going to the center of it all, to Rome (see Photo 55).

The last temptation of Paul might have been to finally acknowledge the power and glory of Rome and to doubt the capacity of the kingdom of God to defeat the evil and supersede the achievements of Rome. The closer Paul got to the heart of the Empire, the farther he was from the Damascus Road. Paul, like Odysseus, heard the seductive call of the Sirens of Rome perhaps better than many others. Like Odysseus, Paul was not fooled. He knew that the beautiful melody was deadly. Like Odysseus, he was bound voluntarily, not to the mast of the ship, but to the cross of Jesus. But Luke gives a clue that Paul was struggling, for when he later met the brothers from Rome on the Appian Way, Luke wrote in Acts 28:15 that "he was encouraged."

We were not encouraged when we passed by the island of Capri into the Bay of Naples and encountered the most congested sailing of any place in the Mediterranean. Hundreds of powerboats roared by. Ferries charged back and forth. Sailboats crisscrossed the bay. We dodged them all, but when we arrived in Pozzuoli, we were told for the first time on the voyage that there was absolutely no room for us in any of the many marinas, nor any place in the town harbors, not even a place to anchor overnight. After spending a day at sea, there is nothing more discouraging. We eventually were granted permission by a sympathetic military officer to anchor in a restricted military anchorage several miles from Pozzuoli. Like Paul, we were saved by the Roman military and were grateful. That night we decided to sail back to Salerno and return by train in the morning to explore the city of Pozzuoli.

So we headed back down past Capri, along the beautiful Amalfi Coast, and into Salerno, tying up at the very same berth we had left two days earlier. We were delighted to learn, when the phone rang shortly after we had docked, that Byron, Virginia, and Roanna Gingrich were in the area. We arranged to meet them for pizza, and for Byron to go with us to Pozzuoli the next day.

The following morning we were at the train station in time to catch the 8:30 train to Naples. In Naples we caught the metro to Pozzuoli and spent the day there, poking around Paul-related sites. The woman at tourist information was extremely helpful, giving us all of the information she had on Paul, contacting people for us, and making photocopies of articles written by locals. We walked around the oldest part of the city to the harbor, the site of the commercial harbor the day Paul arrived in Puteoli in the spring of 60 A.D.

Pozzuoli was the most important port for Rome until the completion of the harbor of Ostia closer to Rome. The large, natural bay had three harbors when Paul arrived—a military harbor, a harbor for wealthy Romans on holiday, and the main commercial harbor. While very few ruins in Pozzuoli date back to the time of Paul, we visited a large amphitheater that held 20,000 spectators built during Nero's reign (see Photo 56), and an elaborate market area also from the first century. Both indicate the wealth and success of the Pozzuoli sea port when Paul landed.

We took the metro back to Naples and walked around that noisy, dirty, multi-lingual circus, then continued on to Salerno, which seemed so tranquil and clean by comparison. Now we were ready for the 30-hour sail back to Tropea.

Mike Eberly, a graphic artist from EMU who had designed the *SailingActs* Web site, arrived the following forenoon. Soon everything was stowed and we eased out of our free slip and over to the fuel dock, happy to be underway. The Gingrichs dropped by to bid us farewell, and we pulled away from the dock, waving and waving, enjoying the only moment on the entire journey that our guests saw us off.

The wind was favorable as we left the dock, the waves were moderate, and we were ready to show Mike just how fun and relaxing sailing could be. At nightfall I reduced sail and started the motor. Janet took the watch from 10:00 in the evening until 2:30 in the morning while I slept. At the unearthly hour of 2:30, she woke me, and I dragged myself out of the bunk and up to the cockpit. Once awake, the next several hours were wonderful as the almost-full moon set, the stars became more brilliant, and I savored one last time of reflection alone on our small boat on a dark and peaceful sea.

At 4:30 I gradually became aware of a gentle knocking noise somewhere in the engine compartment and spent the next hour searching for the source. Everything looked normal, so we continued. At 7:00 Mike woke up and joined me in the cockpit, and I decided to catch a short nap while I had the opportunity. It was very short. A sudden cessation of the knocking woke me up and I sprang into the cockpit as the motor whirred quietly. A quick look into the engine compartment revealed that the propeller shaft had broken loose from the transmission. For the next several hours, I tried everything, from duct tape to wire, to temporarily repair the propeller shaft, but with no success. We would have to sail the remaining 30 miles to Tropea and then enter the marina without a motor. Our biggest concern was to reach Tropea before dark.

Fortunately, a rare, favorable wind began to blow at just the right speed, and gradually we realized that we would reach Tropea well ahead of nightfall. As we approached, we called the marina, explaining our situation, and as we entered the harbor under sail, we were met by a small boat that pushed and pulled us into our berth. We made it!

Mike left early the following morning. Earlier Janet and I decided that I would walk the Appian Way into Rome alone while she'd stay on the boat in the picturesque seaside town of Tropea and get some much-needed rest. A few days later, I packed a small day pack containing the few things I needed to hike on the Appian Way to Rome, then took the night train out of Tropea toward Rome. Arriving three hours late the next morning at Rome's vast train station, I immediately obtained maps and information on the Appian Way and purchased a train ticket to Velleti, a town south of Rome. The modern Appian Way, built on the route of the ancient road, runs through this town. I arrived in Velleti in the early afternoon and began hiking immediately for Rome (see Photo 57). The traffic was light, and the countryside, beautiful.

I thought of Paul walking this stretch of road in public as a prisoner. He was certainly out of shape after sitting in a prison cell in Caesarea for two years, then on ships, and finally on the small island of Malta. He had walked Roman roads for years before his imprisonment, but now he was walking the most famous of them all. He had seen the presence of Rome throughout the Mediterranean, but now he was walking on Roman turf. This was a new experience for him, and I can imagine it was not altogether pleasant.

I took a short break in mid-afternoon for a piece of pizza in the sleepy village of Genzano di Roma. The old man behind the pizzeria counter looked at me quizzically when I entered. *This establishment will never make it into* Frommer's, I thought as my eyes adjusted to the dark interior. I pointed, and the old man sliced off a piece of pizza. "*Caldo?*" he asked.

"*Si.*"

The power and glory of Rome are not visible in Genzano di Roma at 3:00 in the afternoon. The tired Empire, it seemed in that sleepy little town, was taking a long lunch break.

On and on I walked. There were no other pedestrians, but the road gradually became busier with sleek Italian and German cars whooshing by, and the occasional snarling motorcycle cutting so close that the draft made me wonder whether the actual motorcycle was brushing my clothes. I was soaked with sweat. My feet ached. As the sun sank lower in the west, I began looking for a hotel along the route. But after another hour of walking, I saw none. In Castel Gondollo, I began asking people. "Yes," several said encouragingly. "Just five kilometers up the road is a hotel."

So I slogged on and, sure enough, an hour later I found one, a nice hotel set back off the road among trees. I wandered in, trying my best to look like a tourist and not a tramp. The place seemed empty except for two staff behind the desk. Yes, I could have a room for 60 euros for the night. No, they would not give me a discount because I was walking the Via Appia. In fact, they seemed to recoil a little when I explained what I was doing. "Is there another hotel nearby?" I queried after deciding to move on.

"Another several kilometers, Park Hotel," the man said. "Maybe a little cheaper. Not as nice as ours."

Another hour of walking brought me to Park Hotel. It, too, seemed empty, but the old man behind the desk told me that he had room for me for one night only.

"How much?"

"Forty-five euros."

"Breakfast?"

"No."

"Restaurant?"

"No, only sleeping."

I considered walking farther, maybe even finding a secluded field with some bushes and sleeping in the open, but I was just too tired. "Okay."

The man took my passport. I found the small, simple room with a shower that leaked everywhere when I used it. It felt like sheer luxury. Nero himself, I was sure, never enjoyed his sumptuous baths more than I did the shower in Park Hotel. The man at the desk directed me to a nearby kiosk that sold pork sandwiches when I asked him about a restaurant. Semi-drunk workers sat on crude tables under the trees, swigging gigantic bottles of beer. It was the right choice for dining on the Via Appia. I imagined myself at Three Taverns, one of the sleazy roadhouses that lined Via Appia, eating the evening meal with Paul on his way to Rome. I walked back to Park Hotel in the darkness, went to bed, and was instantly sleeping.

At 7:00 the next morning, a Sunday, I paid the bill and walked out the door when the old man behind the desk came trotting out with my passport. I couldn't believe we had both forgotten it. *You would think that returning passports would be routine*, I thought. *But maybe they only collect passports from Americans, and with so few Americans traveling in out-of-the-way places these days, returning passports might not be something Park Hotel has to do very often.*

The Via Appia Nuova, the modern Appian Way, was gradually becoming a busy, four-lane road with a shoulder so narrow that I began to fear for my life every time a vehicle passed, which was now almost continuous. I stopped at a fuel station, for I had neither coffee nor food yet that morning and I was famished. The fuel station had some vending machines which dispensed four tablespoons of strong coffee in a plastic cup, and a bland pastry in a plastic wrapper. I wolfed both down in seconds and continued on toward Rome, setting, I imagined, some kind of record for fast-food consumption on the Appian Way.

According to the map, I was getting close to the intersection where the Via Appia Antica begins. Within minutes I arrived at what appeared on the map to be the correct intersection. There were no other roads. I worried a little as I saw a sign for Santa Maria della Mole, which was completely out of the way, but I assumed that the right road branched off from it. So with confidence, I began walking in the wrong direction, something that didn't become clear to me until I had reached Santa Maria della Mole. When I began asking people how to get to the Via Appia Antica, they looked at me as if walking there was impossible. With the guidance of maps on signs in the center of the village, I worked my way out to the countryside. I did not want to retrace my steps back out to the busy Via Appia Nuova several miles back. I would go forward. I walked for hours, at least eight miles extra in order to find the beginning of the Via Appia Antica. But it was worth, it for I was walking in rural Rome, through scenery straight out of the first century. I came upon a tangle of blackberry bushes and feasted on the sweet, warm berries.

At 10:30 I was finally at the beginning of the Via Appia Antica. This is a stretch of ancient road that has been preserved complete with ruins, pavement, curbstones, and statues, an incredibly satisfying way to approach Rome for the final eight miles. There were no cars, just the occasional bicyclist, and I could almost imagine myself walking with Paul over the ancient pavement as Rome appeared ahead. The Appian Way of Paul's day was lined with statues, villas, and, most significantly, with tombs of the wealthy. Because burying people inside the city walls was not permitted, the wealthy would arrange to have their elaborate tombs erected along the Appian Way as it approached the city, as a way to be remembered and admired by the public after their death.

Paul would have seen these and he would have recognized that Rome, with all its power and glory, could not give life even to its most successful citizens. Rome could not, in fact, give life to anyone at all. Rome could promise the "good life" to some, and death to those who dared to defy it, but it could not give life. Paul, a prisoner on the Appian Way, had experienced two out of the three things Jesus had promised his followers—abundant life, suffering, and eternal life. And because he had seen Jesus on the Damascus Road, Paul was convinced that he would not end up in a tomb somewhere like the richest and most powerful Roman citizens. I believe Paul's confidence and encouragement grew as he drew closer to Rome, thinking about the kingdom of God.

I kept walking. Traffic on the Via Appia Antica increased as I drew within several miles of the city. Italians were walking and cycling, and as I approached the end at San Sebastian Gate, non-Italian tourists were also on the Appian Way.

I trudged past the church and catacombs of San Sebastian. Both were closed but it did not matter; I had been there before. I was going to Rome. The catacombs of San Sebastian mark the place where, according to some written and material evidence, both Paul and Peter were originally buried after their martyrdom. Peter's remains were removed to where St. Peter's Cathedral now stands, and Paul was buried along the Ostian Way where St. Paul's Cathedral stands. I would visit the latter site later. I continued on the Appian Way through San Sebastian Gate, up the shady Viale delle Terme di Caracalla to the Circus Maximus, and then right on the Via di San Gregorio, past Constantine's Arch and the Coliseum swarming with tourists taking pictures of each other under the July sun. Into the Forum, past crowds of tourists huddled under shade trees, drinking their bottled water. Down the Sacred Way, past columns of once-glorious temples and governmental buildings where the most powerful politicians on earth assembled.

SailingActs

And so we came to Rome—Paul and I, sweating, limping, thirsty, and exhausted.

In the blinding sunlight reflecting off the ancient stones on that July afternoon, I thought of Paul the prisoner marching past the Coliseum, the arena of death for the gladiators, and down the Sacred Way through the Forum, a prisoner surrounded by the power and glory of Rome. Earlier he had written to the Corinthians: "For it seems to me that God has put us apostles on display at the end of the procession, like men condemned to die in the arena. We have been made a spectacle to the whole universe . . ." (1 Cor. 4:9). Paul was living his own words, literally.

I limped through the Forum that was once the heart of the Mediterranean world and that still remains a five-acre testament to a power that held a large chunk of the earth in its thrall for five centuries. I shuffled past the temples and the Curia, the senatorial meeting place of the Empire. I thought of the processions that passed by on this very road, triumphant military generals returning from some successful war, leading their shuffling, sad prisoners in chains in front of the cheering throngs. I thought of Paul and the words he had written long before he entered Rome in the scruffy little procession that day: "But thanks be to God, who always leads us in triumphal procession in Christ and through us spreads everywhere the fragrance of the knowledge of him. For we are to God the aroma of Christ among those who are being saved and those who are perishing. To the one we are the smell of death; to the other, the fragrance of life" (2 Cor. 2:14-16).

Where did the smelly/fragrant procession end for Paul that day, coming into Rome? While there is no solid evidence that Paul was incarcerated in the Mamertine Prison while he awaited his first trial in Rome, he was very likely held in this prison, or one like it, until his case was resolved. The Mamertine Prison is next to the Curia, tucked into the northeastern corner of the Forum. Tradition has it that both Paul and Peter were incarcerated in the cell below the church of San Pietro in Carcere just before their martyrdom some years later.

It was in the Mamertine Prison where I chose to end the voyage to Rome. I descended the steps inside the church of San Pietro in Carcere leading down into a simple cave cell (see Photo 58). There were no tourists in Mamertine Prison, just a family of Christian pilgrims from Bulgaria and an Italian couple, holding hands. The Bulgarians reverently touched the altar with the carving depicting Peter and Paul baptizing the prisoners, and discussed in hushed voices the miraculous fountain in the floor that had provided the water for the event. The Italians passionately touched each other and pledged, I think, their love to each other, while I waited patiently for them to leave. That cell, it seemed, was only large enough for Paul and me.

Eventually they all left, and I sat alone in the cool, dark cell of the Roman prison with vivid images of sailing Acts.

I thought of dusty Tarsus and distant Damascus, of Jewish Jerusalem and pagan Caesarea.

I saw the glittering, attractive power and the glory of Rome, and the fearsome power and astounding beauty of the sea.

I smelled the dust and the sweat hiking along Roman roads.

I heard the shrieking of the wind in the rigging, and the roar of the waves smashing against the cliffs of Aegean islands. I heard voices speaking Greek, Hebrew, Aramaic, Arabic, Turkish, Italian, and Maltese. Most were friendly, a few hostile.

I felt the thorn in my foot, the gashes and bruises from the rolling boat, the cold salt spray on my face.

I tasted the oil and wine of the rim of the Mediterranean and the salt of the sea.

I recalled the loneliness of voyaging; the fellowship of voyagers; the helpfulness of strangers; and the friendship of Jews and Greeks, pagans and Christians, Muslims and atheists. I remembered the moments of desperation and fear, and days of living more intensely and joyfully than at any time in my life.

Janet and I had followed Paul from Damascus to Rome. And like Paul, we had fought the good fight; we had finished our course. I do not know how long I spent in the cell with Paul and our memories, but it was dusk by the time I emerged, blinking back tears. I had followed Paul to Rome, and it seemed that I was as close to Paul in the cell as I had been anywhere on the trip. I was ready to move on.

Tomorrow I would see everything I could on foot related to the tradition of Paul in Rome. I also would keep my eyes open for current signs of Paul's faith in Rome. Back at the little pension, I drank several liters of water, took some Advil, and collapsed into bed.

The next morning I checked out early from the little pension and discovered with dismay that they did not serve breakfast. I would have to find some food, lots of food, for after two days of strenuous hiking, I felt semi-famished most of my waking hours, especially in the mornings. I headed toward the train station, Roma Termini, to buy breakfast, but after walking three blocks, I returned to the pension to pick up my passport. Leaving it at the desk two days in a row was a record.

One breakfast was not enough. After eating a "full English breakfast" in one establishment, I moved next door to McDonalds for a cheap cup of coffee and an Egg McMuffin. I was beginning to plot the route of my walking itinerary for the day when I decided to buy one more cup of coffee. It would be a long day.

A few minutes earlier, I had noticed a young African man slip into a seat near the window next to where I was sitting. On the west side of the train station in Rome, large groups of Africans, as well as people from India and the Philippines, often cluster. The guidebooks warn about illicit street vendors, drug traffic, and pick-pocketing. However, this is also the cheapest place for a visitor to eat, and while somewhat gritty, it is a fascinating side of Rome, especially for those traveling on a limited budget.

I observed that the young African did not order anything, which was the case for a number of Africans sitting near the street end of the restaurant. *McDonalds must be the place to sit and rest for a while,* I concluded, and wondered what it would be like to be an African in Italy.

I got up to get another cup of coffee, then in a flash of generosity I asked, "I'm getting myself a cup of coffee. Could I bring you something to drink as well?"

His eyes widened, then narrowed with suspicion. "You will buy me a drink?"

"Sure," I said, feeling a little like a Salvation Army worker out of uniform.

"Okay, I'll take orange juice." I brought him back a large juice, set it on his table, and returned to studying the map.

He sipped the juice. "Where are you from?"

"America."

"Really?" He could not believe it. "Why did you give me this drink?"

"I don't know. I just thought you might be thirsty," I tried to explain, but I knew deep down it had something to do with eating two breakfasts and drinking three cups of coffee while someone sat next to me without enough money to buy even one drink at McDonalds.

"I think God sent you to me."

Uh-oh, I thought, *now what is coming—a request for sponsorship to the United States?* I knew the pattern. But this was not the case.

"What is life like in America these days?" he asked.

"It has been so long since I've lived there, I am not sure," I explained. "But from what I hear and see here in the Mediterranean, Americans seem fearful and suspicious of almost everyone in the rest of the world. Have you noticed that there are very few Americans traveling in Europe, except in groups and in places like Rome where they feel safe? When I traveled in Europe in the '70s, there were Americans everywhere."

"Yes," he said. "I have never met an American before."

"What is it like for an African in Italy?" I asked. What followed was an incredible tale of woe and hope.

SailingActs

There were Africans in Rome at the time Paul visited—many of them were slaves. Slaves and slave owners were among some of the first Christians. As I finished my McDonalds coffee, I realized that the world has not changed much in 20 centuries.

Out on the streets again, the July heat was beginning to climb. The pilgrims and tourists were emerging from their hotels, clutching their guidebooks, maps, and bottles of water. I hiked down to the Forum, stopping to take some pictures of the huge statues of Castor and Pollux that dominate the entrance to the Campidoglio, the elegant square at the northern end of the Forum area. The twin gods Castor and Pollux, the Gemini, were considered to be the guardians of ships and seafarers. Paul had spent many days looking at the backside of these two gods on the Alexandrian grain ship that had transported him from Malta to Puteoli (Acts 28:11).

I retraced my route of the previous day through the Forum, past the Coliseum, the Circus Maximus, out the San Sebastian Gate, but this time I turned right and walked along the outside of the city wall toward St. Paul's Gate, then south along the Ostian Way toward the San Paolo fuori le Mura, St. Paul's Church. St. Paul's is a massive and imposing structure from a distance, but when I got closer it had a look of semi-abandonment and dereliction. *Have they closed St. Paul's?* I worried as I approached. But then I saw the small door at the end was ajar, and I gratefully entered the vast, empty, cool darkness of St. Paul's (see Photo 59).

Paul's burial place in the catacombs on the Appian Way was only temporary, it seems, and his remains were soon moved next to the Ostian Way. A large slab of stone with the words "PAULO APOSTOLOMART" (Paul, apostle, martyr) was discovered and a church erected over the spot. Unlike St. Peter's Basilica, no crowds of people fill the vast empty area around the church. Stepping into the huge, hollow, almost vacant walk-in mausoleum, I was struck by the awesome magnitude, the ornate emptiness. Paul, dead, I concluded, does not seem to attract many people other than the occasional group of reverently excited nuns and whispering, photographing pilgrims. No disorderly women speaking in tongues, no one prophesying, no healings. Everything in this museum of departed church authority was done decently and in order.

Two gigantic statues, one of Peter and one of Paul, flank Paul's grave. High around the top of the columned cathedral are painted 36 scenes from Paul's life. The portraits of every pope, from Peter to the late John Paul II, gaze down upon the visitors. I stared up at the huge statue of Paul. As usual, this one, too, depicted Paul holding a sword in his left hand and a Bible in his right, demonstrating the source of Saul's authority before he met Jesus on the Damascus Road, and of Paul's after that experience.

A small group of idle, uniformed guards sat chatting near the front of the cavernous hall. Clearly their job of guarding Paul was not as demanding as when he was alive, stirring up controversy, exciting the crowds, ruining image businesses, and preaching the resurrection of Jesus. I sauntered over to them. Perhaps they would let me get a closer look at Paul's grave. I wanted to see the slab of stone with the "PAULO APOSTOLOMART" carved on it. "I've been following Paul's journeys since Tarsus and Damascus," I explained. "Rome is the end of the journey."

"Really?" The guard with a good command of English did not believe me. I pulled a *SailingActs* bookmark out of my day pack and showed it to the guard. These bookmarks, our "business cards," gave a short description of the project and the main itinerary. I showed him the final destination on the bookmark itinerary: July—Rome.

"Okay, I believe you," the guard said. "Come with me." He led me toward Paul's grave, took down the rope that kept visitors some distance away, and instructed me to look down through a hole in the floor below the altar. I stretched out face-down on the marble and peered through the hole. It was dimly lit below the altar, and I was pretty sure that what I saw was, indeed, the famous "PAULO APOSTOLOMART," and I thanked the guard profusely.

"What do you think of Paul?" he asked.

"My admiration for him has grown tremendously during this project," I replied. "I almost feel like I know Paul personally."

The guard was suddenly very serious. "If you are so close to Paul, please say a prayer to him for me."

This was not the first time in my life that someone has asked for prayer, but it was the first time someone had requested me to direct a prayer toward Paul. I sat down on a nearby bench and prayed to God as Paul would have done, but I did wonder if Paul was listening in.

By now it was afternoon. The heat was building, driving Italians and tourists alike toward any available shade. I, however, was following Paul in Rome, and heat, blisters, and aching muscles only made the quest for understanding Paul more authentic. I continued south on foot away from Rome toward the Abbazia delle Tre Fontane, the traditional site of Paul's martyrdom. The Church of Tre Fontane (Three Fountains) is so named because Paul's head was said to have bounced three times when it was severed from his body (early church history is not for the squeamish), and at each place it touched the earth, a fountain of water sprang forth. I finally found the shady, peaceful compound with three small chapels hidden in a modern neighborhood just off of Via Laurentina.

As I moved among the fountains, the metal heads with eyes closed in death, the graphic paintings of the beheading, and the pillar, it occurred to me that this was not an especially important place in Paul's life. Paul's life was so full of travel and adventure, triumphs and suffering, friends and enemies, ships and prisons, roads and riots, that his death can be seen as just another feature of his abundant life. Paul had downplayed his own death, and standing there at Tre Fontane, his death seemed almost irrelevant, a death completely unlike the death of Jesus. Paul's execution was nothing compared to his conversion on the Damascus Road.

I was pondering why Roman Catholic religious art seems so focused on the death, suffering, and the crucifixion of Christ as I left the collection of three chapels of Tre Fontane. When I first arrived in the compound, I had noticed a small sign advertising a gallery of religious art with the name "Jehoshu'a," which made me curious. Why the variation of the Hebrew name of Jesus for a shop in Rome? Entering the shop, it was instantly clear that the name was not the only unusual feature. The shop itself was striking, for it contained none of the usual crucifixes of an emaciated Jesus, or objects of veneration of the Virgin Mary. Giovanne, the artist and proprietor of the gallery, specialized in jewelry crosses with different themes, and hundreds were on display in the cases.

I noticed one of Giovanne's creations was an Armenian cross. Why? Was Giovanne Armenian perhaps? "No," he said when I asked. *"Mia Mama, Hebraisch, Jerusalem. Mia Papa, Katholic, Italia."*

With a Jewish mother, Giovanne was legally Jewish. Giovanne was a Jewish/Roman/Christian maker of empty crosses! I had come to visit the site of Paul's death but had met a living demonstration of his life and teaching. I selected a "St. Paul's" cross for myself and an Armenian cross for Janet before trudging back toward the center of Rome.

My last stop of the day was in the historical Jewish quarter of Rome. I found the street where, according to medieval Christian pilgrims, Paul lived for two years in his own rented house. Weary, hungry, and aching, I stood in the street for a long time. Janet and I had traveled so far and so long following Paul to Rome: 3,656 nautical miles, 79 days at sea out of 205 days of voyaging in two seasons, 815 hours at sea, 31 harbors, 21 anchorages, and 16 marinas. We had traveled thousands more miles on public transportation, in rented cars and scooters, and walked the dusty ruins and Roman roads shimmering with heat. This was where Acts, and our journey, ended.

I stood in the narrow Roman street as the sun set. The boutiques and shoppers faded, and time returned to 62 A.D. I imagined myself asking for directions to Paul's house. I glanced into an open doorway and saw Paul surrounded by a group of people, including Romans and Jews, men and women, rich and poor, slaves and citizens. He looked so ordinary for someone whose travels, trials, and triumphs are legendary. When I knocked, he glanced quickly in my direction with a look of welcome and motioned me to join the discussion. I took my place with the others and listened with amazement and gratitude as Paul, boldly and without hindrance, preached the kingdom of God and taught about the Lord Jesus Christ.

Epilogue

August 8, 2005, Tropea, Italy

I am sitting at the chart table, my daily place of work for six months, on *SailingActs*, our home for the past 15 months. It is another beautiful day in Tropea, Italy, where we are moored, and the musical voices of Italian sailors preparing to leave the harbor for another day of boating, sailing, and swimming drift through the open gangway and portholes. I cannot think of anything I would rather do than untie the dock lines and sail out on the fantastic blue waters of the Mediterranean. But it will be a long time before Janet and I will sail again.

This afternoon we will finish the last tasks of getting *SailingActs* ready for winter. We are quiet and subdued, knowing that one of the most challenging and rewarding periods of our lives has come to an end. Tonight we will take the overnight train to Rome and spend tomorrow wandering about through the diminished power and faded glory of Rome, that greatest of all first-century cities.

In two days, we will board the Lufthansa flight to Munich, Germany, for our final destination of Washington, D.C. I don't know what Paul felt like when he finally left Rome after his two-year house arrest, which concludes the book of Acts. I imagine Paul left Rome with a mixture of celebration and sadness. We, too, will be leaving Rome, once the most powerful city on earth, and flying to Washington, D.C., presently the most powerful city in the world. Like Paul, we are aware more than ever that this great nation, like the Roman Empire, is not the kingdom of God.

I realize with sudden delight that our 15-month voyage of sailing Acts with Paul is not really ending at all. Like Paul, we are not yet home.

Glossary

battens
Thin pieces of flexible material such as fiberglass or wood inserted into pockets sewn into the sail. These give the sail its proper shape for maximum efficiency.

berth
The designated space along the wharf or in a marina for boats to tie up.

bilge
The space below the floorboards in the boat's cabin. All liquids (seawater, engine oil, rain, spilled vinegar, etc.) inside the boat end up in the bilge no matter where they originate.

bosun's chair
Contraptions in which someone sits in complete discomfort and dubious safety in order to go up to the top of the mast to fix things like broken lights. Bosun's chairs are generally attached to the rope (halyard) that is used to raise the sail, and are hoisted up by someone on deck cranking the winch. If that "someone" on deck is the wife of the person in the bosun's chair, she is usually not muscular enough to crank her heavier husband up which, as you can imagine, is not a pretty sight and generally requires marriage counseling following the trip up the mast.

CRQ anchor
A type of plough anchor popular in the Mediterranean. Invented by G.I. Taylor, an English professor at Cambridge University and named "CRQ" for unknown reasons.

fenders
Rubber bumpers dangled by ropes along the sides of the boat to protect the hull from inept charter boaters trying to squeeze into a berth, or from things like concrete wharfs when tied alongside in a harbor. Fenders are stowed when sailing.

forestay or front stay
The cable that holds the mast from falling backwards, something you don't want to happen.

GPS
Short for "Global Positioning System," a world-wide navigation system using orbiting satellites. The GPS unit is a small electronic device that magically tells you your exact position, distance to go, speed, course, estimated time of arrival, and much more, allowing complete idiots to sail with confidence.

genoa
The large, light headsail used in gentle winds (see diagram on page 323).

halyard
The ropes that are used to raise and lower the sails.

"heave-to" or "hove-to"
A way of adjusting the sails and rudder in open water in such a position that the boat slowly drifts sideways. This gives the crew time to do things like calm down when trying to figure out how to keep the boat from sinking.

jacklines
Strong straps used to attach yourself to a sailboat in stormy weather. The person who needs to work out of the cockpit puts on a safety harness, attaches one end of a six-foot-long tether to the harness and the other end to a jackline. The tether slides along the jackline, allowing both freedom of movement on deck and relative safety, although the thought

of being towed along in mountainous waves by an out-of-control sailboat was always enough to make me hang on for dear life.

keel   The boat's backbone at the bottom of the boat. The keel is generally very heavy on a sailboat in order to give it stability. The keel also keeps the boat from being pushed sideways when the wind is coming from the side.

launch   A power boat used as a ferry between land and a boat at anchor.

mast spreaders   Horizontal bars part-way up the mast that hold the stays (the cables holding the mast upright) in the proper position. Can also be used to rest on the way up the mast in a bosun's chair when the bosun's wife is doing the winching.

mizzen mast   On a ketch (like *SailingActs*) the mizzen is the smaller of the two masts and is located toward the back end of the boat.

mooring lines   The ropes used to tie the boat to the wharf.

port (side)   The left side of the boat facing forward in the boat.

portholes   The small, opening windows in the boat's cabin designed to seal out water when tightened—but known to fail after 28 years of neglect.

quay   The concrete structure at the edge of the water that boats can tie up to. You do not want to ram into quays with boats.

roller furling   A system that allows the headsail to be rolled up, let out, and adjusted with ropes leading to the cockpit.

sea cock   A valve fitting in the hull of the boat that lets water in or out of the boat.

slip   A berth for a boat in a marina.

snubber rope   A safety rope attached from the boat to the anchor chain so that if the windlass brake gives way, the boat will still be held by the anchor.

spray hood   A canvas awning above the entrance into the cabin from the cockpit that keeps rain and seawater spray from showering down into the cabin.

starboard   The right side of the boat facing forward in the boat.

stern   The back end of the boat.

"stern-to"   To be tied to the wharf by the stern of the boat.

storm jib   The smallest, strongest headsail, used when it is very windy, as in "storm."

sunshade   Awning used in port or at anchor to keep the cockpit shady and cool.

VHF radio   A Very High Frequency (VHF) radio system for ship communication.

"weigh anchor"   To pull up the anchor.

wharf   A dock or other structure for boats to tie up.

windlass   A special chain winch that pulls up or "weighs" the anchor.

working jib   The medium-sized headsail for normal sailing conditions.

Diagrams of *Sailing Acts*

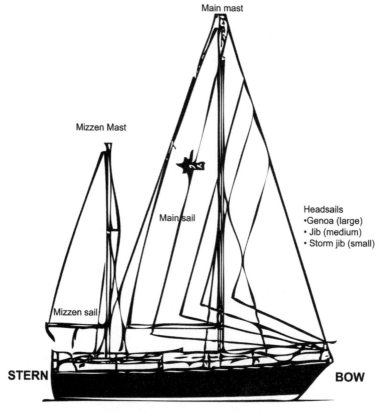

Main mast

Mizzen Mast

Main sail

Headsails
•Genoa (large)
• Jib (medium)
• Storm jib (small)

Mizzen sail

STERN

BOW

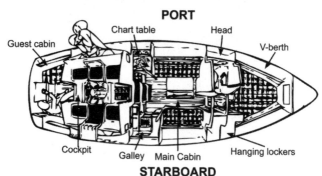

PORT

Guest cabin

Chart table

Head

V-berth

Cockpit

Galley

Main Cabin

Hanging lockers

STARBOARD

Statistics

Sailing days:	79 (out of 205 days in two summer sailing seasons)	
Nights at sea:	9	
Hours at sea:	815	
Hours using motor:	379	
Diesel used:	300 gal. (1,137 liters)	
Season One:	343 hours	1,546 nautical miles (1,779 statute miles)
Season Two:	472 hours	2,110 nautical miles (2,429 statute miles)
Totals:	815 hours	3,656 nautical miles (4,208 statute miles)
Hours seasick:	5	
Harbors:	31	
Anchorages:	21	
Marinas:	16	
Miles by motor scooter:	450	
Miles by foot:	250	
Miles by public transportation:	1,250	
Miles by rental car:	1,720	
Countries:	8	Greece, Turkey, Cyprus, Israel, Syria, Lebanon, Malta, Italy (plus Jordan, for a brief vacation)
Guests:	persons	75
	overnights	135
	meals served	350 (approximate)
Items lost overboard:	7	hat, barbecue piece, Swiss Army knife, new unused screwdriver, U.S. flag, 2 welcome mats)
Persons lost overboard:	0	

Boat Specifications, Equipment, and Repairs

Boat

Westerly 33, built 1979

Length: 33 ft. 3 in.; beam: 11 ft. 2 in.; draft: 5 ft. 6 in.

Sail area: 635 sq. ft.

Displacement: 15,000 lbs.

Ballast: 6,050 lbs.

Engine: Mercedes OM 636 42 h.p. diesel

Fuel capacity: 35 gal.

Fresh-water tank: 40 gal.

Equipment with Boat

Refrigerator (220v)

Radar (defective)

Depth sounder

VHF radio

Inverter

Tomas outboard motor (3 h.p.)

Wind generator

Life raft (defective)

2 Anchors – 45 lb.CRQ, Danforth

New Equipment

3-person dingy

Spray hood

Hot-water heater (electric/engine heated)

Pressure-water system

4 12-volt batteries

Head (toilet bowl with hand pump)

Water-pressure pump and tank

Mizzen sail

Mainsail

Working jib

Roller furler and headsail

Sail covers

Outboard and windlass covers

6 fenders

All halyards, ropes, and dock lines

Auto Helm ST3000

Garmin 12 GPS

Safety Equipment

Inflatable safety harnesses

Emergency tiller

Jacklines

Throw ring and floating rope

Floating MOB light

6-person life raft

Repairs

Replaced 3 lifeline holders

Replaced forward cabin hatch

Replaced cable steering

Serviced engine, replaced all belts

Rebuilt alternator

Refurbished electric windlass

Removed non-functional radar

Built storage shelves in lockers

Repaired auto helm – worked one season

Modified galley

Replaced damaged propeller

Serviced galley stove

Repaired fans in cabin

Removed and resealed all portholes

Transmission broke on final day of sailing—replaced over winter of 2005

Recommended for Further Reading

Cahill, Thomas. *Sailing the Wine-Dark Sea: Why the Greeks Matter* (New York: Nan A. Talese/Doubleday, 2003).

Cannon, James. *Apostle Paul: A Novel of the Man Who Brought Christianity to the Western World* (Hannover, NH: Steerforth Press, 2005).

Casson, Lionel. *Travel in the Ancient World* (Baltimore: The Johns Hopkins University Press, 1994).

Cimok, Fatih. *Saint Paul in Anatolia and Cyprus: A Travel Companion* (Istanbul: A Turizm Yayinlari Ltd. Sti, 1999).

Crossan, John Dominic and Jonathan L. Reed. *In Search of Paul: How Jesus' Apostle Opposed Rome's Empire with God's Kingdom* (San Francisco: HarperCollins, 2005).

Fant, Clyde E. and Mitchell G. Reddish. *A Guide to Biblical Sites in Greece and Turkey* (New York: Oxford University Press, 2003).

Gill, David W. J. and Conrad Gempf, eds. *The Book of Acts in its First-Century Setting*, Vol. 2 (Grand Rapids, MI: Eerdmans, 1994).

Horsley, Richard A. and Neil Asher Silberman. *The Message and the Kingdom: How Jesus and Paul Ignited a Revolution and Transformed the Ancient World* (Minneapolis: Fortress Press, 2002).

Jewett, Robert. *A Chronology of Paul's Life* (Minneapolis: Fortress Press, 1979).

Ramsay, William M. *St. Paul: The Traveler and Roman Citizen* (London: Hodder & Stoughton, 1925; Grand Rapids, MI: Kregel Publications, 2001).

Wangerin Jr., Walter. *Paul: A Novel* (Grand Rapids, MI: Zondervan, 2000).

White, Jefferson. *Evidence & Paul's Journeys* (Hilliard, OH: Parsagard Press, 2001).

About the Author

Linford Stutzman was born in the logging community of Cascadia, Oregon. He learned many of his carpentry and mechanical skills by working alongside his father who was a farmer, logger, and pastor of the community church. Linford's teenage years were spent in the remote interior of British Columbia, Canada. There he worked for the Canadian forestry service, at fisheries, at a hunting lodge, and in mining exploration while his parents served in a ministry assignment with First Nations people.

Linford and his wife, Janet, have served in various ministry roles over 20 years in Jerusalem, Israel; Munich, Germany; and in Perth, Australia. They have two grown sons, David and Jonathan.

Linford holds a Ph.D. from The Catholic University of America, a master's degree in religion from Eastern Mennonite Seminary, and a bachelor's degree in Bible from Eastern Mennonite University. Since 1993 he has been teaching courses in religion, culture, and mission at Eastern Mennonite University.

Together, Linford and Janet have led Eastern Mennonite University's cross-cultural study semester to the Middle East numerous times, as well as summer-study programs to Albania, Lithuania, Greece, and Turkey.

In the summers, they continue to explore the Mediterranean aboard *SailingActs*.